PELICAN BOOKS

FOUR CLASSICAL ASIAN PLAYS

FOUR CLASSICAL ASIAN PLAYS

IN MODERN TRANSLATION

COMPILED AND EDITED BY
VERA RUSHFORTH IRWIN

PENGUIN BOOKS
BALTIMORE, MARYLAND

Penguin Books Inc., 7110 Ambassador Road, Baltimore, Maryland 21207, U.S.A.
Penguin Books Ltd, Harmondsworth, Middlesex, England
Penguin Books Australia Ltd, Ringwood, Victoria, Australia

—

This translation of *Ikkaku Sennin* first published in *Player's Magazine* 1965
These translations of *The Vision of Vasavadatta, Narukami* and *The West Chamber* first published 1972
This collection first published 1972
Library of Congress Catalog Card No. 73-163460
ISBN 0 14 021249 3

—

Made and printed in The United States of America
Set in Monotype Bembo

CONTENTS

LIST OF PLATES

PREFACE

THIS anthology is an introduction to the classical drama and theatre of Asia. The plays selected are examples of Indian, Chinese, Noh and Kabuki theatre; they are also theatre pieces which have been successfully presented by English-speaking actors in America. With the exception of *Ikkaku Sennin*, which appeared in *Players* (March 1956), the translations in this collection appear in print for the first time.

Critical essays by scholars, and production comments based upon interviews, correspondence and observations made by myself at rehearsals, are included in order to help the reader understand the concept of 'total theatre'. Total theatre is the theatrical experience which occurs when dialogue, movement and song are blended – a characteristic of Asian drama.

It is hoped that, after reading these plays and their accompanying critical introductions, the reader will be encouraged to study in greater detail one or all of the examples of Asian theatre in this volume. To assist those interested, a selected bibliography of critical studies and play collections is included. In addition a selection of Asian plays in translation has been included, which are cross-referenced to enable the reader to find the sources listed in the bibliography.

Without the encouragement and assistance of numerous friends and colleagues, this volume would not have been possible. I would like to extend my particular gratitude to Professor John Mitchell, president of the Institute of Advanced Studies, who granted me the privilege of studying at the

Institute as a production observer, and to Professor John Alphonso-Karkala and Judson S. Lyon, who encouraged me to share with others my interest and experience in Asian Theatre. In addition to the contributions of those listed in the Contents, I am indebted to Professor Perry Baisler and Charles Scott who supplied me with secretarial assistance, to Professor Alfred Marks who gave unsparingly of his time in checking the Japanese material, and particularly to Professor Lawrence Sullivan for his invaluable suggestions during the writing process and his inexhaustible patience in reading the manuscript.

V.R.I.

New Paltz, N.Y.
March 1970

INTRODUCTION

It is several hundred years since the literature of the Orient was first introduced to the West, but it is only recently that anyone other than scholars has begun to understand and appreciate the intellectual and emotional values of Asian theatre. No longer do we accept the idea that the Orient is something quaint and charming – an idea which influenced the decorative arts of England, France and America in the late seventeenth and early eighteenth centuries. The romantic appeal of strange and far-off places was to be found not only in the design of our furniture, wallpaper and china, but also in theatre productions of this period. Although these productions reflected interest in the Orient, little or no attention was given to the study of Asian dramatic literature, of theories of dramatic criticism, or of production techniques. Differences in dramatic style, form and artistic intent were then, and for many years after, traditionally identified with the great periods of Western drama, such as Classical, Elizabethan, or Neo-Classic; with classics of various countries, such as England, Spain or France; or with writings of great dramatists such as Aristophanes, Shakespeare or Racine.

It was not until the late nineteenth century that serious interest in the art of Asian theatre began. This interest, which came about during the period of the French Symbolist movement, was a natural outgrowth of the theatre artist's search for new forms. At the same time that other creative artists were finding the accepted forms a restraining influence upon their work, so too the theatre artist sought and explored new ways of expressing his reactions and attitudes towards the human condition. Many playwrights, seeking to break away from the commercialism and narrow limitations of the realistic and naturalistic theatre, did so in the belief that the theatre had become too rigid, too confining and too illusionistic. Western theatre had now become a sociological, psychological and philosophical theatre – a theatre of ideas expressed through the written word. In addition, the creation of the fourth wall, demanded by the accepted forms of representational theatre, assisted in creating a theatre isolated both from its audience and from the glories of its theatrical past. The magnitude and beauty of the Greek and Elizabethan theatre of poetry, song, dance and music had disappeared.

Among the playwrights of this period, William Butler Yeats, searching for a dramatic form which was to be 'indirect and symbolic,' turned not only to Maeterlinck and the French Symbolist poets, but also to the Noh for inspiration. On reading Pound and Fenollosa's '*Noh*,' or *Accomplishment*, Yeats wrote concerning the possibilities inherent in the Noh which he felt were applicable to Western drama. Though some critics felt Yeats never really understood the art of the Noh, it cannot be denied that he turned to Asia in search of a new dramatic form.

It was not only playwrights such as Yeats and, later, Claudel who looked to the East; directors, too, in their explorations and desire for new forms, found in the purity, theatricality and symbolism of Asian theatre an answer to what they believed theatre should be. Directors such as Artaud and Capeau revealed their indebtedness to this stylized theatre in their productions and their critical and theoretical writings. This movement towards the release from the theatre of realism has continued, and today we find dramatists such as Brecht, Genet and Wilder also acknowledging their interest and use of the non-illusionistic conventions of the Asian theatre. *The Caucasian Chalk Circle*, *The Good Woman of Setzuan*, of Brecht; *The Balcony*, *The Blacks*, and *The Screens*, of Genet; and the American classic, *Our Town*, of Wilder – are all illustrations of the influence of Asian dramatic forms and styles of acting upon both contemporary playwrights and directors. The influence of this interest is also revealed in the works of such scenic artists as Edward Gordon Craig, Robert Edmond Jones, and Lee Simonson who, with other European and American designers, sought release from the picture-frame stage and the illusion of visual reality.

Although in the last half-century the artist and scholar have been influenced by the beauty and profundity of the theatre of Asia, it has only been in the last few years, especially after the Second World War and the American occupation of Japan, that the majority of ordinary theatre-goers have broadened their appreciation of drama beyond Western drama.

It is natural that the theatre of Asia should be the last of the Oriental arts with which we are familiar. Because of the nature of the art – a visual, auditory one that requires the total participation of all the senses, and because of the paucity of translations, Asian theatre has been a relative latecomer in attracting interest. Fortunately more and more translations are now becoming available, as are films and recordings. Some of the isolationism as regards world theatre has also been removed by university programs, government-supported cultural exchanges, productions presented by universities and professional schools such as the Institute of Advanced Studies in the Theatre Arts, and by the touring of national troupes such as the Grand Kabuki, which has recently appeared in America for the second time.

The stylization and totality of Asian theatre has become absorbed into our contemporary theatre and has, as Leonard

Pronko so aptly stated in *Theatre East and West*, 'created new areas of sensitivity, and has invited us to enjoy the feast of total theatre from which we have been excluded too long'.

It is hoped that this volume will contribute in some small way to greater understanding and pleasure, which can be found in the beautiful and exciting theatre of Asia.

THE VISION OF VASAVADATTA

An Introduction to

THE VISION OF VASAVADATTA

By Henry W. Wells

The Vision of Vasavadatta is a play which can be taken as in many ways representative of ancient Sanskrit dramatic literature. Although it is comparatively early and short, it contains much of interest. It includes the largest number of features, or conventions, of Sanskrit drama – a literary genre which developed extensively and which was written and performed for at least twelve centuries. *The Vision of Vasavadatta* has been translated many times and into several languages, quite often produced in recent years and much used as a text in courses devoted to the Sanskrit language; and it is generally accepted to be the finest work by the first dramatist from whom a considerable number of plays have survived.

Actually, nothing definite is known of either author or date. The play was among a dozen others recovered in several manuscripts by the scholar Pandit Ganapati Sastri in 1912. He reported discovering them at Trivandrum, the southernmost city in India, and hence designated the collection as the 'Trivandrum Plays'. His ascription of them to 'Bhasa', though supported by elaborate argument, is by no means conclusive; most scholars accept it as a convenience only. There was apparently more than one playwright of this name. Little is known, however, about any such man; and nothing clearly assigns this work to such a person. A few scholars suppose all thirteen Trivandrum Plays to be by one hand, but internal evidence seems much to favour the view that they were written by several playwrights. *The Vision of Vasavadatta* itself, however, is dramatically and stylistically a unified piece throughout. Certainly there is no reason to presume that this is a work by several hands.

The dating is equally problematical. Scholars, however, generally agree that the Trivandrum Plays are all early works, presumably written even before the beginning of the Christian era, possibly as early as the fourth century B.C. The comparatively simple rhetoric, and the absence of the euphuism which characterizes much of the later surviving Sanskrit drama, lead to this conclusion. A hypothesis (which neither dissents from this opinion nor necessarily supports it) is that all the Trivandrum Plays are acting versions, which were originally conceived with no special emphasis on strictly literary value. This plausible view does not deny the plays' literary worth but merely sets them apart from the most famous Sanskrit plays, which are of highly conscious literary value and, as in the case of works by Kalidasa, the most celebrated of Indian dramatists, works of pure poetry. *The Vision of Vasavadatta* is not only a true dramatic poem; it is a fine acting play too.

Like almost all famous Sanskrit plays, it gives a strong impression of being court drama. Indeed, it gives the impression of sophistication of taste and of culture. It may, as already suggested, seem slightly primitive when compared to other Sanskrit dramas, but it is none the less a good example of one of the most mature and self-conscious schools of drama and theatrical art. It is more elegant and aristocratic than plays of the Chinese classical theatre – which is not to say that it is intrinsically finer, but that it is a mature work when seen in the context of the theatrical art of the world. In some other literary traditions the earliest works known to us are, apparently, already mature; in Sanskrit drama there are no extant primitive works. *The Vision of Vasavadatta*, although early, is nevertheless highly developed. Earlier works will probably never be known; however one can hardly believe that such plays were written in the infancy of a nation's dramatic history.

It is no surprise that classical Indian theatre is closer to that of the West than to that of China or Japan. Some intercourse between the Sanskrit and the Graeco-Roman theatres is plausible, although there is no evidence to prove that it took place. The greatest distinction between the theatres of East and West is the differing proportions of naturalism and stylization; in the West, the emphasis is on naturalism, in the East, on stylization. The Japanese Noh theatre is the most highly stylized that is known. The Chinese stage is only a little less permeated by a conventional symbolism. The Indian theatre is still strongly Eastern, yet on the whole more easily approachable to the West than the drama of eastern Asia. This applies especially to performance, but is true, too, of the written text of Sanskrit drama. In comparing Western and Indian theatre, we shall first look at the ways in which they differ.

The principles, usages and conventions of classical Indian drama are discussed in many treatises; the most impressive is the *Natyasastra*, ascribed to the sage Bharata. Scholars are virtually unanimous in believing that the theoretical treatises followed the oldest extant plays by several centuries; in other words, the rules and formulation of the aims were apparently written down many generations after the dramatists had written their plays and seen them performed. The theatre was universally considered the summation of the arts. The *Natyasastra* laid down elaborate prescriptions for the building of theatres of many types and sizes, for the rituals to precede the performances and the benediction to conclude them, for the appropriate preludes to the individual acts and the handling of the major and minor characters, as well as the instrumental music, the gestures, the costumes and the color symbolism. The aims of the theatre are given as reflections of the intense spiritual life of India. A play is described as a spiritual exercise lifting the human spirit above emotional involvement in the struggles of the world; not, however, lifting it out of sight of this world and its physical aspects. It thus enables a man to approach half-way to the Indian ideal of ultimate religious detachment. This does not imply a separation of art from morality. On the contrary, the play is to avoid all vulgarity, to present heroes distinguished by strength and goodness and to offer on the whole a strongly idealized image of life. Tragedy and satire are not, however, excluded; but humor is preferred to satire and the criticism of life is to be made more in terms of the psychological than the social. (We are far indeed from the world of Confucian morality.) Drama is described as the delight of all social classes or, as the Indians were more likely to say, all castes; however the caste distinctions were to be observed. (A possible exception is the recommendation that the manager of the troupe, who takes part in the prologues of the plays, shall be a man of mixed caste, so that he may better understand all classes.) The hero is usually to have as his foil and inseparable companion a comic character, the *vidusaka*, who is in many respects ambiguous. He is a poor Brahman, stupid, ignorant, lascivious, greedy, lazy and timid, in all respects as unlike the hero as possible. Yet he is the hero's friend, at times showing a shrewd judgement and having several remarkable abilities, such as a sure sense for prophecy. He enjoys the privileges of the ruling or Brahman class. He is bald, dirty, clumsy and walks with aid of a crude cane. This character appears, as would be expected, in *The Vision of Vasavadatta*. Like all characters in that play, he must be understood as a theatrical convention.

The *Natyasastra* also describes the appropriate subject-matter for the plays. The dramatist has considerable freedom of choice. He may select, for example, the political, the erotic, or a conjunction of the two; but whatever his choice, he must remain within the confines imposed by it. There are certain moods, with their numerous subdivisions, which he must observe. The play must express these moods, both in its parts and its totality. It requires an action or plot, but, according to Indian thinking, the development of the mood is the more important. The aesthetic prescribed by Indian doctrine for the arts is much closer to Western conceptions of music than of the stage.

Indian drama is extremely self-conscious in all matters of technique. Virtually every gesture or word must conform with conventions fully understood. The hero is required to speak in Sanskrit, as are gods and certain other eminent figures, but the heroine and lesser characters speak only in the popular form of Sanskrit, or rather a vernacular dialect known as Prakrit. Again, the play is written in both verse and prose. A full-length play may have almost any number of verse passages, ranging, say, from fifty to over five hundred. The verse passages must exemplify the wide variety of metres of Sanskrit lyric poetry. Precisely how the words were originally rendered on the stage will never be known; but it seems clear that the prose was spoken in a comparatively colloquial manner and the verse in a more formal manner, though not strictly with a singing voice. Many Sanskrit plays commence with a prayer to the goddess of Speech and Learning. The classical Indian stage was less operatic than the Chinese or the Noh. It was emphatically a literary drama. None the less, in the many centuries of its development some changes in this regard were made. The plays ascribed to Bhasa are less lyrical than those written by the masters of the later Sanskrit drama, such as Kalidasa, Sudraka, Harsa and Bhavabhuti. The verse passages in such a play as *The Vision of Vasavadatta* do not stand out from the play's text as a whole with as much of the integrity of lyric poetry as those in the later dramatists. The Bhasa plays stand closer to narrative or fiction; the later plays to pure poetry. Perhaps, with the years, the Indian theatre became less theatrical; that it became more lyrical cannot be denied. The works of the greatest period of the Indian theatre, those of Kalidasa – most notably his masterpiece, *The Recovery of Sakuntala* – were also those of greatest poetical genius. Unfortunately for those incapable of reading Sanskrit a barrier is created by this very refinement. Much less is lost in translating *The Vision of Vasavadatta* than in translating *The Recovery of Sakuntala.* But there is also less to lose. Bhasa's play has long been recognized as the simpler work. In courses in Indian universities dealing with Sanskrit literature, Bhasa's work is often included for undergraduate study, Kalidasa's for the more advanced or graduate classes.

The plot of *The Vision of Vasavadatta,* like those of a very large number of Sanskrit dramas, is derived from Indian epic story-telling. Indian playwrights delighted in plots that were plots in both senses of the word, that is, both stories and the intrigues of shrewd politicians. The milieu of a court drama is indicated. The most active figure in *The Vision of Vasavadatta,* the man who propels the action, is Yaugandharayana, the incredibly wily prime minister of the king, Udayana, who is a conventional character. He attains his ends by the most devious means. Soothsayers have foretold that King Udayana, ruling in his capital, Kausambi, will attain success and security for his kingdom by Padmavati, a princess of the neighboring kingdom, Magadha. Udayana is in a precarious position. He has eloped with Vasavadatta, princess of another neighboring state, Ujjain, and hence lies at least under a suspicion of bad relations with that realm. The king, according to custom, might easily have two wives; but how can Udayana, who is passionately devoted to Vasavadatta, be persuaded to perform his duty as a statesman-king and marry Padmavati? The minister finds a devious answer. He can take the loyal and devoted Queen Vasavadatta at least in part into his confidence but not the king. On an occasion when the king is in the countryside on a royal hunt the minister arranges to have a village burnt to the ground and a report circulated that in it Vasavadatta has been burnt to death and he himself also lost in the flames while attempting her rescue. These events, which precede the play's action, are recounted in Act One. This act describes a meeting taking place in a sacred grove. The minister comes there disguised as a Buddhist hermit-priest, the queen disguised as his sister-in-law. To this grove, with its colony of ascetics, comes also Padmavati, princess of Magadha, destined as Udayana's second wife. The minister persuades her to undertake the care of the disguised Vasavadatta, who thereupon becomes one of the maids in Padmavati's court circle. The two women go to Magadha. The ministers at Kausambi persuade Udayana to go there, too. Convinced that Vasavadatta is dead. Udayana accepts Padmavati as his wife. Vasavadatta withstands the many disheartening and embarrassing situations occasioned by the new courtship and wedding ceremonies. But the inevitable enlightenment occurs in a manner that even the witty minister has not foreseen, Vasavadatta's parents, at last fully reconciled to their daughter's irregular marriage, send Udayana two portraits as gifts, one of her and one of him. When these gifts are unveiled it is clear to Padmavati and others that the portrait of the queen is also the likeness of the new maid-in-waiting in Padmavati's entourage. The ubiquitous minister is at hand. There is mutual forgiveness. Political events have meanwhile proved the good judgement in the minister's strategy. Even Vasavadatta takes no exception to having another queen bestowed on Udayana. By a sequence of incidents she had been thoroughly convinced that Udayana, even when believing her dead, has never ceased to love her. In conclusion there is magnanimity, forgiveness and happiness for all.

The plot is, of course, scarcely plausible in terms of political affairs and of a complexity only less great than that of Bhasa's preceding play with much the same characters, *The Minister's Vows*. But it is admirably contrived to evoke the mood of pathos and the sentiment of magnanimity, which are the aims of this Indian dramatist.

The beauty or fascination of the play is not and never can have been in its plot. Its charm, its value, both morally and aesthetically, lies in the evocation of certain sentiments or emotions. Some critics maintain the characters lack what Westerners term 'characterization'. They are particularized. Udayana is the conventional hero; Vasavadatta, the wife ever loyal under misfortunes and apparent cruelty; Padmavati, merely a perfect queen and wife; the minister, merely the conventional intriguer whose plots invariably succeed. Yet no figure is actually wooden or even stiff; this is because the playwright handles both words and situations with delicacy. Great pathos is achieved in the scene depicting Vasavadatta weaving a wedding garland for the woman who is, to all appearances, to succeed her as Udayana's queen. Vasavadatta's joy on hearing her husband's avowal of his preference for her leads her to a situation where she obviously experiences the most intense joy but must show this to the audience more through gestures than words. The play's most striking scene, the episode of the 'vision' or dream, gives further poignant evidence of the love of both husband for wife and wife for husband. As in the preceding episode, restraint in expression becomes a necessary and most important factor. The typical sentiment of the play, however, is even better exhibited in the episode of the last act when the king first recovers his lost lute – of whose loss nothing has been heard earlier – and then, within a few moments, recovers his lost queen. It has, however, already been stated that Udayana won his bride by teaching her the lute. The instrument seems almost a person. It has a name, 'Ghoshvati.' Bhasa's words virtually personify the lute and identify it first with Udayana and second with Vasavadatta. Both lute and girl have been lost in the forest. In playing it, Vasavadatta clasped it to her breast as though it were her husband; when clasping Vasavadatta to his chest Udayana has felt an analogy with his own playing of the lute. Thus the physical relations of man and woman in love are symbolized by the relations of the musician to his instrument. This episode, quite as much as the earlier dream incident, demonstrates the peculiar force and maturity of Sanskrit poetic drama. This drama is rich in symbolism. Yet nothing seems forced. We are perhaps carried away by the beauty of the symbolism, while scarcely conscious that such symbolism exists. The greatest Sanskrit plays, those by Kalidasa, Sudraka and Bhavabhuti, are merely very developed forms of the art shown in greatest simplicity and purity in the best of the Bhasa plays.

Kalidasa has been loosely called the Shakespeare of India. This statement probably does no more than express the view that each author is the supreme poetic playwright of his country. But, playwrights aside, particular English plays do offer an analogy to *The Vision of Vasavadatta.* These are the once highly popular and justly admired works by Beaumont and Fletcher, *The Maid's Tragedy* and *Philaster*, with their unhappy heroines, Aspatia and Euphrasia. The heroines of these English masterpieces are obvious companions to Bhasa's Vasavadatta. The suffering of an injured heroine is in each instance depicted with the finest pathos, her story in each case told with faultless art.

Unlike a book, the theatre is a social institution. The techniques of theatrical production are commonly much colored by the country in which the play is produced. The techniques of the Sanskrit stage are far from those of the Elizabethans – though they are certainly much closer to the Elizabethan than, say, to the naturalistic theatre of the West in the nineteenth century. But the flower of the theatre, its poetic essence, is not insular, parochial or national. A really good play is always 'relevant'.

Perhaps there is a way in which Bhasa's play can be considered finer than those by Beaumont and Fletcher. The Indian play is the richer in symbolism. The garland scene is symbolical; there are, however, comparable episodes in English plays. But the English plays contain no episodes similar to those of the dream-scene or the lute-scene. Udayana remains uncertain whether he has beheld his love in dream or in reality, as vision, ghost or woman. The episode of the lute is pure poetic symbolism, very finely wrought. The result is an essentially metaphysical type of drama, one natural in the land that produced such great religious works as the *Upanishads* and the semi-dramatic poetic dialogue, the *Bhagavad-gita*. Sanskrit theatre also presents amazingly effective stage business. This is best exhibited in its masterpiece, *The Recovery of Sakuntala*. There is an old saying in Sanskrit criticism that two opinions at least are right: the best play in Sanskrit is *The Recovery of Sakuntala* and the best scene or act is Act Four, the ritualistic robing of the heroine as a bride and therefore a future mother. But this is merely to observe commonplaces of the Sanskrit theatre as a whole. Dramatic realities are more clearly and simply presented in Bhasa's masterpiece, *The Vision of Vasavadatta*. It is the subtlety of their metaphysic that makes the Indian plays not only seem distinguished but especially attractive to students of drama in the latter years of the twentieth century.

THE VISION OF VASAVADATTA
(SVAPNAVASAVADATTAM)

Attributed to

BHASA

Translated into English by

NIRANJAN BHAGAT

1. *The Vision of Vasavadatta:* from a performance at Indiana University.

THE VISION OF VASAVADATTA

CAST

(In order of appearance)

STAGE MANAGER (Sutradhara), Prologue and Epilogue only

TWO GUARDS, one called Shambhashaka, both belonging to Princess Padmavati's retinue

YAUGANDHARAYANA, chief minister of Udayana, King of the Vatsas

VASAVADATTA, Princess of Ujjain (Avanti), daughter of King Pradyota Mahasena and Queen Angarvati. Married to King Udayana, and when the play begins, supposed to have been burnt alive and appears in Magadha disguised as Avantika, Lady of Avanti

KANCUKI, Chamberlain, from Magadha in the retinue of Princess Padmavati

PADMINIKA, MADHUKARIKA — Maidens from Magadha in the retinue of Princess Padmavati

PADMAVATI, Princess of Magadha, sister of King Darsaka, second Queen of Udayana, King of the Vatsas

HERMIT-WOMAN

STUDENT of theology

NURSE of Padmavati

VASANTAKA, jester of King Udayana

UDAYANA, King of the Vatsas

CHAMBERLAIN of the Vatsa King at Kausambi

VIJAYA, door keeper (portress) at Kausambi

RAIBHAYA, Chamberlain from the Avanti court at Ujjain

VASUNDHARA, nurse of Vasavadatta from Ujjain

Characters which are referred to but do not appear

MAHADEVI, widowed Queen of Magadha, mother of King Darsaka and Princess Padmavati

PRADYOTA *or* MAHASENA King of Ujjain } Parents of Vasavadatta
ANGARVATI Queen of Ujjain }

SON OF PRADYOTA, whose father sends a message to King Darsaka of Magadha for the hand of his sister Princess Padmavati

KUNJARIKA, a maid

KING DARSAKA, King of Magadha, brother of Princess Padmavati

VIRACHIKA, a maid with whom Udayana had an affair, incurring the anger of Vasavadatta

RUMANVAN, minister of King Udayana, who plotted with Yaugandharayana to save Kausambi

ARUNI, usurper of the throne of Vatsas

GOPALAKA } sons of Mahasena, brothers of Vasavadatta
PALAKA }

The play first produced in this translation by IASTA, New York, in September 1964.

PROLOGUE

At the end of the invocation, enter the STAGE MANAGER.

STAGE MANAGER: May the arms of Balarama protect you,
arms of the colour of the newly risen moon,
arms languorous with the drinking of wine,
arms luminous with the awakening of beauty,
arms with the enchantment of the newly budded spring,
I wish to announce to the worthy gentlemen that . . . how now! even as I begin to make the announcement I believe I hear a noise. Well, let me see!
[*Inside*]
Make way, make way, gentlemen, make way! Yes, now I know
The trusted servants of the king of Magadha
who are escorting the princess
impolitely turn away
the people gathered in the hermitage.
[*Exit the* STAGE MANAGER.]

END OF PROLOGUE

ACT ONE

The Ashram

[*Enter two* GUARDS.]

TWO GUARDS: Make way, make way, gentlemen, make way!

[*Enter* YAUGANDHARAYANA *in the disguise of a wandering ascetic and* VASAVADATTA *in the disguise of Avantika, a lady of Avanti.*]

YAUGANDHARAYANA [*listening*]: What! Even here are people turned away! Why

scare these quiet and honourable gentlemen
who dwell in the hermitage, clad in barks and
content with the fruits of the forest?
O, who is this insolent and impolite fellow
blinded by fickle fortune
who by his command
turns the peaceful penance-grove into a village street?

VASAVADATTA: Sir, who is this that turns us away?

YAUGANDHARAYANA: My lady, one who turns himself away from the Right Path.

VASAVADATTA: No, sir, I didn't mean that. But I am one to be turned away!

YAUGANDHARAYANA: My lady, even deities, when unrecognized, are disobeyed.

VASAVADATTA: Sir, the fatigue does not cause such pain as this humiliation.

YAUGANDHARAYANA: These things your ladyship has once enjoyed but has now given up. Let it not trouble you. For

once you too walked according to your own sweet will.
Your lord's victory will enable you to walk the worthy way again.
With the course of time

the turning cycle of worldy fortune revolves
like the spokes in a wheel.

TWO GUARDS: Make way, gentlemen, make way.

[*Enter* KANCUKI.]

KANCUKI: No, Shambhashaka, no! You must not turn these people away! Look

Bring no ruin to the reputation of the king.
Show no harshness to those who dwell in the hermitage.
These high-minded men come to the forest to escape
the humiliations of the city.

TWO GUARDS: So be it, sir.

[*Exeunt the two* GUARDS.]

YAUGANDHARAYANA: Ah, he seems to be a man of discretion. Let us approach him, my child!

VASAVADATTA: Very well, sir.

YAUGANDHARAYANA [*approaching*]: Why are people being turned away?

KANCUKI: O, ascetic!

YAUGANDHARAYANA [*to himself*]: Ascetic! It is indeed an excellent title. But being unfamiliar it does not appeal to me.

KANCUKI: Listen gentlemen! This is Padmavati, the sister of our great king, named by his *gurus*,* Darsaka. After visiting the queen mother, Mahadevi, who has made this hermitage her home, with her permission, she is on her way to Rajagriha. So today she desires to stay here in this hermitage. Therefore

fetch from the forests at your pleasure
holy water and fuel and flowers and darbha grass –
the treasures of the hermits.
Piety is dear to the king's daughter.

---

*Elders.

Never would she hinder your pious duties.
Such is the tradition of her family.

YAUGANDHARAYANA [*to himself*]: So, this is Padmavati, the Magadha princess, who, as the seers Pushpaka, Bhadraka and others have predicted, is destined to be my master's queen.

Aversion and admiration both spring from our
desires. Because I wish to see her wedded to
my noble lord, I feel great affection for her.

VASAVADATTA [*to herself*]: Hearing that she is a princess, I feel almost a sisterly affection for her.

[*Enter* PADMAVATI *with her retinue and a* MAID.]

PADMINIKA: Come this way, come this way, princess! Be pleased to enter the ashram.

[*A* HERMIT-WOMAN *is observed seated.*]

HERMIT-WOMAN: Most welcome, princess!

VASAVADATTA [*to herself*]: So this is the princess. Her beauty truly becomes her noble birth.

PADMAVATI: Revered lady, I salute you.

HERMIT-WOMAN: May you live long! Come in, child, come in! A hermitage is indeed a guest's own home.

PADMAVATI: So it is! I feel reassured. I am grateful to you for your courteous words.

VASAVADATTA [*to herself*]: Not only her looks but her words also are sweet indeed.

HERMIT-WOMAN: Good maid, has no king proposed to this sister of our gracious king?

MADHUKARIKA: Yes, there is king Pradyota of Ujjayini; he sends messengers on behalf of his son.

VASAVADATTA [*to herself*]: Well, well. She has now become one of our own.

HERMIT-WOMAN: Her beauty well deserves this great

honor. I have heard that both the royal families are of great nobility.

PADMAVATI: Sir, have you found any hermits willing to favor us? Please invite all the ascetics in order to give them what they want, and ask, 'Does anyone here desire anything?'

KANCUKI: As you please, my lady. O ascetics, dwellers of the ashram, listen, sirs, listen! Her ladyship the princess of Magadha, who is gratified by your warm regard, invites you to accept the gifts bestowed as a religious duty.

Who wants a pitcher? Who needs a garment?
Does anyone who has completed his studies
want anything to offer his teacher?
The princess, who is a friend to the pious,
asks as a personal favor
that, whosoever desires anything, let him speak out,
What shall be given today and to whom?

YAUGANDHARAYANA [*to himself*]: Ah, I see an opportunity. [*Aloud.*]

Sir, I ask a favor.

PADMAVATI: Happily my visit to this hermitage is fruitful.

HERMIT-WOMAN: All the holy men in this hermitage are well contented. This must be some stranger.

KANCUKI: Sir, what can we do for you?

YAUGANDHARAYANA: This is my sister. Her husband has gone abroad. I wish her ladyship to look after her for some time.

I seek not wealth, nor pleasures, nor raiments.
Nor do I wear a hermit's robes to make a living.
This young lady is wise and knows the path of duty.
She will be able to protect the virtue of my sister.

VASAVADATTA [*to herself*]: So, the noble Yaugandharayana wishes to leave me here. Let it be so. He will not act rashly.

KANCUKI: My lady, his expectation is great indeed. How can we consent?

It is easy to part with wealth
or life or ascetic power.
Everything else is easy
but hard is the guarding of a lady.

PADMAVATI: Sir, after first making the proclamation, 'Does anyone here desire anything?' it is now improper to hesitate. Please do as he says.

KANCUKI: These words are worthy of you, my lady.

PADMINIKA: Long live the princess who keeps her word.

HERMIT-WOMAN: May you live long, my child.

KANCUKI: As you wish, my lady.

[*Approaching.*]

Sir, her ladyship accepts the guardianship of your honor's sister.

YAUGANDHARAYANA: I am indebted to her ladyship. Approach her, my child.

VASAVADATTA [*to herself*]: What is to be done? I will go. Unfortunate am I!

PADMAVATI: Well, well. Now she is one of my own.

HERMIT-WOMAN: Her looks make me feel she also is a princess.

MADHUKARIKA: Well said, madam. I too think she has known better days.

YAUGANDHARAYANA [*to himself*]: Ah, half my task is done! Things are turning out just as it was planned with the ministers. When my lord is reinstated and Vasavadatta restored to him, her ladyship, the princess of Magadha, will be my surety for her.

Those who first foretold our present calamity
predicted Padmavati was destined to be my master's queen.

Relying on their words have I done this,
for fate never transgresses the well-considered words of the seers.

[*Enter a* STUDENT.]

STUDENT [*looking upwards*]: It is midday. I am very tired. Where shall I rest now?

[*Walking about.*]

Good, I know. This must be a hermitage all around.

Serenely the fawns are grazing
unafraid and feeling safe.
All the trees nursed with tenderness
have their branches laden with fruits and flowers.
Here also abound these great herds of tawny kine;
and no soil is tilled on any side.
This smoke rises aloft from many places.
This undoubtedly is a hermitage.
I will walk in.

[*Entering.*]

Hallo, here is a person, out of keeping with a hermitage.

[*Looking in another direction.*]

But here are some ascetics also. There is no harm in approaching them. O, womenfolk!

KANCUKI: Walk in freely, sir, freely. The hermitage is common to all.

VASAVADATTA: Hum!

PADMAVATI [*to herself*]: Ah, this lady shuns the sight of strangers. Well, it will not be difficult to look after my ward.

KANCUKI: Sir, we were here before you. Please accept the hospitality due a guest.

STUDENT [*sipping water*]: Enough, enough! My fatigue is gone.

YAUGANDHARAYANA: Sir, where do you come from and where are you going? Where do you live?

STUDENT: Sir, listen! I live in Rajagriha. But I have been staying in Lavanaka, a village in the country of the Vatsas, to specialize in Vedic studies.

VASAVADATTA [*to herself*]: Ah, Lavanaka! At the mention of Lavanaka my anguish is renewed.

YAUGANDHARAYANA: And have you completed your studies?

STUDENT: No, not yet.

YAUGANDHARAYANA: If you have not finished your studies why have you returned?

STUDENT: A terrible calamity has occurred there.

YAUGANDHARAYANA: What was that?

STUDENT: There lives a king named Udayana.

YAUGANDHARAYANA: I have heard of his honor Udayana. What about him?

STUDENT: He passionately loved his wife Vasavadatta, the daughter of the king of Avanti.

YAUGANDHARAYANA: Possibly. Then?

STUDENT: Then while the king was away hunting she perished in a village fire.

VASAVADATTA [*to herself*]: This is false! This is false! I am alive. Unfortunate I!

YAUGANDHARAYANA: Then? Then?

STUDENT: Then a minister named Yaugandharayana, who sought to rescue her, plunged into the same fire.

YAUGANDHARAYANA: Did he really? Then? What then?

STUDENT: The king, on his return, hearing the news, was so distracted at the separation that he sought to end his life in that very fire. The ministers held him back with great difficulty.

VASAVADATTA [*to herself*]: I know, I know my noble lord's tenderness for me.

YAUGANDHARAYANA: Then? Then?

STUDENT: Then the king, pressing to his heart the half-burnt remnants of the ornaments that adorned her body, fell unconscious.

ALL: Alas!

VASAVADATTA [*to herself*]: The noble Yaugandharayana is now satisfied, I hope!

PADMINIKA: Princess, this lady is in tears.

PADMAVATI: She seems to have a soft heart.

YAUGANDHARAYANA: Quite so, quite so. My sister is sympathetic by nature. Then? Then?

STUDENT: Then gradually he regained consciousness.

PADMAVATI: Happily he is alive. When I heard that he fell into a swoon, there was a void in my heart.

YAUGANDHARAYANA: Then? Then?

STUDENT: Then the king suddenly stood up – his body stained with dust from rolling on the ground – and lamented, 'O Vasavadatta! O Princess of Avanti! O darling! O beloved pupil!' and so on and so on. In short,

no love birds ever lamented so,
nor even those parted from fairy-women.
Blessed is the woman so loved by her lord
though consumed by fire, she lives for ever
through the love of her husband.

YAUGANDHARAYANA: But sir, did some minister not seek to console him?

STUDENT: There was a minister named Rumanvan who tried his utmost to console his honour. He too,

abstains from food,
his face is wasted by ceaseless weeping.
Sorrowing with his master
he neglects the care of his person,
day and night he waits on the king with diligence.

Should the king perchance suddenly give up his life,
he too would die.

VASAVADATTA [*to herself*]: Happily my noble lord is in good hands.

YAUGANDHARAYANA [*to himself*]: O, Rumanvan bears a heavy responsibility.

The burden I bear has lightened.
His toil is constant.
Everything depends on him
on whom the king himself depends.

[*Aloud*.]

Well, sir, is the king now consoled?

STUDENT: That I do not know. The ministers departed from the village taking with them, after great effort, the king, who lamented, 'Here I laughed with her! Here I talked with her! Here I sat with her! Here I quarrelled with her! Here I spent the night with her!' With the departure of the king the village lost all its splendor like the sky when the moon and the stars have set. Then I, too, came away.

HERMIT-WOMAN: He must indeed be a virtuous king who is so praised, even by a stranger.

MADHUKARIKA: Princess, will another woman win his hand?

PADMAVATI [*to herself*]: My heart was asking just the same.

STUDENT: I would take leave of you, Pray, let me go.

PADMAVATI *and* MADHUKARIKA: Go and fare you well.

STUDENT: Thank you.

[*Exit the* STUDENT.]

YAUGANDHARAYANA: Well, I too wish to go, with her ladyship's permission.

KANCUKI: He wishes to go, with your ladyship's permission.

PADMAVATI: Your honor's sister will be lonely in your absence.

YAUGANDHARAYANA: She is in good hands. She will not be lonely.

[*Looking at* KANCUKI.]

Pray, let me go.

KANCUKI: Go then, sir. May we meet again!

YAUGANDHARAYANA: Let it be so!

[*Exit* YAUGANDHARAYANA.]

KANCUKI: It is time now to retire.

PADMAVATI: Revered lady, I salute you.

HERMIT-WOMAN: Child, may you get a husband worthy of you!

VASAVADATTA: Revered lady, I too salute you.

HERMIT-WOMAN: May you also find your husband soon.

VASAVADATTA: I am grateful to you.

KANCUKI: Come along then. This way, this way, my lady. For now,

the birds have returned to their nests.
The hermits have plunged into the streams.
The fires are lit and shine brightly.
The smoke spreads from the hermit's groves.
And lo! descended down from high
the yonder sun with rays drawn in,
turns his chariot and slowly alights
on the peak of the Western Mount!

[*Exeunt all.*]

END OF ACT ONE

ACT TWO

The Palace Garden

Interlude

[*Enter* PADMINIKA.]

PADMINIKA: Kunjarika! Kunjarika! Where, O where, is the princess Padmavati? What do you say? 'Here is the princess playing ball near the jasmine bower!' Well, I will go to her.

[*Turning and looking around.*]

Ah, here comes the princess playing ball. Her earrings are tossed up and her face though tired and perspiring looks charming in its fatigue. I will go and meet her.

[*Exit* PADMINIKA.]

End of Interlude

[*Enter* PADMAVATI *playing ball, accompanied by* MADHUKARIKA *and* VASAVADATTA.]

VASAVADATTA: Here is your ball, my dear.

PADMAVATI: Now that is enough, madam.

VASAVADATTA: Playing ball too long has made your hands so red that they do not seem to belong to you at all.

MADHUKARIKA: Play on, princess, play on. Enjoy these charming days of maidenhood while you may.

PADMAVATI: Madam, why do you look at me as though to tease?

VASAVADATTA: Not at all, not at all, my dear. Today you

look unusually beautiful. And today I see your beautiful face from every angle.

PADMAVATI: Away with you! Please do not make fun of me.

VASAVADATTA: I will keep quiet, O future daughter-in-law of Mahasena!

PADMAVATI: Who is this Mahasena?

VASAVADATTA: There is a king of Ujjayini named Pradyota, who because of his vast army is known as Mahasena.

MADHUKARIKA: The princess does not desire alliance with that king.

VASAVADATTA: Whom does she desire then?

MADHUKARIKA: There is the king of Vatsas named Udayana. The princess is fascinated by his virtues.

VASAVADATTA [*to herself*]: She desires my noble lord as her husband.

[*Aloud.*]

Why?

MADHUKARIKA: Because he is so tender-hearted.

VASAVADATTA [*to herself*]: I know. I know. I too fell in love with him like that.

MADHUKARIKA: Princess, if the king be ugly?

VASAVADATTA: No, no, he is handsome.

PADMAVATI: How do you know, madam?

VASAVADATTA [*to herself*]: Partiality to my noble lord has made me transgress the bounds of propriety. What shall I do now? Yes, I see . . .

[*Aloud.*]

The people of Ujjayini say so, my dear!

PADMAVATI: That is so. Indeed he is no rare sight in Ujjayini. And beauty fascinates the mind of all.

[*Enter a* NURSE.]

NURSE: Victory to the princess! Princess, you are betrothed!

VASAVADATTA: To whom, good lady?

NURSE: To Udayana, the king of Vatsas.

VASAVADATTA: Is the king well?

NURSE: He arrived here quite well. He has accepted the princess.

VASAVADATTA: What an outrage!

NURSE: What outrage?

VASAVADATTA: Oh, nothing. His grief was so great and now he is indifferent!

NURSE: Madam, the hearts of great men, dominated as they are by sacred precepts, easily find consolation.

VASAVADATTA: Good lady, did he ask for her hand himself?

NURSE: No, no. He came here on some other purpose. It was our king, who, finding in him nobility, learning, youth and beauty, offered her hand.

VASAVADATTA [*to herself*]: So! Then my lord is not to blame.

[*Enter* PADMINIKA.]

PADMINIKA: Make haste, madam, make haste! Our queen declares, 'The stars are auspicious today. The ceremony of marriage must take place this very day.'

VASAVADATTA [*to herself*]: The more they hasten, the deeper the gloom in my heart.

NURSE: Come, princess, come!

[*Exeunt all.*]

END OF ACT TWO

ACT THREE

[*Enter* VASAVADATTA, *deep in thought.*]

VASAVADATTA: I have left Padmavati behind in the ladies' court which is filled with the festive wedding guests and come alone to this pleasure garden. Here I can give vent to the sorrow which is my fate.

[*Walking about.*]

O, what a calamity! My noble lord now belongs to another, Let me sit down.

[*She sits down.*]

Blessed indeed is the *cakravaka*, the bird of love which parted from her mate ceases to live. But I do not die. Desolate as I am I cling to life in the hope of seeing my noble lord again.

[*Enter* MADHUKARIKA *carrying flowers.*]

MADHUKARIKA: Where has the noble lady of Avanti gone?

[*Walking about and looking around.*]

Oh, there she is, seated on a stone bench under the *priyangu* creeper. Dressed in a graceful garment unadorned and completely preoccupied, she looks like the crescent moon obscured by mist. I will go to her.

[*Approaching.*]

Noble Avantika, I have been searching for you so long.

VASAVADATTA: Why?

MADHUKARIKA: The queen says, 'Avantika comes of a noble family. She is loving and skilful. So let her make this wedding garland.'

VASAVADATTA: And for whom am I to make it?

MADHUKARIKA: For our princess.

VASAVADATTA [*to herself*]: O, the gods are cruel indeed, to make this part of my duty!

MADHUKARIKA: Madam, do not think of other things now. The bridegroom is bathing in the jewel-inlaid room. So make the garland quickly, madam!

VASAVADATTA [*to herself*]: I can think of nothing else!

[*Aloud.*]

Have you seen the bridegroom, my dear?

MADHUKARIKA: Yes, I have seen him. I was curious and I love the princess.

VASAVADATTA: What is he like?

MADHUKARIKA: Madam, I tell you I have never seen anyone like him before.

VASAVADATTA: Tell me, tell me, my dear, is he handsome?

MADHUKARIKA: He is the god of love himself without the bow and arrows.

VASAVADATTA: Enough!

MADHUKARIKA: Why do you stop me?

VASAVADATTA: It is wrong to listen to the praises of another's husband.

MADHUKARIKA: Then hurry with the garland, madam!

VASAVADATTA: I will do it at once. Now let me have the flowers.

MADHUKARIKA: Here, madam!

VASAVADATTA [*discarding some flowers and examining others*]: What herb is this?

MADHUKARIKA: It is 'Keep-off-widowhood'.

VASAVADATTA [*to herself*]: I will use plenty of them both for myself and for Padmavati.

[*Aloud.*]

What herb is this?

MADHUKARIKA: It is 'Kill-thy-rival'.

VASAVADATTA: This must not be used.

MADHUKARIKA: Why not?

VASAVADATTA: His wife is dead, so it is useless.

[*Enter* PADMINIKA.]

PADMINIKA: Make haste, madam, make haste! The matrons are conducting the bridegroom to the inner chamber.

VASAVADATTA: There, take it!

PADMINIKA: How lovely! I must go.

[*Exeunt* PADMINIKA *and* MADHUKARIKA.]

VASAVADATTA: They are gone. Alas! What a calamity! My noble lord now belongs to another. I will go to bed. It may soothe my sorrow if I can sleep.

[*Exit* VASAVADATTA.]

END OF ACT THREE

ACT FOUR

Interlude

[*Enter* VASANTAKA.]

VASANTAKA [*joyfully*]: O, how fortunate to have seen the auspicious and happy marriage of his honor the king of Vatsas! Who could have known that after being flung into such a whirlpool of disaster we should rise again to the surface? Now we live in palaces, bathe in the tanks of the inner court and eat dainty and delicious sweetmeats – thus I am enjoying a stay in Paradise – but for the company of heavenly nymphs. But there is one great drawback. I do not digest my food well. I cannot sleep even on a bed furnished with fine coverlets. I see the wind and blood disease all around. O, there is no happiness without good health and without good food.

[*Enter* PADMINIKA.]

PADMINIKA: Where has the noble Vasantaka gone?

[*Walking about and looking around.*]

Oh, here he is.

[*Approaching.*]

Worthy Vasantaka, I have been looking for you for such a long time.

VASANTAKA [*observing*]: Why have you been looking for me, my dear?

PADMINIKA: Our queen asks, 'Has the son-in-law finished his bath?'

VASANTAKA: Why does she want to know?

PADMINIKA: So that flowers and scents may be brought to him.

VASANTAKA: His highness has finished his bath. You may bring everything except food.

PADMINIKA: Why except food?

VASANTAKA: Unfortunate that I am, my inside is rolling around like the eyes of a cuckoo.

PADMINIKA: May you always be like that!

VASANTAKA: Get away, my dear. Now I will go to his honor.

[*Exeunt both.*]

End of Interlude

[*Enter* PADMAVATI, *accompanied by her retinue*, PADMINIKA, MADHUKARIKA *and* VASAVADATTA *dressed as a lady of Avanti.*]

PADMINIKA: What has brought the princess to the pleasure garden?

PADMAVATI: My dear, I want to see if the *shephali* clusters have blossomed.

MADHUKARIKA: Princess, they have indeed blossomed. They are laden with flowers like pendants of pearls interspersed with coral.

PADMAVATI: If that is so, why do you delay, my dear?

MADHUKARIKA: Let the princess sit for a moment on this stone bench while I gather some flowers.

PADMAVATI: Shall we sit here, madam?

VASAVADATTA: Yes!

[*Both sit down.*]

MADHUKARIKA [*having gathered flowers*]: Look, princess, look! My hands are filled with *shephalika* flowers that shine like the crystals of arsenic.

PADMAVATI [*observing*]: Look, lady, look. What a variety of colors these flowers have!

VASAVADATTA: Oh, what lovely flowers!

MADHUKARIKA: Princess, shall I gather more?

PADMAVATI: No, no, my dear, no more.

VASAVADATTA: Why do you stop her, my dear?

PADMAVATI: If my noble lord comes here and sees this wealth of flowers, I will be so honoured.

VASAVADATTA: You love your husband so much?

PADMAVATI: I know not, madam. But when he is away from me, I feel lonely.

VASAVADATTA [*to herself*]: How difficult it is for me! Even she speaks thus!

PADMINIKA: With what dignity the princess has said, 'I love my husband.'

PADMAVATI: I have only one misgiving.

VASAVADATTA: What is it, what is it?

PADMAVATI: Was my noble lord as much to Vasavadatta as to me?

VASAVADATTA: Even more.

PADMAVATI: How do you know?

VASAVADATTA [*to herself*]: Ah! Partiality to my noble lord has again made me transgress the bounds of propriety. I know what I will say.

[*Aloud.*]

If her love was less, she would not have forsaken her own people.

PADMAVATI: Possibly.

PADMINIKA: Princess, tell your husband gently that you too would learn to play the *vina*.*

PADMAVATI: I did tell my noble lord.

---

*Lute.

VASAVADATTA: And what did he say?

PADMAVATI: Nothing. He sighed deeply and kept silent.

VASAVADATTA: What do you think that meant?

PADMAVATI: I think that he remembered the virtues of Vasavadatta and out of courtesy did not weep in my presence.

VASAVADATTA [*to herself*]: Blessed am I if that be true!

[*Enter King* UDAYANA *and* VASANTAKA.]

VASANTAKA: Aha, how lovely the pleasure garden looks with a thin sprinkling of *bandhujiva* flowers, fallen while being gathered. This way, my lord!

UDAYANA: My dear friend Vasantaka, here I come.

When I went to Ujjayini
and saw the daughter of Avanti's king,
I was thrown into an indescribable state of mind.
The god of Love wounded me with all his five arrows.
Of these the pain I still bear in my heart
and here I have been struck again.

Kama has but five arrows, how could he let fly a sixth?

VASANTAKA: Where has her ladyship Padmavati gone? Has she gone to the creeper bower? Or to the stone bench called 'Crest of the Hill' which is so strewn with *asana* flowers that it seems to be covered with a tiger's skin? Or to the groves of the seven-leaved trees with powerful pungent fragrance? Or to the wooden pavilion adorned with the frescoes of birds and beasts?

[*Looking up.*]

O, see, my lord, the flight of cranes advancing steadily along the clear autumnal sky as lovely as the outstretched arm of Baladeva.

UDAYANA: I see it, friend.

Now stretched in a line,
now broken apart;

now soaring high, now sinking low;
in its twists and turns
crooked like the figure of the Great Bear;
like a boundary line,
it divides in twain the sky;
bright like a serpent's belly
when it sheds its slough.

PADMINIKA: Look, princess, look at this flight of cranes advancing steadily, white and lovely like a garland of rose-tinted lotuses. O, the king!

PADMAVATI: Ah! My noble lord! Madam, I shall avoid meeting my lord for your sake. Let us enter this bower of *madhavi* creepers!

VASAVADATTA: Let us!

[*They act accordingly.*]

VASANTAKA: Her ladyship Padmavati must have come here and gone away.

UDAYANA: How do you know that?

VASANTAKA: Just look at these *shephalika* clusters from which the flowers have been plucked.

UDAYANA: O Vasantaka, what a variety of colors these flowers have!

VASAVADATTA [*to herself*]: The utterance of the name Vasantaka takes me back to Ujjayini once more.

UDAYANA: Vasantaka, let us sit down on this stone here and wait for Padmavati.

VASANTAKA: Very well, sir.

[*Sitting down and rising up again.*]

Hi, hi, the heat of the scorching autumn sun is unbearable. So let us enter this bower of *madhavi* creepers.

UDAYANA: Very well. Lead the way.

VASANTAKA: Yes!

[*Both walk about.*]

PADMAVATI: The noble Vasantaka is about to spoil everything. What shall we do now?

PADMINIKA: Princess, shall I keep my lord away by shaking this hanging creeper swarming with bees?

PADMAVATI: Yes, do so!

[PADMINIKA *acts accordingly*.]

VASANTAKA: Help! Help! Keep away, your honor, keep away!

UDAYANA: Why?

VASANTAKA: I am plagued by these damnable bees.

UDAYANA: No, no, do not say that! We must not frighten the bees. Look –

Intoxicated with honey and closely embraced by their love-sick mates
our footsteps will annoy the melodiously humming bees,
and like us they too will be parted from their sweethearts.
So let us stay here.

VASANTAKA: All right!

[*Both sit down*.]

MADHUKARIKA: Princess, we are imprisoned.

PADMAVATI: Happily my noble lord is seated here.

VASAVADATTA [*to herself*]: I am glad to see my noble lord in good health.

MADHUKARIKA: Princess, the lady's eyes are filled with tears.

VASAVADATTA: My eyes water because of the pollen of *kasha* flowers set flying by the wantonness of the bees.

PADMAVATI: Quite so!

VASANTAKA: O, this pleasure garden is deserted. There is something I want to ask. May I?

UDAYANA: Gladly.

VASANTAKA: Whom do you love – her ladyship Vasavadatta that was, or Padmavati of today?

UDAYANA: Now why do you put me in such a very awkward predicament?

PADMAVATI: Oh dear, my noble lord is in such a predicament,

VASAVADATTA [*to herself*]: And I too, unfortunate I!

VASANTAKA: Frankly, tell me frankly. One is dead, the other is nowhere near.

UDAYANA: No, my friend, no. I shall not answer. You are too talkative.

PADMAVATI: My noble lord has said everything!

VASANTAKA: O, I swear truly. I will not tell anyone. Here, I bite my tongue.

UDAYANA: My friend, I dare not speak.

PADMAVATI: O, how indiscreet he is! Even after that he does not understand his heart.

VASANTAKA: You will not tell me? If you do not, you shall not stir a single step from this stone bench. Your honor is my prisoner.

UDAYANA: What, by force?

VASANTAKA: Yes, by force.

UDAYANA: Well, then, we shall see!

VASANTAKA: Forgive me, your honor, forgive me! In the name of our friendship I ask you to tell the truth.

UDAYANA: What is to be done?

> By reason of her beauty, virtue and sweetness,
> much as I admire Padmavati
> she has not won my heart
> which is bound to Vasavadatta.

VASAVADATTA [*to herself*]: So may it be for ever. That is my reward for all my suffering. Ah, even my disguise is of value.

PADMINIKA: Princess, indeed my lord lacks courtesy.

PADMAVATI: Not at all, my dear, not at all! My noble lord does possess courtesy, for even now he remembers the virtues of noble Vasavadatta.

VASAVADATTA: Dear child, your words are worthy of your birth.

UDAYANA: I have spoken. Now you must tell me who your favorite is – Vasavadatta that was or Padmavati of today!

PADMAVATI: Now my noble lord plays Vasantaka's part.

VASANTAKA: What is the use of my idle talk? I admire both the ladies greatly.

UDAYANA: Fool, you made me speak and now you do not.

VASANTAKA: What, me too, by force?

UDAYANA: Yes, of course, by force!

VASANTAKA: Then you will never hear it.

UDAYANA: Forgive me, O great Brahmin, forgive me! Speak at your own sweet will, at your own sweet will.

VASANTAKA: Then listen, your honor! I admire her ladyship Vasavadatta greatly. Her ladyship Padmavati is young and beautiful, without anger and without conceit, affable and courteous. And there is one other great virtue. She comes to me with delicious dishes saying, 'Where can the noble Vasantaka have gone?

VASAVADATTA [*to herself*]: All right, Vasantaka, all right! Remember what you've said just now!

UDAYANA: Very well, Vasantaka, very well, I shall tell all this to Queen Vasavadatta.

VASANTAKA: Alas, Vasavadatta! Where is Vasavadatta? Vasavadatta is dead long ago.

UDAYANA [*sadly*]: So it is. Vasavadatta is no more!

With that jest you bewildered my mind
and by force of old habit these words escaped me.

PADMAVATI: Truly a charming romance is spoilt by this wretch.

VASAVADATTA [*to herself*]: Well, well, I am reassured. Ah, how sweet to hear such words and not to be seen!

VASANTAKA: Courage, your honor, courage! Destiny cannot be challenged. It is just so!

UDAYANA: Friend, you do not understand my condition. It is hard to forget a deep-rooted passion.

By constant memory one's sorrow is renewed.
Such is the way of life that the mind gains peace
only after cancelling the debt with tears.

VASANTAKA: His honour's face is wet with tears. I will fetch some water to wash it.

[*Exit* VASANTAKA.]

PADMAVATI: Madam, my noble lord's face is hidden in a veil of tears. Let us slip away meanwhile.

VASAVADATTA: Yes. Or rather you stay here. It is wrong for you to go away leaving your husband in a reminiscent mood. I will go alone.

MADHUKARIKA: What madam says is right. Let the princess go to him.

PADMAVATI: Should I really go to him?

VASAVADATTA: Yes, my dear, go!

[*Exit* VASAVADATTA.]

VASANTAKA [*entering with a lotus leaf filled with water*]: Here is my lady Padmavati.

PADMAVATI: My good Vasantaka, what is this?

VASANTAKA: . . . This is that . . . or that is this . . . !

PADMAVATI: Speak, speak, sir, speak!

VASANTAKA: My lady, the pollen of *kasha* flowers, wafted by the winds, got into the eyes of his honor and his face is wet with tears. Take him this water to wash his face, my lady!

PADMAVATI [*to herself*]: Ah, the courteous master has a courteous man!

[*Approaching* UDAYANA.]

Victory my noble lord! Here is water for washing the face.

UDAYANA: Ah, Padmavati! Vasantaka, what is this?

VASANTAKA [*whispering in his ear*]: It is like this –

UDAYANA: Good, Vasantaka, good.

[*Sipping water.*]

Padmavati, be seated!

PADMAVATI: As my noble lord commands,

[*She sits down.*]

UDAYANA: Padmavati,

my face is wet with tears
from the pollen of the *kasha* flowers
white as the autumnal moon
and wafted by the winds, fair lady.

[*To himself.*]

This young girl is newly wed;
should she hear the truth she would be hurt.
No doubt she has courage,
but a woman is by nature easily alarmed.

VASANTAKA: This afternoon his honour the king of Magadha will receive his friends, giving you, sir, the place of honor. Courtesy returned by courtesy begets affection. So let your honor rise.

UDAYANA: Yes, indeed. An excellent idea!

[*Rising.*]

It is easy to find in this world
men of eminent virtues and constant courtesy.
But it is difficult to find
those who can appreciate them.

[*Exeunt all.*]

END OF ACT FOUR

ACT FIVE

Interlude

[*Enter* PADMINIKA.]

PADMINIKA: Madhukarika! Mahdukarika! Come here. Quick.

[*Enter* MADHUKARIKA.]

MADHUKARIKA: Here am I, my dear. What do you want me to do?

PADMINIKA: Do you not know that princess Padmavati is ill with a headache?

MADHUKARIKA: Alas!

PADMINIKA: Run quick, my dear, and call madam Avantika. Just tell her that the princess is suffering from a headache and she will come of her own accord.

MADHUKARIKA: What will she do, my dear?

PADMINIKA: By telling pleasant stories she will relieve the headache of the princess.

MADHUKARIKA: That's true. Where is the bed of the princess made?

PADMINIKA: The bed is made in the Pavilion of the Sea. Now do go. I shall look for the noble Vasantaka so that he may inform my lord.

MADHUKARIKA: Yes.

[*Exit* MADHUKARIKA.]

End of Interlude

PADMINIKA: Now where shall I find the noble Vasantaka?

[*Enter* VASANTAKA.]

VASANTAKA: On this extremely joyful and auspicious occasion, fanned as it were by his marriage with Padmavati, the fire of love burns brighter than ever, in the heart of his honor the king of Vatsas, tortured by separation from his queen.

[*Observing* PADMINIKA.]

Hello, Padminika! What's the news?

PADMINIKA: Noble Vasantaka, do you not know that the princess Padmavati has a bad headache?

VASANTAKA: No, truly I do not know it, lady!

PADMINIKA: Well, then inform my lord about it. Meanwhile I will hurry up with the ointment for her head.

VASANTAKA: Where is the bed of Padmavati made?

PADMINIKA: The bed is made in the Pavilion of the Sea.

VASANTAKA: Go along, lady. I will tell his honor.

[*Exeunt both.*]

[*Enter* UDAYANA.]

UDAYANA:

Once again, in the passage of time
I bear the burden of married life.
But, to the virtuous daughter of Avanti's king,
to the one whose slender frame was burnt
by flames at Lavanaka,
like the lotus withered by frost,
my thoughts return.

[*Enter* VASANTAKA.]

VASANTAKA: Quick, your honor, come quick.

UDAYANA: Why?

VASANTAKA: The lady Padmavati has a bad headache.

UDAYANA: Who told you so?

VARANTAKA: Padminika.

UDAYANA: O, alas!

My sorrow today is as though softened
by a beloved endowed with grace
and beauty and other virtues.
Yet after my first experience of pain
and the former wound still rankling
I fear to meet the same fate with Padmavati.

Where is Padmavati?

VASANTAKA: The bed is made in the Pavilion of the Sea.

UDAYANA: Then show me the way.

VASANTAKA: Come, your honor.

[*Both walk about.*]

This is the Pavilion of the Sea. Enter, your honor.

UDAYANA: You go in first.

VASANTAKA: Oh, all right!

[*Entering.*]

Hello! Help! Stand back, your honor, stand back.

UDAYANA: Why?

VASANTAKA: The light of the lamp reveals the form of a cobra wriggling on the ground.

UDAYANA [*entering and looking around with a smile*]: O, this is what the idiot thinks to be a serpent.

Fool, you mistake for a serpent
the dangling wreath dropped from the portal arch
and lying stretched along the ground.
Swayed by the gentle evening breeze
faintly resembling the movement of a serpent.

VASANTAKA [*looking attentively*]: What your honor says is right. This indeed is not a cobra. Her ladyship Padmavati must have come here and gone away.

UDAYANA: Friend, she could not have come.

VASANTAKA: How does your honor know?

UDAYANA: What is there to know? Look!

The bed is unpressed and as unruffled as when made,
the quilt undisturbed and the clean pillow
unstained with cures for the aching head.
No decorations are placed
to divert the patient's gaze.
No person who goes to bed through sickness
is likely to leave it so soon and willingly.

VASANTAKA: Then let your honor sit down on the bed for a while and wait for her ladyship.

UDAYANA: Very well.
[*Sitting down.*]
Friend, I feel sleepy. Tell me a story.

VASANTAKA: I will tell you a story. Let your honor respond with a 'hum'.

UDAYANA: Very well.

VASANTAKA: There is a city called Ujjayini. It is said that in it there are delightful swimming pools.

UDAYANA: What, did you say Ujjayini?

VASANTAKA: If you do not like this story, I will tell you another.

UDAYANA: Friend, it is not that I do not like it. But
I sadly remember the daughter of Avanti's king,
who at the time of leaving thought of her people
with tears of love which clung to the corner of her eyes,
and dropped on my chest.
Moreover,
again and again during her lessons
she fixed her gaze on me.
And, dropping the bow, her hand
played in the air.

VASANTAKA: Well, I will tell you another. There is a city called Brahmadatta. There lived a king called Kampilya.

UDAYANA: What, what?

[VASANTAKA *repeats what he has just said.*]

Fool, say rather 'King Brahmadatta and Kampilya city'.

VASANTAK: What, King Brahmadatta and Kampilya city?

UDAYANA: That is so.

VASANTAKA: Then let your honor wait for a moment while I remember it. 'King Brahmadatta, Kampilya city.'

[*Repeating it several times.*]

Now listen, your honor! Why, his honor is asleep. The hour is very chilly. I will go fetch my shawl.

[*Exit* VASANTAKA.]

[*Enter* VASAVADATTA, *in the disguise of Avantika, a lady of Avanti, and* MADHUKARIKA.]

MADHUKARIKA: Come, madam, come. The princess has a severe headache.

VASAVADATTA: Alas! Where is the bed of Padmavati made?

MADHUKARIKA: The bed is made in the Pavilion of the Sea.

VASAVADATTA: Then lead the way.

[*Both walk around.*]

MADHUKARIKA: This is the Pavilion of the Sea. Enter, madam. Meanwhile I will hurry up with the ointment for her head.

[*Exit* MADHUKARIKA.]

VASAVADATTA: O, cruel are the gods to me. Even Padmavati, who was a source of comfort to my noble lord distracted by his bereavement, has fallen ill. I will go in.

[*Entering and looking around.*]

O, the carelessness of the servants! Padmavati is ill and they have left her with only a lamp to keep her company. There she lies asleep. I will sit down. But if I sit elsewhere it will seem as though I had but little love for her. So I will sit on the same bed.

[*Sitting down.*]

Why is it that now I am sitting with her my heart seems to thrill with joy? Happily her breathing is easy and regular. She must be free from her headache. Occupying just one side of the bed she seems to invite me to embrace her. I will lie by her side.

[*Proceeds to lie down.*]

UDAYANA [*talking in his sleep*]: O Vasavadatta –

VASAVADATTA [*rising suddenly*]: Ha! It is my noble lord and not Padmavati. Have I been seen? The great vow of Yaugandharayana is frustrated by my being seen!

UDAYANA: O daughter of Avanti's king!

VASAVADATTA: Happily my noble lord is only dreaming. There is no one about. I will stay here for a while and gladden my eyes and my heart.

UDAYANA: O darling! O beloved pupil! Answer me!

VASAVADATTA: I am speaking, my lord, I am speaking.

UDAYANA: Are you angry?

VASAVADATTA: O no! O no! I am only unhappy.

UDAYANA: If you are not angry why have you given up your ornaments?

VASAVADATTA: What is the use after this?

UDAYANA: Are you thinking of Virachika?

VASAVADATTA [*angrily*]: O no! Even here Virachika?

UDAYANA: I pray forgiveness for Virachika.

[UDAYANA *stretches out his hand.*]

VASAVADATTA: I have stayed too long. Some one might see me. I must go. But first I will put back on the bed my lord's hand that is hanging down.

[*She does so, and exits.*]

UDAYANA [*rising suddenly*]: Vasavadatta! Stay, stay! Alas!

Rushing out in my confusion
I struck against a panel of the door,
and now I know not clearly

if this vision was a reality.

[*Enter* VASANTAKA.]

VASANTAKA: Ah, his honor is awake.

UDAYANA: Friend, I have joyful news! Vasavadatta is alive.

VASANTAKA: Alas! Vasavadatta! Where is Vasavadatta? Vasavadatta is long dead.

UDAYANA: Nay, not so, friend!

As I lay asleep on this couch
after waking me, friend, she disappeared.
Rumanvan deceived me
when he said she perished in the fire.

VASANTAKA: Alas! It is impossible, is it not? Ever since I talked about the swimming pools, you were thinking of her ladyship. You saw her in a dream.

UDAYANA: So I saw only a dream.

If that be a dream
would that I had not been awakened;
and if that perchance be an illusion
may the illusion last for ever.

VASANTAKA: My dear friend! Don't be ridiculous! In this city dwells a fairy named Avanti Sundari. Maybe it is she whom you saw.

UDAYANA: No, no.

At the end of my dream when I woke up
I saw her face,
with eyes without collyrium,
and the long unbraided hair of one
who is still guarding her virtue.
Moreover, look, friend, look!
This arm of mine
clasped by the queen in her agitation
has the hair still standing on end
though it felt her touch only in a dream.

VASANTAKA: Do not imagine absurdities now. Come, your honor, come. Let us retire to the inner court.

[*Enter the* CHAMBERLAIN *of the Vatsa king at Kausambi.*]

CHAMBERLAIN: Victory unto my noble lord! Our sovereign king Darsaka sends this message, 'Your honor's minister Rumanvan has arrived with a large force to attack Aruni. My own victorious army with elephants, horses, chariots and soldiers is equipped and ready.' Let your honor therefore arise. Moreover,

your foes are divided.
Your subjects still faithful to you for your virtues
have gained confidence.
Arrangements are made to protect the rear
when you advance.
All that is needed to crush the foe
I have accomplished.
Forces have crossed the Ganges;
the kingdom of Vatsa is in your hands.

UDAYANA [*rising*]: Excellent! Now

I will assail that Aruni
adept in dreadful deeds,
and on the battlefield,
surging like a mighty ocean
with elephants and horses,
with a lashing spray of arrows
I will destroy him.

[*Exeunt all.*]

END OF ACT FIVE

ACT SIX

Interlude

[*Enter the* CHAMBERLAIN *of the Vatsa king at Kausambi.*]

CHAMBERLAIN: Hey there! Who is on duty here at the door of the golden arch?

[*Enter* VIJAYA.]

VIJAYA: Sir, it is I, Vijaya. What may I do?

CHAMBERLAIN: Good woman, take a message to Udayana, whose glory is enhanced by the capture of the Vatsa kingdom. Tell him, 'The Chamberlain of the Raibhya clan, has come here sent by Mahasena and with him Vasavadatta's nurse, Vasundhara, sent by her ladyship Angarvati. They are waiting at the door.'

VIJAYA: Sir, this is not the time and place for the message.

CHAMBERLAIN: How is this not the time and place?

VIJAYA: Listen, sir. Today someone in the Suryamukh Palace of my lord was playing on the *vina*. Hearing it my lord said, 'I seem to hear the sound of Ghoshvati.'

CHAMBERLAIN: Then? Then?

VIJAYA: Then going up to him soneone asked whence that *vina* came. He said, 'I saw it lying in a thicket on the banks of the Narmada. If it is of any use, take it to the king.' When they took it to him, my lord placed it on his lap and then fainted. When he came to himself, with his face stained with tears, my lord said, 'I have found you Ghoshvati. But she is nowhere to be seen.' Sir, that is why the hour is not suitable. How can I take the message?

CHAMBERLAIN: Lady, announce us. This also has something to do with the same matter.

VIJAYA: Sir, I will announce you at once. Why, here comes my lord descending from the Suryamukh Palace. I shall tell him here.

CHAMBERLAIN: Yes, madam.

[*Exeunt both.*]

End of Interlude

[*Enter* UDAYANA *and* VASANTAKA.]

UDAYANA:

O sweet-sounding *vina*,
you did repose on the breasts
and in the lap of the queen.
How did you then dwell
in that dreadful forest
where flocks of birds fouled
thy strings with dust?

And you are unfeeling, Ghoshvati. You do not remember the wretched queen –

How she pressed you to her side
as she held you on her hip.
How she softly embraced you
between her breasts when she was weary.
How she bewailed the loss of me
when from me she was parted.
How she smiled and chattered
in the intervals of playing.

VASANTAKA: Enough now of this excessive sorrow, your honor!

UDAYANA: Nay, not so, my friend!

My passion long suppressed
is reawakened by the *vina*.
But I see not that queen
to whom Ghoshvati was so dear.

Vasantaka, take Ghoshvati, to an artist, have it restrung and bring it back to me at once.

VASANTAKA: As your honor commands.

[*Exit* VASANTAKA *taking the vina.*]

[*Enter* VIJAYA.]

VIJAYA: Victory to my lord! A chamberlain of the Raibhya clan, sent by Mahasena, and Vasavadatta's nurse, the noble Vasundhara, sent by Queen Angarvati are waiting at the door.

UDAYANA: Then call Padmavati.

VIJAYA: As your lordship commands.

[*Exit* VIJAYA.]

UDAYANA: How now! This news is learnt by Mahasena, so soon!

[*Enter* PADMAVATI *and* VIJAYA.]

VIJAYA: Come, princess, come!

PADMAVATI: Victory to my lord!

UDAYANA: Padmavati, did you hear that the chamberlain of the Raibhya clan, sent by Mahasena, and Vasavadatta's nurse, the noble Vasundhara, sent by her ladyship Angarvati, have arrived and are waiting at the door?

PADMAVATI: My noble lord, I will be glad to hear the good news about my relatives.

UDAYANA: It is worthy of you to look upon the relatives of Vasavadatta as your own. Padmavati, be seated. Why will you not be seated?

PADMAVATI: My noble lord, would you want me to be seated by your side when you receive these people?

UDAYANA: What harm is there?

PADMAVATI: It may seem like indifference, as I am the second wife of my noble lord.

UDAYANA: It would be a greater fault to deprive such persons who deserve to meet my wife of the opportunity of seeing her. Be seated therefore.

PADMAVATI: As my noble lord commands.

[*Sitting down.*]

My lord, I am quite uneasy as to what the father or the mother would have to say.

UDAYANA: Just so, Padmavati,

My heart misgives me
as to what he will say.
I stole away his daughter
and failed to protect her;
through fickle fortune have I brought about
the ruin of the fair name I had acquired.
Like a son who has roused
his father's wrath, I am afraid.

PADMAVATI: There is no help when it is the hour of doom.

VIJAYA: The chamberlain and the nurse are waiting at the door.

UDAYANA: Conduct them here at once.

VIJAYA: As your lordship commands.

[*Exit* VIJAYA.]

[*Enter the* CHAMBERLAIN *of the Vatsa king, the* NURSE *and* VIJAYA.]

CHAMBERLAIN: Oh!

Great is my joy
on visiting this allied kingdom.
But when I recall the death of the princess
sorrow overtakes me.
O Fate, could you not have been content
to have the kingdom seized by enemies
and the queen spared?

VIJAYA: Here is my lord, Sir; approach him.

CHAMBERLAIN: [*approaching*]: Victory to my noble lord!

NURSE: Victory to my lord!

UDAYANA [*respectfully*]: Sir,

that king
who commands the rise and fall of royal dynasties,
that king
whose alliance I have sought,
is he well?

CHAMBERLAIN: Why, yes, Mahasena is well. He also inquires if here all be well.

UDAYANA [*rising from the seat*]: What are the commands of Mahasena?

CHAMBERLAIN: This is worthy of the son of Vaidehi. But let your honor be seated and hear the message of Mahasena.

UDAYANA: As Mahasena commands.

[*He sits down.*]

CHAMBERLAIN: Glory to you for recovering the kingdom seized by enemies. For

the timid and the weak
are incapable of enterprise,
and only the energetic
as a rule enjoy kingly glory.

UDAYANA: Sir, it is all due to the might of Mahasena. For

aforetime when I was vanquished
he fondled me along with his sons.
I stole away his daughter by force
and I have failed to protect her.
Now hearing about her death
he still shows me the same affection.
The king indeed is the cause
of my regaining the land
of my lawful subjects the Vatsas.

CHAMBERLAIN: This is the message of Mahasena. This lady here will convey the message of the queen.

UDAYANA: Ah, mother!

The chief among the sixteen queens,
the holy goddess of the city, my mother,
so afflicted was she with grief
at my departure, is she well?

NURSE: The queen is well. She inquires if your honor and all be well here.

UDAYANA: If all be well here! Mother, well, in this way!

NURSE: My lord! Do not torment yourself thus!

CHAMBERLAIN: Be strong, my noble lord! Mourned thus by my noble lord, the daughter of Mahasena, though dead, is yet not dead. But

whom can anyone protect
in the hour of death?
When the rope breaks
who can save the pitcher?
The same law holds for men and trees:
in season they perish,
in season they spring.

UDAYANA: Nay, not so, sir,

Mahasena's daughter,
my pupil and my beloved queen,
how can I help remembering her
even in births to come?

NURSE: The queen says thus, 'Vasavadatta is no more. You, who are to me and to Mahasena as dear as our Gopalaka and Palaka, have been from the first the son-in-law we wished for. For that purpose we brought you to Ujjayini. Under the pretext of learning the *vina* we gave her to you, with no ritual fire as witness. In your impetuosity you eloped without celebrating the wedding rites. So then we had the portraits of you and Vasavadatta painted on a panel and celebrated the marriage. We send you the portraits. May the sight make you happy!'

UDAYANA: Ah, extremely kind and worthy are the words of her ladyship.

These words are more precious
than the conquest of a hundred realms.
For I am not forgotten in her love
despite my grave offences.

PADMAVATI: My noble lord, I would like to see the portraits of the elders and pay my homage to them.

NURSE: Look, princess, look!

[*She shows her a picture-board.*]

PADMAVATI [*to herself on seeing it*]: Hum! Truly she bears a striking likeness to madam Avantika.

[*Aloud.*]

My noble lord, is this a good likeness of the queen Vasavadatta?

UDAYANA: It is not a likeness. It is her own self. O, alas!

How could cruel calamity befall
this charming complexion?
How could fire ravage
the sweetness of this face?

PADMAVATI: Looking at the portrait of my noble lord I will be able to tell if the other one is a good likeness of her ladyship or not.

NURSE: Look, princess, look!

PADMAVATI [*seeing it*]: The portrait of my noble lord shows a good likeness, I am convinced the other one is a good likeness of her ladyship.

UDAYANA: O queen, after looking at the portraits, I notice you seem delighted, but perplexed. How is that?

PADMAVATI: My noble lord, there lives here in this palace one who closely resembles this portrait.

UDAYANA: What? Of Vasavadatta?

PADMAVATI: Yes.

UDAYANA: Then bring her here at once.

PADMAVATI: My noble lord, before my marriage a certain Brahmin left her with me as a deposit, saying that she was his sister. Her husband is away and she shuns the sight of strangers. So observe her in my company, and you will know who she is.

UDAYANA:

If she be a Brahmin's sister
it is clear she is someone else.
One does come across persons
who resemble one another closely.

[*Enter* VIJAYA.]

VIJAYA: Victory to my lord! Here is a Brahmin from Ujjayini who says he placed his sister as a deposit in the hands of the princess and is waiting at the door to claim her back.

UDAYANA: Padmavati, is he the same Brahmin?

PADMAVATI: It must be.

UDAYANA: Offer the Brahmin welcome at once with the formalities proper to the inner court.

VIJAYA: As your lordship commands.

[*Exit* VIJAYA.]

UDAYANA: Padmavati, do you bring her here.

PADMAVATI: As my noble lord commands.

[*Exit* PADMAVATI.]

[*Enter* YAUGANDHARAYANA *and* VIJAYA.]

YAUGANDHARAYANA [*to himself*]: Ah!

I concealed the queen
in the king's interest.

Truly, only for his good
I did what I did.
Yet even when my task is fulfilled
my heart misgives me
as to what the king will say.

VIJAYA: Here is my lord. Approach him, sir!

YAUGANDHARAYANA [*approaching*]: Victory to your honor, victory!

UDAYANA: It seems I have heard this voice before. O Brahmin, did you leave your sister as a deposit in the hands of Padmavati?

YAUGANDHARAYANA: Why, yes.

UDAYANA: Then bring his sister here at once, at once!

VIJAYA: As your lordship commands.

[*Exit* VIJAYA.]

[*Enter* PADMAVATI, *accompanied by her retinue, and* VASAVADATTA *as Avantika.*]

PADMAVATI: Come, madam, come. I have good news for you.

VASAVADATTA: What is it? What is it?

PADMAVATI: Your brother has come.

VASAVADATTA: Happily he still remembers me.

PADMAVATI [*approaching*]: Victory to my noble lord! Here is the deposit.

UDAYANA: Padmavati, render her back. A deposit should be returned in the presence of witnesses. The worthy Raibhya and this good lady here will act as witnesses.

PADMAVATI: Sir, receive this lady!

NURSE [*looking at* VASAVADATTA *closely*]: O, this is princess Vasavadatta!

UDAYANA: What, the daughter of Mahasena? O queen, go into the inner court with Padmavati!

YAUGANDHARAYANA: No, no. She shall not go in, Assuredly she is my sister.

UDAYANA: What does your honor say? Assuredly she is the daughter of Mahasena!

YAUGANDHARAYANA: O king!

Born in the house of Bharatas
you are self-controlled, enlightened and pure,
To take her by force is unworthy of you,
who are a model of kingly duty.

UDAYANA: Well, let us see then the likeness of form. Draw the curtain aside!

YAUGANDHARAYANA: Victory to my lord!

VASAVADATTA: Victory to my noble lord!

UDAYANA: Ah, this is Yaugandharayana. This is the daughter of Mahasena.

Is it reality
or but a dream
that I see her once again?
I saw her before like this
and was deceived.

YAUGANDHARAYANA: Will my lord forgive me for taking away the queen?

[*He falls at the feet of* UDAYANA.]

UDAYANA [*raising him*]: You are Yaugandharayana assuredly!

Through feigned madness,
through wars,
through plans
prescribed by the codes of polity,
through your exertions
you lifted me up when I was sinking.

YAUGANDHARAYANA: I do not follow the fortunes of my lord.

PADMAVATI: Ah, this is the queen. Your ladyship, in treating you as a companion, I have unknowingly overstepped the bounds of propriety.

VASAVADATTA [*raising* PADMAVATI]: Rise up, rise up, O fortunate lady, rise up. The suppliant herself is to blame.

PADMAVATI: I am grateful to you.

UDAYANA: Friend, what was your purpose in taking away the queen?

YAUGANDHARAYANA: My only purpose was to save Kausambi.

UDAYANA: Why did you leave her as a deposit in the hands of Padmavati?

YAUGANDHARAYANA: The seers Pushpaka and Bhadraka had predicted that she was destined to be your lordship's queen.

UDAYANA: Did Rumanvan also know this?

YAUGANDHARAYANA: My lord, they all knew.

UDAYANA: Oh, what a rogue Rumanvan is!

YAUGANDHARAYANA: My lord, let his honor the noble Raibhya and her ladyship return this very day to announce the news of the safety of the queen.

UDAYANA: No, no! We will all go, taking the queen Padmavati.

YAUGANDHARAYANA: As your lordship commands.

END OF ACT SIX

EPILOGUE

STAGE MANAGER: This earth, stretching up to the sea,
with the Himalaya and Vindhya as her ear-drops;
marked with the symbol of a sovereign sway
may our lion-like lord rule over this earth.

PRODUCTION COMMENTS

An Interview with Mrinalini Sarabhai

The Vision of Vasavadatta, a prime example of Bhasa's historical plays, revolves around the legendary heroes Udayana, Pradyota and Darsaka, whose dates have been accepted as the sixth century B.C. Bhasa deals with king Udayana, the hero of a thousand legends, and his beloved queen, Vasavadatta.

In the interpretation of this play, the Western director must keep in mind the differences between the dramatic literature of the West and that of India. Unlike Western drama, which concentrates upon action or character, or on social, psychological, and philosophical themes, Indian drama is centered upon mood or moods which are called *rasas*. The Sanskrit play is not classified as a comedy, tragedy, melodrama, or farce, but is defined according to one of the *rasas*. The theory of *rasa* or aesthetic flavour is a deep, unifying aspect of all Indian art and difficult to interpret. Art in India has always been a state of being, slowly evolving, leading to the final merging with God. Numerous techniques contributed towards this aspiration; and the states of being were divided into Dominant moods (*stayi*) from which arose a multitude of Transitory (*vyabicari*) states, and these were again divided into various emotional qualifications. However the main *rasas* or sentiments are nine in number – *sringara* (the erotic), *hasya* (the humorous), *karuna* (the pathetic), *raudra* (the terrible), *vira* (the heroic), *bhayanaka* (the fearful), *bibhatsa* (the odious), *abhbuta* (the wondrous), and *santa* (the peaceful).

Bhasa was the master of all nine *rasas* of Indian drama, and in *The Vision of Vasavadatta* he employed a number of these: *sringara*, the main theme, is the sentiment of love and is divided into *sambhoga*, the union of lovers, and *vipralamba sringara*, the separation of lovers, as depicted in the love of Udayana and Vasavadatta; *hasya*, the sentiment of humor, is folly exploited in Vasantaka's character; *karuna*, the sentiment of pathos, is embodied in Vasavadatta, alone in her grief; and the heroic sentiment, *vira*, is found in the character of Udayana, who throughout the play exhibits strength in his struggle between reality and illusion.

Superficially, the characters may be thought of as conventional; but it is in performance that their depth and human qualities can be drawn and developed. The psychological effects of love upon the king and queen, bringing him to near-madness at the end, demonstrates Bhasa's insight into the complexities of human nature and his sense of the dramatic. The king is conventionally to be portrayed as a handsome, artistic, intelligent and sensitive person; that is, as the ideal king. Vasavadatta, his queen, is shy, sensitive, musical, and now suffers humiliation in the new role she must play. The young princess, Padmavati, is innocent, vivacious, and conscious of her responsible position. She shows no jealousy toward Udayana in his love for his lost queen, but loves him all the more.

In this play Vidusaka, the most ancient character found in Indian drama, is intelligent, courteous, and a constant companion to the king. He is a jester who amuses and advises, with a presence of mind that is popular with everyone.

However in this, as in all classical plays of India, it is the actor's psychological insight, his movement and gestures, costume and make-up, song and speech which are really responsible for the play's interpretation. Little or no scenery is used with only the necessary properties found on stage. The sense of harmony and serenity within the play is created in rehearsal. In the beginning, emphasis is placed upon the art of expression, or *abhinaya*, which is a very ancient Indian art. The gestures, or *hastas*, and their meanings are set down by Bharata in the book *Natyasastra*, written about the second century B.C. to the third century A.D. In this treatise, which is still available, the body and each of its parts must assume certain positions for the *abhinaya* which is as integral a part of acting as that of speech. Another treatise used by dancers today is the *Abhinaya Darpana* by Nandikeshvara which is a detailed exposition of the technique of expression.

I begin the actors with the chanting of a 'sacred' syllable which we pronounce 'OM'; a mantra which has been practiced for thousands of years. The Mundaka Upanishad tells us that 'the OM is the bow, the arrow is the self; Brahman the SELF is the mark. With concentration is IT to be penetrated; one should become one with IT as the arrow in the target.' When spoken, this particular sound leads to concentration, mental peace, clarity of voice and correct breathing. The actors then perform exercises for the use of various parts of the body. I taught them the *surya namaskars*, perhaps the best exercise for the body and mind.

We classify the major and minor limbs as the *angas* and the *pratyangas*. These two categories cover the entire body. Then there are the various features, the *upangas*, which include the eyes, eyebrows, cheeks, nose, lips, etc. Bharata has given detailed instruction for the usage of each feature. For instance, a gesture of the head is *adhomukha*, the head bent downwards to be used to denote shyness, sorrow, greeting, etc. The actor learns each movement separately and then makes use of them according to the mood of the character in the drama. After the actor has learned to exercise each particular part of his body, he then must learn how to control the whole body. After mastering these various movements, the actor learns the language of the hands called *hasta mudras*. This is a complicated process, but I used only those movements necessary in *The Vision of Vasavadatta* and did not emphasize the religious meaning of each hand symbol. For the Western actor, training in the use of the hands takes a great deal of time since the actor must learn that each finger has a life of its own, and that the shoulder, the elbow, and the fingers are alive and separate. The actor must become aware that his fingers have life, his eyes have life, his mouth has life, that every part of his body has life and is separate from the whole, As the actor perfects the movements and gestures, which reveal the relationship between the Inner Divine self and the outer human form, a quality of understanding and sensitivity essential to Indian drama, then the aesthetic aspects of the player and play reach significant form.

In the staging of the play, the costumes, make-up, and jewelry should be as authentic as possible to assist in the creation of the visual feeling or atmosphere of India. *Abhinaya*, the art of expression, has four divisions, namely, *angika*, *vachika*, *aharya* and *sattvika*. *Aharya* is decoration, the costumes and make-up, *sattvika* is interpretation of the subject. In classical drama it is usual to show the social status of the character, the geographic locale or origin, and this historical period through the use of costume. Unless the role calls for special footwear, the actor is barefoot. This is traditional since the characters would remove their footwear in the home or in the temple. As the actor becomes familiar with the play, he will begin to realize Bhasa's command of language both in poetry and prose, a command which led Jayadeva (A.D. 1200) to say that the playwright was the 'laughter of poetry.'

The director, through reading Bhasa's plays and critical

studies of his works, becomes aware of his simplicity of style, psychological insight, sharpness of characterization, deep love of nature, and use of dramatic irony. With this knowledge, and understanding the intertwining of music, speech, and movement in Indian drama, the director will be able to present a significant production of *The Vision of Vasavadatta*, the most poetic of Bhasa's plays. Actor and audience will then experience one of the most sophisticated forms of world theatre.

THE WEST CHAMBER

An Introduction to Yüan Drama and

THE WEST CHAMBER

By Daniel S. P. Yang

IT is often said that the history of the Chinese theatre can be traced back to the twelfth century B.C. or so; actually the Chinese theatre as a mature dramatic form started rather late, The first extant Chinese play, entitled *Chang Hsieh chuan-yüan* 'Chang Hsieh, the Doctor of Letters,' is placed by most scholars in the early thirteenth century – a much later date than the Greek theatre and the Sanskrit theatre. The full-fledged Chinese drama did not appear until the Yüan dynasty (1234–1368) when China was under the control of the Mongols.

There are reasons why Chinese drama developed so late. The most essential one can be attributed to the puritanical view of orthodox Confucianists who looked upon anything playful with absolute disdain. The Chinese term for 'drama' is unfortunately synonymous with 'playfulness,' thus none of the early scripts were listed in any of the bibliographical sections of dynastic histories. This being the temperament of Confucianists with regard to drama, the only chance for the development of Chinese drama occurs at a time when orthodox scholarship loses its grip on the populace and the society.

In 1234 Genghis Khan's son Ogutai overthrew the kingdom of the Chin and established the Yüan dynasty. Forty-five years later Kublai Khan overthrew the southern Sung empire, putting the whole of China under his control. The early Mongol emperors had a deep suspicion of Confucian scholars, who consistently refused to cooperate with the alien government. The life of Chinese intellectuals during the Mongol reign was most pitiful. Within the ten castes of society the scholars were placed down toward the bottom, only slightlys higher in position than the beggars. The triennial civil examination, hitherto the only avenue for Chinese scholars seeking a career, was discontinued for almost eighty years. This setback to classical scholarship was, however, a blessing in disguise. The literature cherished by the common people gradually gained status and received unprecedented attention and nurture. Vernacular novels, folk songs, and full-fledged dramas were all products of this dark age. The writing of drama, hitherto considered an unworthy occupation by orthodox Confucianists, was now taken seriously by scholars who needed a means of living. The new group of playwrights soon found this literary excursion a way of satisfying their creative desire and at the same time of expressing their disappointment with the new society and rulers. This new form of vernacular literature was further encouraged by the uncivilized Mongol rulers who could at least appreciate drama, music and singing. For these reasons Chinese drama attained full maturity in this period of political disunion.

Yüan drama is governed by strict conventions. A play usually has four acts, plus a 'wedge' in the form of a prelude or interlude. The 'wedge' (*hsieh-tzu* in Chinese), whether placed before the first act or between acts, enables the playwright to include more material without violating the four-act structure of the play. The songs in each act must belong to the same musical scale and follow a definite pattern. The requirements of the music determine the length of the lines as well as the words accented. All the sung passages in the four acts, except the 'wedge,' are given to the principal actor, whether male or female. Occasionally one may find exceptions to this rule. For instance in this very play, as translated by Professor Henry W. Wells for this anthology, both the hero and the heroine sing, and even the maid Hung Niang is given two sung passages – a rare case in Yüan drama.

The Yüan stage employs stock characters – a convention found in all classical Chinese theatre forms. There are two major roles on the Yüan stage: the *mo* (male) and the *tan* (female); each is subdivided into variations of the main role. The protagonist of a play is often impersonated either by the *cheng-mo* (principal male) or the *cheng-tan* (principal female) actor. There are also two minor roles: the *ching* (painted face) and the *ch'ou* (comic). Every role has its individual techniques of acting as well as its own costume and make-up styles. Of the three unities in the Aristotelian sense, only unity of action is followed by Yüan dramatists. There is no rule which calls for the observation of the unities of time and place. The dramatic action in a play often covers a long span of time, switching from one locale to the other. The play is enacted on a platform stage devoid of scenery, a convention still observed in later dramatic forms such as the *K'un-ch'ü* and the Peking opera.

In comparison with writers and poets of other periods in the history of Chinese literature, Yüan dramatists are perhaps the least known. Although over a hundred names of dramatists have come down to us through the effort of a Yüan writer Chung Ssu-ch'eng, who compiled a book in 1330 entitled *Lu kuei pu* or 'A Record of Deceased Personages in the Theatrical Profession,' we are still unable to find enough material for a continuous biography of a dramatist. The total number of Yüan plays is quite impressive. Today we have some 600–700 play titles, of which about 160 are extant. Though the Yüan plays have traditionally been classified into twelve categories since the Ming period, the contemporary scholar

Lo Chin-t'ang reclassified them into eight categories by combining some of the repetitious elements. The eight categories of these extant plays are further classified by Liu Wu-chi (*An Introduction to Chinese Literature*, Indiana University Press, 1966, p. 171.) into six categories: (1) love and intrigue; (2) religious and supernatural; (3) historical and pseudo-historical; (4) domestic and social; (5) murder and lawsuits; and (6) bandit-hero. *Hsi-hsiang chi* or 'The Story of the West Chamber' belongs to the first category and is a supreme example of classical drama.

The authorship of *Hsi-hsiang chi* has long been a heated topic of controversy. A pentalogy, the original play is a series of five parts, each containing four acts. In this respect this play is not a good example of Yüan drama which should have only four acts. According to most scholars, the first four parts were written by Wang Shih-fu and the fifth part by Kuan Han-ch'ing, both of whom were noted playwrights in the thirteenth century. Wang Shih-fu wrote fourteen plays, of which three are still extant. Kuan Han-ch'ing, who has been hailed as the 'Shakespeare of China,' was the author of some sixty plays of which eighteen have survived. The legend says that when Wang was writing this play he concentrated so intensely upon the project that after finishing the first song in Part IV, Act 3, he felt his genius had been exhausted and died of a stroke. After his death his good friend and contemporary Kuan Han-ch'ing completed the play with a conventional happy ending. The legend must have been created by some later admirers of Wang and is highly unreliable. Nevertheless, the fifth and last part, commonly known as the 'continuation,' is definitely inferior in poetry and melodramatic in plot. It is inconceivable that a dramatist of Kuan Han-ch'ing's reputation and magnitude would have written a sequel of inferior quality to the work of a younger contemporary.

Scholars today are generally content to attribute the whole five parts to Wang Shih-fu and to blame the inferiority of the fifth to the old age and failing health of the author.

The story of how the talented young scholar Chang Chün-jui wooed and won the hand of the beautiful Ts'ui Ying-ying had been recorded in two Chinese literary works prior to the play of Wang Shih-fu. The first one was a romantic literary tale entitled 'The Story of Ying-ying' (*Ying-ying chuan*) written by the T'ang poet Yuan Chen of the eighth century. The second one was a long narrative poem 'The Story of the West Chamber' (*Hsi-hsiang chi*) written by Tung Chieh-yüan (i.e. 'Scholar Tung,' *chieh-yüan* being an honorary title given to a scholar), a professional poet in the reign of Emperor Chang-tsung (1190–1208) of the Chin dynasty. In this version, the original story of Ying Ying has been greatly expanded. Besides numerous additions of situations and episodes, Tung made a major change in the last part of his long narrative. Instead of the original pathetic ending – the desertion of Ying Ying by Scholar Chang – Tung brought the romance to a happy ending in which the lovers were finally united. Wang Shih-fu's play followed Tung's version very closely. The great length of Tung's narrative poem also caused Wang to expand his play into a twenty-act pentalogy – an unheard-of length for a Yüan drama.

Hsi-hsiang chi is a masterpiece of plot construction, characterization, and poetry. Professor Liu Wu-chi in his book (p. 172) describes this play as follows: 'The delicate romantic atmosphere is laden with lovers' sighs and tears, the tingling notes of the zither, the fragrance of incense, the moonlight breeze, flowery shadows, and, above all, the yearnings, the expectancy, and the ecstasy of the fulfillment of love.' Against this background of tender love, there are moments of tension and comic relief which together make this play one of the most lively pieces in the Yüan drama repertoire as far as dramatic action is concerned. The play contains much beautiful poetry. The scene of Scholar Chang's first glimpse of Ying Ying, that in which Ying Ying is praying in the garden as Scholar Chang peeps in from behind a wall, and the farewell scene now rank with the foremost pieces of classical Chinese poetry.

Through the creative genius of Wang Shih-fu, Scholar Chang and Ying Ying have since become the archetype of romantic lovers in the mind of Chinese readers and audiences – the talented scholar (*ts'ai-tzu*) and the beautiful maiden (*chia-jen*) – to be depicted over and over again in fiction and drama. But the author's most successful portrayal of a character is Hung Niang, the witty maid and companion of Ying Ying. Wang Shih-fu has written some of the best scenes for her. As the play progresses we see Hung Niang rising in stature, until in certain crucial moments she commands an even more important position than the two lovers. She is, as Professor Liu Wu-chi observes (p. 173), 'as adept in repartee and raillery as in the stratagems of love. She knows how to tell innocent lies, how to prevaricate, to tease, to persuade, to convince, to console, and to defy.' The success of Wang Shih-fu in his depiction of the maid is further proved by the fact that in many regional versions (including the Peking opera version) of *Hsi-hsiang chi*, the title of the play is often changed to *Hung Niang* with the maid playing the lead.

This play has been translated several times into Western languages. The earliest one was a French version by Stanislas Julien, published in *L'Atsume Gusa*, 1872–80. This publication completed the partial translation (of seven acts) which had been made some years before by the same author for *L'Europe Littéraire*. Julien's version was entirely in prose. It contained sixteen acts without the 'continuation.' In 1926 a German version by Vincenz Hundhausen was published. It was a free adaptation with the sung passages rendered into German rhymed couplets. The same version, with its twenty-one wood-engraving plates, was reprinted in 1954. The second French version came out around 1928. Translated by Soulié de Morant, it had the interesting title *L'amoureuse Oriole, jeune fille*. The third French version was a thesis written by Chen Pao-ki at the University of Lyon in 1934.

Two English versions of this play appeared in 1935 and 1936 respectively. The 1935 version, entitled *The Romance of the Western Chamber*, was translated by S. I. Hsiung, a Chinese scholar who had gained quite a reputation with his translation and production of the Peking opera *Lady Precious Stream* (*Wang Pao-ch'uan*). The 1936 version, entitled *The West Chamber*, was made by Henry H. Hart, who also wrote books such as *A Chinese Market*, *The Hundred Names*, etc. In these two versions, spoken dialogues have been rendered into prose and sung passages into free, unrhymed verse. Both versions followed the original quite faithfully and both were highly readable. The Hsiung version has twenty scenes including the 'continuation,' while the Hart version has only fifteen scenes without the much too contrived happy ending. Both versions (and this present translation, too) were mainly based upon the 1956 edition of Chin Sheng-t'an, a slightly tampered with and truncated edition yet considered prestigious by people up to the second half of this century.

The present translation by Professor Henry W. Wells of Columbia University is the third and newest English version of *Hsi-hsiang chi*. It differs from the other two in one major aspect: the whole play has been rendered into English verse and all sung passages rhymed. Yüan drama is poetic drama with a high literary value. All noted playwrights were skilled poets. A play is judged not so much by its plot and prose dialogue as by its lyrical sung passages. The sung passages in

Yüan drama, called the *ch'u*, rank with the Sung *tz'u* and T'ang *shih* as the three leading styles in classical Chinese verse. The writing of these dramatic songs is governed by rigid tonal requirements, and each song follows a prescribed pattern with a rhyming scheme. The songs are then set to music to be sung by actors in performance. Although the scores of these dramatic songs have unfortunately been lost, readers of Yüan drama can still appreciate a good percentage of its musical qualities through the tonal and metrical arrangement of the sung passages. To eliminate the lyrical-musical qualities of a Yüan drama in a free, literal translation is almost as mistaken as to perform the libretto of an opera as straight drama without the music. Unfortunately this seems to be the case in most English translations of Yüan dramas. The Wells translation, therefore, is unique, plausible and praiseworthy in this respect.

Hsi-hsiang chi has held the stage for nearly eight centuries and today it still delights Chinese audiences in various regional theatre forms. We are sure that this third English version will generate a new literary interest among Western readers, and we hope that this fine piece of classical Chinese drama will henceforward grace the Western stage more often.

THE WEST CHAMBER
(HSI-HSIANG CHI)

Attributed to
WANG SHIH-FU

Rendered into English Verse
by
HENRY W. WELLS

2. *The West Chamber:* from a performance in Taiwan, Republic of China.

THE WEST CHAMBER

CAST OF CHARACTERS

MADAME TS'UI, widow of the late Prime Minister
YING YING, her daughter
HUAN LANG, an adopted son
HUNG NIANG, their family servant
CHANG, son of the late Minister of Rites
FA PÊN, abbot of the P'u Chiu Monastery
FA TSUNG, his assistant
HUI MING, a monk
SUN FEI HU, 'The Flying Tiger,' a bandit chief
TU CH'ÜEH CHÜN-SHIH, 'The White Horse General'

Note: In this play, passages which are to be sung by the actors are printed in italic.

Part One

SCENE ONE

[*Enter* MADAME TS'UI, HUNG NIANG, YING YING *and* HUAN LANG.]

MADAME TS'UI: My family name was Chêng, my lord's was Ts'ui.
Once Prime Minister, he grew ill and died.
We had one daughter only, small Ying Ying,
Now in her nineteenth year, a true past-mistress
Of every art appropriate for a girl,
Above all, sewing and embroidery.
Verse she writes with special talent, drawing
The characters with grace. She is well read
In history. She makes her calculations
Accurately on the abacus.
My husband promised me he would betroth
This daughter to my brother's oldest son,
Chêng Hêng. My noble brother also ranked
Among the highest ministers of state.
However, since the time of family mourning
Continues, marriage has not occurred.
This little maid standing at my right side
Has served my daughter from her babyhood.
She is Hung Niang. This small boy at my left
Is Huan Lang, adopted by my husband
So that his family line would still exist.
After my husband's death, I, with Ying Ying,
Have brought his coffin on its final journey
For burial with his parents in Po-ling.

Great troubles have beset us on the way,
Detaining us in Ho-chung Prefecture.
Here we have deposited the coffin
Safely in the P'u Chiu Monastery,
Established by the Empress Wu Tsê-t'ien.
Fa Pên, its abbot, was originally
Mentioned for ordination by my husband.
On this account a guest-house was erected
In the West Wing. There we are resting now.
Quite recently I have dispatched a letter
To Chêng Hêng in the capital requesting
His help to take the coffin to Po-ling.
I well recall that when my husband lived
We entertained in prodigality
With hundreds in attendance. Three or four
Now serve us. This great change has saddened me.

My husband died at his official post;
My affluence conluded with his life.
Here in the monastery bleak distress
Overpowers his daughter and his wife.
Our hope is lost to reach his parents' tomb,
Tears as thick as blood witness our gloom.

Moreover, spring has faded and today
This heavy season brings on weariness.
Hung Niang, go to the Western patio
To find if anyone walks there. If no one,
Escort your mistress on an easy walk
Where she may find an hour of recreation.

HUNG NIANG: I shall in everything obey you, madame.

YING YING: *We have arrived here at the close of spring,*
The monastery gates locked at all hours.
I bear my pains in silence yet I most

Resent the East Wind ruining the flowers.
[*Exeunt.*]
[CHANG *enters on horseback with a* SERVANT *who walks and carries his lute.*]

CHANG: My family name is Chang: my given name
Is Kung, my name in courtesy, Chün-jui.
My birth was near Lo-yang. My honored father,
President of the Board of Rites. As yet
Having no office, I am travelling.
This is the first day of the second month,
The seventeenth year of the period Chêng-yüan.
My prime wish is to reach the capital
To take the highest state examination.
I've had to pass through the prefecture Ho-chung,
Where I have a friend whose proper name
Is Tu, his other names, Ch'üeh and Chün-shih.
He comes from the same city as myself.
As fellow students, we became sworn brothers.
In time he left his literary studies
And in the military examinations
Came out the first. Shortly he was appointed
Chief General in the western operations,
Commander of a hundred thousand men,
Assigned the guardians of the P'u Kuan Pass,
Since I am, happily, near by, I long
To see my elder brother once again,
After which I can reach the capital.
Long have I bent over the classic pages
Lit by fireflies or the moonlight snow.
I wander still by river and lake, not knowing
When I may realize my high ambitions.
My case is stated in an ancient rhyme:
'A sword lies hidden in the autumn stream

That well might serve the empire in its need
While rich caparison of horse and man
Burdens alike the horseman and his steed.'

I travel through the empire to enlarge
My thoughts, from friend to friend and town to town,
Never bound upon a stated path,
Wandering as wind-blown swirls of thistledown.

I raise my eyes to heaven and there I see
The sun on the horizon not so far
Removed from me as I am grieved to find
The Capital and my ambitions are.
On every page a bookworm bores with pain,
Bores in, never to issue out again!

I have taken state examinations
So often and so long that in the hall
My seat never cools off and there my ink-stone,
Though hard as iron, is ground into a ball.

To rise into the official heaven and soar
Like the enchanted p'eng bird in the sky
For ten long years you must labor diligently
Beneath the light of snow and firefly.
These times are bad; vulgarity prevails;
A man of culture naturally fails.

Turning to banality, he proves
Either a trifler in insipid verse
Or else a picker-up of learned fragments
And barren annotations, which is worse!

Why look! while wrapped in melancholy thoughts
I've reached the borders of the Yellow River!
Ah! what panorama it presents!

Where is there any fortress that surpasses
This wall of wind and water girdling in
The separate provinces of Ch'i and Liang,
Separating those of Ch'in and Chin?

Granting protection to the Yü and Yen,
It thrusts its snow-white crests into the sky.
The rapids on its shining surface rival
Cumulus clouds of autumn hastening by.

Floating bridges lashed with bamboo cords
Are jet-black dragons crouching in a pit.
It serves nine states from east to west; a hundred
Streams from north and south pour into it.

That boat upon its breast flies like an arrow
Shot with high vigor from a twanging bow.
Its current is the Milky Way in Heaven,
A cataract whose source no mortals know.

It rises past the clouds to rush unceasing,
Pouring at last into the Eastern Sea,
Watering a myriad flowers that blossom
Along its green-clad banks perennially.
Would I could float where these mad waters run,
Visiting at last the moon and sun!

While pronouncing my encomium
Upon the river, I have reached the town.
Lute-bearer, hold my horse. Let's look about
And call the keeper of this handsome inn.

INNKEEPER: I am the host of this famed hostelry
Located on the Street of Graduates.
We have a neat room here where you may stay.

CHANG: Then give me your best room. – Innkeeper, tell me
What are the leading sites about the city?

INNKEEPER: The famous P'u Chui Monastery is here,
Erected by the Empress Wu Tsê-t'ien
To be a nursery for noble thinking.
Travellers coming from the north or south
Never fail to visit such a temple.
This is the only site we have of interest
Where you may certainly regale yourself.
CHANG: Boy, put down my bags. Unbind my horse.
I shall go afoot to see this abbey.
SERVANT: I shall do precisely as you wish.
[CHANG *and his* SERVANT *go out*, FA TSUNG *enters.*]
FA TSUNG: I'm monk Fa Tsung, disciple of Fa Pên,
The abbot of our temple. He has gone
Elsewhere today to lead a special service
While I remain beside the monastery
So that if any visitor arrives
I may take note of it and then report
To him on his return. I'm at the gate
That overlooks the mountain to perceive
If any traveller should step this way.
CHANG [*entering*]: 'A path winds toward a Buddhist holy place
Where flowers and branches sweetly interlace.'
This must be it!
FA TSUNG: Where do you come from, sir?
CHANG: I have travelled from the region of Lo-yang.
I hear your shrine is tranquil and secluded.
I have come first to worship Buddha's image,
Secondly, to pay honor to your abbot.
FA TSUNG: My master is not here, but I, sir, am
Fa Tsung, the abbot's dutiful disciple.
Come to our hall and drink a bowl of tea.
CHANG: Well, since the abbot is not here, I shall not

Linger for tea, but I should much enjoy
A survey of the architecture.

FA TSUNG: Good, sir,
There I shall certainly delight to aid you.

CHANG: Indeed, this is a noble edifice!

Straying through the halls, I've seen above
Buddha's shrine, the abbot's patio,
This bell-tower in the front, the kitchen west,
While the monks' modest quarters lie below.

The main hall for expounding Buddha's law
Lies northward. I have climbed the sacred stairs
Of your pagoda and to the great Kuan Yin
And all the Arhats offered up my prayers.

But tell me, what is this magnificent
Pavilion? Will you kindly show me in?

FA TSUNG: You must not go in there! Please remain here!
This pavilion serves for the time being
As residence for the family of the late
Prime Minister, his Excellency, Ts'ui.
[YING YING *and* HUNG NIANG *enter.* CHANG *sees them.*]

CHANG: *Suddenly I have perceived a woman*
Whom I have loved five centuries ago,
Blessèd in another incarnation!
Thousands of women have not moved me so!
My eyes are dazzled. My lips refuse to speak.
My soul ascends to heaven's highest peak!

Meanwhile she stands unmoved while thousands gaze.
She seems unconscious, but with perfect grace
Bends her head aside to note a flower
Held in her hand, a smile upon her face.

Can this be Paradise and she immortal?
The heart's Elysium or the heart's despair?
Smiling or sober, she is lovely always,
Flower-bright ornaments decking her hair.

Her eyebrows, arching like the crescent moon,
Touch the hairs that wave behind her ears.
Before she speaks she blushes. From her teeth,
Jade-white, and lips like cherries, her smile appears,
And when this oriole speaks her sweet voice bears
Likeness to the bird whose name she shares.

YING YING: Dear Hung Niang, I wish to see my mother.

CHANG: *Every step she takes moves my affections;*
All the motions of her body please;
She has a thousand wiles and subtle charms,
Like willows swaying in an evening breeze.

[*Exeunt* YING YING *and* HUNG NIANG.]

She treads on fallen petals with noiseless step;
Their rose-sweet, aromatic scents diffuse
Heaven's own perfume, while the dust itself
Is rich from the light pressure of her shoes.

Even without the glances of her eyes
Her gait reveals the secrets of her heart.
Slowly she walks, reaches her door at last
And, smiling, seems reluctant to depart.
She turns to look at me and with her eyes
Confers on me a glimpse of Paradise.

Now she is gone, the door behind her shut,
Her silence richer to me than all words,
I only see the willows blurred by mist
And hear the muted chirping of the birds.

Behind me she has left the scented blooms
Of pear trees, a white wall against the blue;
Against the obduracy of heartless heaven
What is there that a mortal man can do?

Her fragrance, like the lily and the musk,
Still lingers but the tinkling of her jade
Belt-ornaments, that once were softest music,
On her departure now begin to fade.

Still the East Wind sways the willow branches
That touch the petals of the peach in bloom
But now the flower-like face of her I worship
Is hidden, leaving me in utter gloom!

On that side of the fatal wall there dwell
Those of the late Prime Minister's family;
On this side dwells the deity of Mercy,
Küan Yin, the goddess of the Southern Sea.

I strain my eyes with watching; in my throat
I feel the fierce constriction of desire.
Soon the longing of my love will set
The very marrow of my bones afire.

How could I resist her parting glance?
Even if I were made of iron or rock,
My heart would burst into an eager flame
Summoned to life by this celestial shock.

By the pavilion flowers stand as they were,
The sun at zenith marks the height of day.
The shade of the pagoda now is round;
Spring flashes in its rapturous array.
But her I do not see, whose brighter eyes
Turned Buddha's shrine into a Paradise.
[*Exeunt.*]

SCENE TWO

[*Enter* MADAME TS'UI *and* HUNG NIANG.]

MADAME TS'UI: Carry a message for me, Hung Niang.
Go into the temple and inquire
When the abbot wishes to perform
The funeral service for my husband. Then
Return and tell me what the abbot said.

HUNG NIANG: Yes, I shall take the message to him promptly.
[*Exeunt.*]

FA PÊN [*entering*]: I am the aged priest, Fa Pên, the abbot
Of P'u Chiu Monastery. Last night I
Presided at a village ceremony.
I have not heard if we had visitors.
[*He addresses* FA TSUNG, *who in turn enters.*]

FA TSUNG: Last night a Bachelor of Arts arrived
Coming from Lo-yang, who wished to see you.
Having missed you, he may soon return.

FA PÊN: Wait by the mountain gate and let me know
If he comes back.

FA TSUNG: Master, indeed I shall.

CHANG [*entering*]: Since I saw that girl, all night my eyes
Declined to close in sleep. Today I'm going
To see the abbot. I have much to tell him.
[*He bows to* FA TSUNG.]
Show mercy to me, Fa Tsung, in my plight
Or I shall always hold you in despite!

FA TSUNG: Welcome, good sir. This humble priest, however,
Cannot fathom the strange words you uttered.

CHANG: *Please rent me as a guest one half a cell!*
I wish to live next door to her I love
With such distraction. Though I cannot seize
Her jade-like body, I shall be grateful of
The chance to mark her motions and her face,
Lovely as clouds afloat in lucid space.

FA TSUNG: Pardon, I cannot comprehend such words!

CHANG: *Formerly when I saw a powdered face*
I myself would blush with natural shame;
Painted eyebrows piqued me with distrust;
Amorous adornments were the same.
But now that I have finally gazed on her
All my soul and spirits are in a whirr.

FA TSUNG: Excuse me, but I do not grasp your words!
My master has been waiting a long time
Your humble servant hastens to announce you.

CHANG: *I see a man whose head is white as snow,*
Whose eyebrows are like hoarfrost, but whose look
Is of a healthy youth. His voice is strong.
Had I not known him, I had undertook
To think this noble human was instead
Buddha without the halo at his head.

FA PÊN: Enter, sir, in my religious cell.
Last night I was away. So I have failed
To welcome you. Be kind and pardon me!

CHANG: I long have known of your high reputation
And now have come in hope to hear you preach.
Last evening I was sorry to have missed you.
Today on seeing you I am acquiring

Pleasures from three past existences.

FA PÊN: May I ask you, sir, what is your family,
Where do you come from, why do you travel here?
Tell me your surname and two other names.

CHANG: My family home lies westward of Lo-yang.
Chang is my surname, while my second name
Is Kung, and my name in courtesy, Chün-jui.
I am journeying on my way to take
Examinations at the capital.

My master questions me. I shall reply
Frankly exposing to him all my heart.
Lo-yang was my birthplace. I have travelled
Widely through the Empire's every part.

I settled for a while in Hsien-yang.
My father graced the Board of Ceremony;
He died of illness in his fiftieth year,
A just man, leaving me small patrimony.

Your humble servant has no more ambition
Than to have you grant as gracious boon
The gift of your instruction, for your merits
Are pure as air and lustrous as the moon.

Your scholar, travelling lightly as he is,
Has slender means to manifest esteem
But begs you to accept an ounce of silver,
Hoping you will receive it with a smile.

A scholar's gifts are light as scraps of paper.
He is ignorant of money and of trade.
He feels no fear when men observe his weakness
Nor cares for what his conduct may be weighed.

My coming was alone to visit you.
Let not my small gift be misunderstood.

It will not buy you firewood, soup or tea
Nor gain your monastery lavish food.

Provided you shall take the girl inside
My messages, my object will be won.
Whether I myself shall live or die,
I never shall forget your kindness done.

FA PÊN: Why do you talk in such mysterious ways?
Surely you have more definite requests!
CHANG: I cannot study. So I have dared to ask
A room for rent. Down in the noisy inn
Classical reading is too difficult,
But here from dawn to evening I can listen
To your instruction. I shall gladly pay you
Whatever monthly rent is rightly due.
FA PÊN: You have your choice from many vacant rooms,
Or, should you wish, you certainly may share
My cell. Say only what is your desire.
CHANG: *I do not wish a room well stored with incense.*
Nor any decorated panelled hall.
I do not wish a chamber north or east
But merely one beside the western wall.
That location only suits me well.
Breathe no word about your abbot's cell!

HUNG NIANG [*entering*]: My mistress has dispatched me to inquire
When the abbot wishes to perform
The funeral service for her husband, then,
Returning, tell her what the abbot said.
[*She sees* FA PÊN.]
O sir, ten thousand blessings light upon you!
My mistress has dispatched me to inquire
When it is your intention to perform

The ceremonial service for her husband?
CHANG: Ah, what a charming girl her servant is!

Her manners and her language argue her
A maid who serves a noble family.
No one in her conduct can detect
The slightest flippancy or coquetry.

She bows obsequiously before the abbot,
Opening her scarlet lips, from which ensue
Words of the utmost propriety,
Such as grave matrons speak in Liang Chou!

Her face is sweetly round and lightly powdered,
Exuding frankness so that none may doubt her.
She wears a mourning dress of whitest silk;
There is nothing commonplace about her!

This maid has turned her bird-like eyes on me,
Who only long myself to lie beside
Her little mistress with a coverlet
Of mandarin ducks, fit blanket for a bride.

Truly, if we were married I would not
Trouble you to make or fold the bed;
I should pray your mistress and her mother
To free you, and I'd see you richly wed.

FA PÊN: Will you please be seated for a moment
While I step with this young servant-girl
Into Buddha's shrine and then return?
CHANG: What would you say if I should go with you?
FA PÊN: By all means, come!
CHANG: Then let this servant-girl
Walk out in front and I shall follow after.

Can it be she is showing off her charms
Before this old, ascetic monk? If she
Is not, why is it that the girl is dressed
In garments moving us alluringly?
Ha! in the chambers of this monastery
Fortune from Heaven may fall even on me!

FA PÊN [*angrily*]: What right have you to prattle of such things?

CHANG: Blame me not for what I had to say!

If I have violated etiquette,
Injuring Hsüan Tsang's disciple, why aver
That such a wealthy clan as that of Ts'ui
Must send to you a female messenger?
Among their servants can there be no men?
If none, pray take the consequences then!

FA PÊN: Be serious! This well explains the matter.
The daughter of the late Prime Minister, Ts'ui,
Moved at heart by filial piety,
Wishes a memorial service held
And, prompted by complete sincerity,
Sends to me her own domestic servants,
Hung Niang, to ask the date of such a rite.
[*To* HUNG NIANG.]
The place and order of the sacrifice
Are both determined. On the fifteenth day
On the half-moon Buddha receives his offerings.
I have asked the widow and her daughter
To come that day and offer up the incense.

CHANG [*weeping*]: Abbot, this recalls to me my father
And mother and the pains that I have caused them!
I, too, am eager to repay such kindness,
Illimitable as the heavens above!

Even this young girl is moved to thanks
For all the generosity received.
I trust that out of goodness and your mercy
You will accept from me five thousand coppers!
May I share these obsequies to make
Similar memorials to my parents
And so observe the duties of a son?
When pious Madame Ts'ui shall hear of this
I cannot think that she will have objections.

FA PÊN: There will be none. Fa Tsung, prepare the way
For master Chang to join our ritual.

CHANG [*aside to* FA TSUNG]: Will the young girl be there?

FA TSUNG: How could she possibly
Neglect a rite in honor of her father?

CHANG: What an investment for five thousand coppers!

A glimpse of Ying Ying, even in heaven or earth,
Is worth all offerings that ever were!
What do I care if I am far removed
If only I may have the sight of her?

I here renounce all possibility
Of compassing her body, soft as jade –
Though not so cold – or breathing her perfume.
One touch of her, and my unrest would fade!

FA PÊN: Come, all of you, and let us drink some tea!

CHANG: Please forgive me, abbot, just a moment!
[*He retires, but observes.*]
The servant-girl must certainly come here.
I shall be waiting for her when she passes.

HUNG NIANG: I must not drink this tea, for I'm afraid
Madame would scold me if I dared delay.
[*She starts to go but is met by* CHANG.]
CHANG: Good day, my girl!

HUNG NIANG: Ten thousand joys to you!
CHANG: My girl, do you not wait upon Ying Ying?
HUNG NIANG: Indeed I do! Why do you trouble to ask?
CHANG: May I take the liberty to speak?
HUNG NIANG: Words are arrows. Do not let them fly
Without a cause. Once they have pierced the ear
They cannot be removed by any force.
But speak now, if you will, and have no fear.
CHANG: My family name is Chang. My given name
Is Kung, my name in courtesy, Chün-jui.
My home is to the westward of Lo-yang.
My age is twenty-three, and I was born
At the hour of the rat and on the seventeenth day
Of the year's first moon. I am a bachelor.
HUNG NIANG: Who asked you that? I'm no astrologer
Or teller of fortunes. Of what possible use
To me could be this year and month and day?
CHANG: Hung Niang, I have a question. Does your mistress
Often go walking?
HUNG NIANG: Well, what if she did?
You are a scholar and a gentleman.
Don't you remember what Confucius said?
'Never utter an improper word
Nor make a single move without propriety.'
My mistress rules her household rigorously.
Her orders can be cold and hard as ice.
Even if a child were three feet tall
He would not go into her room unsummoned!
You are no relative of hers at all!
Luckily, I merely am her servant
And so I may excuse you. If my mistress
Had any notion you had spoken so,
You could not possibly have been forgiven.

From now on ask me only proper questions
And don't you dare to ask what you should not!
[*Exit.*]

CHANG: This love-desire will surely be my death!

The servant's words burden my soul with sorrow,
Crushing my heart within a cruel vice.
She says I cannot see the girl unsummoned;
She says her mother's heart is hard as ice.

I know that if you fear your mother's anger
It would be wrong of you to turn your head
Or glance at me, but when you walk away
Even the thought of you leaves me half-dead!

If in this life we cannot place our cheeks
Together as twin blossoms but must spend
Bleak years apart, does this, perhaps, presume
In earlier lives I dreamed our love should end?
My true aim is to win you as my prize,
Loved with my heart and worshipped with my eyes.

I have long heard that paradise on earth
Stands as remote as heaven's farthest stars,
But find our union even more removed,
Guarded by a thousand iron bars.

Yet when I met you briefly, I discovered
Myself in paradise seeing your face.
Even now I feel I stand beside you,
My body lingering in an alien place.

My hope is that you tell your love to me;
My fear is you may tell it to your mother.
Surely, you thrill to see the orioles
And butterflies disport with one another!

Hung Niang, you are too timid! Your prognostics
Are surely false, for when did any man
Meet a young girl of equal age with him,
Lovely and fresh, and not devise a plan
How he might marry her and all his life
Pencil the eyebrows of his loving wife?

She, too, will dream that I shall be her husband
And faithful lover, like Chang Ch'ang of old.
To claim that I am courteous, loyal, upright,
Is surely truth nor can it be too bold
To say that she is pure and true in heart,
Perfect in speech and every household art.

Hung Niang, the eyebrows of your little mistress
Are delicately painted while her face
Is lightly tinted, jade-like smooth; her neck
Is white like fragrant powder. What peerless grace!

She wears a silken skirt of emerald green
Where colored love-birds in embroidery meet
Under which there issue golden lilies
That are, in truth, only her tiny feet.

Lifting red sleeves adorned with phoenixes,
She barely shows her fingers, white and fine
As shoots of fresh bamboo. Oh, if I could
Only banish from all thought of mine
This ravishing girl, how lucky I should be
And from what torture I would then be free!

I quite forgot this old religious man.
[*He turns to* FA PÊN *and addresses him.*]
May I ask you now about my room?

FA PÊN: There is a quiet room near the West Chamber
Where you can rest in peace.

[*They walk about.*]
This room is yours.

CHANG: Well then, I shall immediately revisit
The inn and promptly bring my luggage here.

FA PÊN: May I really count on you to come?

CHANG: Yes, I can readily transport my baggage.
But how shall I endure this solitude?
[*Exit* FA PÊN.]

Hung Niang, I am alone in this bare chamber.
I find my mat and pillow cold as frost.
The night-lamp flickers on my books and screen.
I win my leisure at too high a cost.
The goal of learning loses its delight
If I must so endure the live-long night.

I cannot sleep. I shift from side to side.
Rest shuns me, agitation comes instead.
I toss a thousand times upon the pillow,
Pounding tight-clenched fists upon the bed.

She is all delicacy, a speaking flower,
Too briefly seen. Neither can I recall
Her form precisely nor recapture sleep.
I find that I am miserable in all.
Laying my hand upon an aching cheek,
I yearn for one whom I must vainly seek.
[*Exeunt.*]

SCENE THREE

YING YING [*entering*]: My mother sent Hung Niang to ask the abbot
The time for holding the religious rite.
I've waited a long time for her return.

HUNG NIANG [*entering*]: I have reported to the madame. Now
I come to give the word to my young mistress.
He finds the second month, the fifteenth day,
Appropriate for Buddha's ritual.
He bids your mother and you to light the incense.
[*She laughs.*]
Now I can tell you an amusing story.
The scholar whom we saw the other day
Was sitting in the court of our pavilion.
He stepped before me, bowed and promptly asked:
'Young girl, are you Hung Niang, Ying Ying's attendant?'
And then he further said to me, 'I am a scholar;
My proper name is Chang: my other names
Are Kung and Chün-jui. My native home
Is westward of Lo-yang, I am twenty-three,
Born at the rat's hour, on the seventeenth day,
Of the first month, and I am still unmarried.'

YING YING: Who ever ordered you to ask him questions?

HUNG NIANG: Who asked him? He just gave the information!
Besides, he spoke your name and further asked
If ever you went walking to relax.
For all this talk I gave him a good scolding.

YING YING: You should not have scolded him at all!
HUNG NIANG: I can't say what on earth the fellow thought!
    I didn't believe such silly fools existed.
    Tell me, should I not have scolded him?
YING YING: Did you tell my mother this or not?
HUNG NIANG: I have not said a word to her about it.
YING YING: Then do not breathe a word of it to her.
    Twilight has come. Go quietly, bring the incense
    And we shall burn it in the flower-garden.

    What vague emotions fill my heart with gloom,
    Leaning above the fire, watching the moon!
    [*Exeunt*].

CHANG [*entering*]: I have moved into the monastery
    And taken quarters by the Western Chamber.
    Asking questions of the monk, I learn
    That every evening in the flower-garden
    The girl burns incense. Luckily this garden
    Is separated from my quarters only
    By this low wall, so that when she emerges
    I can await her by the sacred stones
    To feast my eyes upon her. – Ah, what joy! –
    Now it is late. The world lies fast asleep.
    I am alone. Air's pure; the moon shines bright.
    At leisure I can converse with the abbot,
    Or better, looking toward the Western Chamber,
    Compose a poem under this radiant moon.

    The sky is clear, without a trace of cloud;
    Heaven's River is a starry waterfall;
    The silver moon is mistress of the night;
    Flower-shadows clamber up the western wall.

When through her silken sleeves she feels the cold
She must discover that the hour is late.
I listen closely, walk with lightest tread,
Hidden in shadows of the court, and wait.

The first watch long ago has run its course
In utter silence. When I see her pace
The pavements by her door I shall confront her,
Holding her tenderly in my embrace.

I shall complain our meetings are too few
And far too short, while on the contrary
Our separations are too many and long.
Life is a shadow, no reality!

[YING YING *enters, with* HUNG NIANG.]

YING YING: Open the gate; carry the incense out.

CHANG: *All at once I hear an opening door.*
A breeze in brushing past her brings a scent
Of rich perfume. I stand on tip-toe, gazing
Upon her with a growing wonderment.

When I first saw her she was wonderful
But haste then left her image in a blur.
Now that I watch her quietly, I conclude
The goddess of the moon must bow to her.

It's easily imagined that this girl,
Weary of her conventional confinement,
Has taken this occasion to escape,
Much as the goddess of the silver moon
Contrived escape out of her bright moon-palace.
She stands there silently and without motion,
Her long sleeves, her silk garments hanging loose.
She is like the imperial concubine Hsiang Ling
Bending low before the crimson portal

Of the great temple of the Emperor Shun,
Or like the goddess of the River Lo,
Who prayed the Prince of Ch'ên to sing her praise.

Slowly she walks along the garden path,
Impeded by the smallness of her feet.
As she approaches me I see more clearly
Until her total splendor stands complete.
Truly, when any man has seen her whole
Who could escape her conquest of his soul?

YING YING: Dear Hung Niang, carry the incense here.
CHANG: I shall learn what prayers the lady makes.
YING YING: On lighting the first incense I petition
That my beloved father, who has died,
May soon be born again in highest heaven.
In burning this, the second I humbly pray
That my dear mother live a hundred years.
And for this third . . .
[*She hesitates.*]
HUNG NIANG: Why are you always silent
When you are coming to the third petition?
Let your maid, Hung Niang, pray for her mistress:
I pray that my young mistress wins a husband
Unsurpassed in literary genius,
Highest in the highest examination,
Handsome in body, with distinguished mind,
Noble, yet gentle in his disposition.
May the two live as one a hundred years!
[YING YING *adds the third stick of incense.*]
YING YING: All the yearnings of a woman's breast
Inspire my final act of adoration.
[*She bows low.*]

CHANG [*aside*]: Lady, what are you hiding in your heart,
Sighing and leaning there against the altar?

The hour is late. Thick incense fills the court;
The gentle western wind that earlier swayed
The screens has paused. Her prayers are at an end.
Sighing she leans against the balustrade.

The moon's smooth disc shines mirror-like and round.
Ascending incense makes its face appear
Shrouded in fog. I hear the two girls sigh
But the two figures are no longer clear.

Surely, the mistress spoke from her own heart!
Though I, perhaps, am not the famous lover
Ssu-ma Hsiang-ju, she still may be Wên-chün.
I shall compose a poem and read it to her:

[*Recites.*]
The moon shines with her keenest glow tonight.
Shadows of spring flowers are on the wall.
Gazing at her disc, I see distinctly
The great Moon Goddess in her silver hall.

YING YING: Hush! Someone in the corner of the court,
Hiding from us, is reciting verses.

HUNG NIANG: The voice is of that dolt of twenty-three,
That idiot who doesn't have a wife.

YING YING: Nevertheless his poetry is delightful!
I shall compose a poem to rhyme with his:
[*Recites.*]
My chamber harbors solitude and silence.
No fragrant blooms of spring flower by its wall.
I trust the poet I heard will show some pity
To one whose sighs interminably fall!

CHANG: How promptly she has answered to my poem!

At first I noticed an exterior
Of charms, the rouge and powder on her face,
But now I find the spirit and the heart,
Replying to my poem with perfect grace.

She took my verse and promptly answered it
In perfect tune. Her feelings were expressed
Completely; words and rhymes were fresh and pure.
She is the oriole, who sings the best.

If you should look on me and I on you
We could persist till dawn in answering chime
By one side of the wall and by the other
While every moment yielded blissful rhyme.

Shall I come across the wall to meet you?

I would like to lift my silken robe
And vault the wall. If so, perhaps she might
Welcome me kindly. Ah, my dear Hung Niang,
You have been hostile. – Come now, do me right!

Ah, suddenly I hear a startling sound!

HUNG NIANG: We must go, or Madame will chastise us!

[*Exeunt* YING YING *and* HUNG NIANG, *shutting the garden gate.*]

CHANG: *Sleeping birds, disturbed by this alarm,*
Have left their boughs and at the self-same sound
A thousand blossoms, quivering in the shadow,
Have fallen on the crimson-littered ground.

Now on the emerald moss a cold dew gleams.
Moonlight sifts through shadows of the flowers.
The live-long day I had been sick at heart.
Then hope came with night's enchanted hours.

Your screen was lowered and your door was shut.
If I had breathed you might have answered me.
In the pure moonlight of the second watch
We missed our fairest opportunity.
Now I seem the wretched victim of
A destiny inimical to love.

On my returning I have paused a moment.
The Dipper and the Bushel shift their place.
Reading the constellations of the sky,
Stars tell me misery may end in grace.

Bamboo limbs are waving in the breeze.
Omens are shifting. – If she does not care
For me, then for what person does she care?
She would speak her love but does not dare.

Ah, tonight how can I sleep and dream?

My lamp burns low and flickers. The battered screen
Fails to keep off the wind. The night is cold,
The pillow lonely, the coverlet is grim
With misery, the window-paper old,
It rattles. Men of iron would concur
To pity me, since I cannot dream of her!

I'm restless. I can neither sit nor sleep.
There's no man I can hate and none revile,
And yet I trust at another time
Fortune herself will turn to me and smile.

Beneath the willows, in a mist of flowers,
Shrouded in clouds, when night is far advanced,
No man about, with sea and hills to witness,
We shall be together and entranced!

Tonight my better fortune came to light.
My poem and her reply prove this to me.
I shall no longer dream of her by night
But clasp my love beneath a flowering tree.
[*Exit.*]

SCENE FOUR

CHANG [*entering*]: This is the second moon and fifteenth day.
The aged abbot asks me to burn incense.
I shall proceed at once into the temple.
A soothing rain of holy eloquence
Pours from the abbot's sermon down to earth.
Like rippling waves the gentle springtime breeze
Rustles the pages of the sacred books.

The full moon shines above the monastery,
High at its zenith, cold and far aloof.
Clouds of auspicious smoke laden with perfume
Soar toward it, high above the green-tiled roof.

[FA PÊN *enters followed by a train of monks.*]

FA PÊN: This is the second month, the fifteenth day
When Sakyamuni entered in Nirvana,
When Mañdjusri and Auysman Cunda then
Laid out the offerings for the sacrifice.
If pious men and faithful women offer
Worship today, their prayers will be accepted.
Chang has already come, so now the priests
Can loudly sound their sacred instruments.
[*The instruments are sounded with great vehemence.*]
When the full dawn has come, summon the lady
Together with her daughter to burn incense.

CHANG: *Smoke from our incense pours in massive clouds.*
Murmur of chanted prayers is like the dashing
Of waves. The swaying of huge banners casts
Vague shadows. Cymbals and drums are loudly crashing.

The roar throughout each crevice of the hall
Rivals thunder in the months of spring.
The clangor and the clamour of the bells
Are like the whistling when the storm-winds fling
Clouds and rain against the serried lines
Of madly waving, tempest-driven pines.

No priest may knock at the pavilion door
Where the late Minister's family has its home.
Hung Niang, the maid, has not yet given word
When Madame and her daughter are to come.
All my ardent spirits are ablaze
To see her, never to revert that gaze.

FA PÊN: Sir, light your incense first. Should Madame Ts'ui
Object, tell her you are my relative.
[CHANG *burns the incense.*]

CHANG: *May all who live on earth enjoy long lives!*
May all the dead obtain felicity
In heaven! May all my noble ancestors
Be one with the Buddhist Trinity!

Once more I offer incense, but this time
I pray in secret from my inmost soul.
May Hung Niang be no more my enemy!
May Madame not obstruct my true love's goal,
And, holiest of holy Buddhas, hark!
When I approach my love, let no dog bark!

[MADAME TS'UI, YING YING *and* HUNG NIANG *enter.*]

MADAME TS'UI: Let us enter the religious shrine.
We shall burn incense, as the abbot asks.

CHANG: *She seems a spirit from the upper air*
But actually is a tender maid.
She comes to make a pious sacrifice
Who is herself a goddess cut in a jade.

I am indeed a wretched sufferer,
An object of inestimable pity.
How can any heart resist the spell
Of one who well might overthrow a city?

You proffer peach and cherry at your lips;
Your jade-like nose is chiselled and justly spaced;
Your cheek is whiter than an almond bud;
You are a swaying willow about the waist.
The girl has every beauty and every grace
Alike in excellence of form and face.

FA PÊN: Madame, this old priest has a word for you.
This scholar, a poor relative of mine,
Goes on a journey to the capital
To take the highest of examinations.
After his parents' death he had no means
Of showing his devotion but through prayer,
So I included him in your devotions
But fear my noble lady may resent it.
MADAME TS'UI: How can you possibly incur displeasure
Wherever filial piety is shown?
Kindly ask the man to come to see me.

CHANG: *The lecherous abbot from his lofty throne*
Eyes the young girl. He is a fool as well.
He beats the bald head of his acolyte
Blandly believing it to be a bell.

The old and young, the ugly and the lovely,
Are cast together in a mad confusion,
Worse even than a New Year's celebration
Making piety itself delusion.

Today desire becomes reality.
The lovely girl whom I alone adore,
Afraid that others may detect our love,
Casts her tear-filled eyes upon the floor.

Insatiable desire has fired my heart.
She is a bird who warbles at all hours,
The oriole from which she takes her name.
Her teeth are like fresh dew upon the flowers.

I hate the pious abbot and his mummery,
Covering his face in grief for the deceased!
I hate the acolyte who lights the candles!
I hate the odious, incense-burning priest!

The incense smoke is rising to the clouds;
The candle-flames into their cups return.
Through looking too intently at Ying Ying
Their lights are blurred and finally cease to burn.

YING YING [*to* HUNG NIANG]: That student has been fuming all the night.
The handsome man is at his height of youth.
His mind must be alert, his knowledge great.
He paces back and forth, swaying his limbs,
Showing manly virtues by his gait.

Evenings he makes a stir beside our window.
At midnight, when about to go to bed,
Rather than reading from his book in hand
He heaves a hundred heavy sighs instead.

CHANG: *My face is the betrayer of my mind.*
Well she knows the passion in my heart!
Equally true it is that I detect
Reciprocal devotion on her part.

You priests and novices intoning texts,
Your clashing cymbals and incessant peal
Of trumpets only aggravate my pain
But no way quench the agony I feel.

It is far worse to love than not to love.
I, whom all the agonies pursue
That belong to love, am miserably assailed
By free and loveless spirits such as you!

FA PÊN: The dawn has come. I must request you, Madame,
Together with your daughter, to retire.
[MADAME TS'UI, YING YING *and* HUNG NIANG *go out.*]

CHANG: I have again enjoyed a fruitful day,
But where will it all leave me in the end?

I have been agitated all the night.
The moon has set. The bell announces day,
The cock has crowed. Pale daylight has returned,
The beautiful young girl has gone away.

The ritual service now has reached its end.
Its pious congregation has dispersed.
The monks have all departed to their cells.
Now day on the horizon rim has burst.
[*Exeunt.*]

SCENE FIVE

[SUN FEI HU *enters with a crowd of soldiers.*]

SUN: I am Sun, the Flying Tiger. At the present
The Empire stands in total disarray.
Ting Wên Ya, the nominal commander,
Is utterly incompetent to rule.
I lead a squadron of five thousand soldiers,
With sturdy cavalry, to guard Ho-Ch'iao.
I recently have ascertained Ying Ying
The black-browed daughter of the Minister Ts'ui,
With face as lovely as a springtime lotus,
Is living in the Temple of P'u Chiu,
Where for a time her father's body rests.
There, on the second month and fifteenth day,
A special service for his soul was held
Where many people witnessed to her beauty.
Now when I observe that my superior
Follows no laws of conduct, why should I? –
Soldiers and officers, obey my orders!
All of you, keep your tongues from idle chatter,
March by day and night to Ho Chung Fu,
Forcibly capture Ying Ying for my wife
And so fulfil the passion of my life!
[*Exit, with his followers.*]

FA PÊN [*entering, alarmed*]: A great calamity has fallen on us!
Who would suppose the bandit Sun Fei Hu,
The Flying Tiger, with five thousand soldiers,
Would thunder at the monastery gates

Enclosing us as if in iron rings?
Gongs roar, drums rattle, while the bandits shout,
Waving their flags. Their chief himself demands
The tender girl, Ying Ying, to be his wife.
I must tell the mother and the daughter.

MADAME TS'UI: What is there we can do? What frightful danger! –
Good abbot, we must talk about the matter
Somewhere apart, outside my daughter's room.

[FA PÊN *and* MADAME TS'UI *go out. Enter* YING YING *and* HUNG NIANG.]

YING YING: Ever since I looked at Master Chang
Two days ago, at the memorial service,
My spirits have been so desperately strained
That I can neither eat nor drink. Besides,
These airs of later spring inspire my soul
With even greater love and melancholy.
The poet has expressed my feelings clearly:
'The pure moon fills a lover's heart with pity;
I bear my sorrow through long, silent hours.
How can I help from grieving when I see
The East Wind casting down the early flowers?'

The sadness of the season wears me thin.
Soon the days of spring will be no more.
The robe of gauze is hanging from my limbs.
How many sunsets must my heart endure?

Chill wind blows clouds of incense smoke about
So that I may not raise my chamber blind.
My door is shut against the falling blossoms.
Air on the balcony becomes unkind.

Fierce rain has drowned the ruddy blooms. Last night
I dreamed of spring but with the dawn's faint ray

White moths like snowflakes lit on faded flowers
And all the gaudy spring fell to decay.

Fallen flowers compose the swallow's nest,
Plastered with mud and leaves. My waning strength
Leaves me dejected when I recollect
My lover absent but a garden's length.

How history instructs us of the past!
Beauties of the Six Dynasties and Three
Provinces have also known distress,
Languishing in an equal misery.

HUNG NIANG: Young mistress, you look overwhelmed with grief.
I'll sprinkle perfumes on your colored quilt.
That may help you, dear, to rest and sleep.

YING YING: *My sky-blue spread grows cold, my bed is crushed,*
Do not waste the perfume, for though thrown
In wild profusion none could do me good.
No lover can be warm who sleeps alone.

Last night your poetry wrapped me in delight.
Today he is lost from me, for all his wit.
A few steps only, and I feel fatigue.
I find that I can neither stand nor sit.

Were I to trust your word, I would be lying
Upon my marriage bed. But, mother, I find
Even you shadow me with observation.
Now, above all, you prove to me unkind!

Well you know that when I saw a stranger,
And if he stood near to me, I was distressed.
If such a man was of my family
My modesty was even more oppressed.

But when I saw this man the other night
Every inhibition was undone.
Both our poems were natural and unforced,
Their words were different but the meaning one.
Who now will cross the wall and tell him of
My depth and my intensity of love?

He is as rich in learning as in passion.
His mind is cultured and his body strong.
He is amiable and kind by nature.
Why has he to wait for fame so long?

[MADAME TS'UI *and* FA PÊN *enter and knock at* YING YING'*s door.*]

HUNG NIANG: Mistress, your mother comes to us. She brings
The abbot. They are just beside the door.
[MADAME TS'UI *and* FA PÊN *come into the room.*]

MADAME TS'UI: My child, have you been told what has occurred?
Sun, the Flying Tiger, has surrounded
The monastery with five thousand men.
The bandit mocks us, calls your eyebrows black
And shining, says your face is like a flower,
With beauty that can overwhelm a city,
Comparable to the courtesans of old.
He intends to fetch you to his camp
And there compel you to become his mistress.
My child, whatever is there we can do?
Death is not sad for one of sixty years.
You, dear child, are young and still unwed.
Now that such disaster overwhelms us,
What is there possibly that we can do?

YING YING: Give me, then, into the bandit's hands
So that all our family may be saved.

MADAME TS'UI: No man in our family violated
A law; none of our women married twice.
How can I give you to a bandit chief?
That would cast our family in disgrace.

YING YING: Dear mother, do not brood over your daughter!
There are five blessings in this sacrifice:

It saves my father's widow from destruction.
The monastery will not be consumed.
Its priests will still remain in quietness.
My father's coffin will not then be doomed.
My adopted brother, though not yet a man,
Will be enabled to renew our clan.

Otherwise, by thinking of myself
And by refusing those whom I abhor,
The monastery would be turned to ashes,
All its monks spattered with blood and gore.

My father's body brought to common dust,
Pitiful death for my adopted brother,
And then, to my unbearable remorse,
Ignoble death to my beloved mother!

Perhaps a wiser thing for me to do
Would be to wind this scarf, stopping my breath,
Give a dead body to the robber chief.
And that way save my family from death.

FA PÊN: Come, go together to the Council Hall,
Asking the priests and laymen gathered there
In two divisions, what judicious plan
They find the best to save us from disaster.
[*They all go to the temple.*]

MADAME TS'UI: My child, what can we do? I have a plan.
It will be difficult to give you up,
My daughter, but the need confronts us now.
If any of you here on either hand,
Priest or layman, can induce the bandits
Merely to retire, then I, your mother,
Will willingly present you as his wife,
And in addition many wedding gifts,
And though his social rank were less than ours,
Such matrimony clearly would be better
Than falling into the vile bandit's hands.
Abbot, announce my offer with loud voice
Throughout the hall. – My child, it's you who suffer.
FA PÊN: This is at least a wiser course to steer.

YING YING: *Dear mother, you think only of my good,*
Though to tell others of it would require
More words than time allows. Do not be troubled
Nor think too much of what I may desire.

It is small matter who my husband is
Provided that he overpower the foe
And you are truly generous to provide
So rich a dowry for his doing so.

[FA PÊN *commences to promulgate the offer, when* CHANG *enters.*]
CHANG: I have a plan for driving out the bandits.
Why do you not consult me in your trouble?
FA PÊN: Madame, this is my relative, the scholar
Who joined us in our pious ritual,
Held in the middle of the second month.
MADAME TS'UI: Tell us, sir, what is your strategy?
CHANG: I beg to tell you, Madame, that I believe
The highly generous reward you offer

Will surely bring you a courageous man.
Provided you are faithful to your promise
My device is certain of success.

MADAME TS'UI: I have informed the abbot that I offer
My daughter as the bride of any man
Who drives the vicious robber band away.

CHANG: This being so, I have the remedy.
But first I must request the abbot's help.

FA PÊN: This aged Buddhist cannot kill in battle.
I beg you, sir, to call on someone else!

CHANG: Don't be alarmed. Assuredly I would not
Suggest that you should fight. Merely go out
And tell the bandit chief that Madame Ts'ui
Reminds him that her daughter still is wearing
Mourning garments for her honored father.
So if the general wants her as his wife
He should lay by his armor and his arms,
Retiring from the monastery walls
The distance of an arrow's farthest flight.
He should wait there three days until the rites
Of mourning are completed. Then at once
Her mother would dispatch her daughter to him.
If she should go to him wearing the robes
Of mourning, it would be an evil augury
For all his army. You must tell him this.

FA PÊN: What is to happen after the three days?

CHANG: I have a loyal friend whose name is Tu,
His second name is Ch'o. He bears the title
Of General Riding the White Horse. He now
Commands a hundred thousand loyal men,
Guarding the P'u Kuan Pass. We are sworn brothers.
When he receives my letter he will surely
Fly in a moment to us for our rescue.

FA PÊN: Madame, if the General really comes
We need not fear a hundred Flying Tigers. –
My lady, you may set yourself at rest.

MADAME TS'UI: Truly, I thank this honorable scholar.
Hung Niang, escort your mistress to her room.

YING YING: Hung Niang, we are indeed indebted to him!

Every monk is cowering for his life;
No one of our kith or kin will dare
To rescue us; only this total stranger
Makes our safety his especial care.
He is no pedant lavish of advice
But saves himself with us in stormy weather.
Jade and stones, he believes, should not at once
In molten conflagration burn together.
No near relation pities our distress.
Our fate itself hangs wholly on his pen.
One brush-stroke in his letter saves our lives,
Sweeping away five thousand fighting men.

[YING YING *and* HUNG NIANG *go out.*]

FA PÊN [*calling loudly*]: I summon your commander to a parley.

SUN [*entering, with some soldiers*]: Send Ying Ying to me immediately!

FA PÊN: Calm your anger, General! Hear the message
Which Madame Ts'ui requests that I should give.

[FA PÊN *whispers in* SUN'*s ear.*]

SUN: Well then, I grant you the three days' delay.
But if you fail to send her afterwards
I swear that every man of you shall die. –
Tell Madame the good-natured son-in-law
That I shall make. She will accept me gladly.

[SUN *goes out, with his soldiers.*]

FA PÊN: [*to* CHANG]: The robbers have gone off. Now, my good sir,
Kindly write the letter that you promised.

CHANG: The letter has been written in advance.
I only need a messenger to take it.

FA PÊN: I have a pupil in the kitchen named
Hui Ming, whose chief delights are wine and fighting.
If you simply ask him to convey
A message, he will flatly tell you, no,
But if you arouse his fighting spirit
Nothing on earth will keep this man from going.

CHANG [*speaking loudly*]: Here is a letter that I wish to send
To the White Horse General. I cannot allow
Hui Ming of your kitchen staff to take it,
But who among the other monks will dare
To go on such a perilous adventure?

HUI MING [*entering*]: I am Hui Ming, and I demand to go!

I never could digest the Lotus Sutra;
The King of Lang's Repentance moves my mirth;
I've cast my monk's hood to the roaring winds
And thrown my monkish cassock to the earth.

Thirst for slaughter animates my soul.
Killing brings the joy that cannot fail.
I swing an iron poker in my fist
As a black dragon swings his vicious tail.

I am not vain nor greedy. I know well
That in Buddhistic worship I'm a fool.
But I can brave a tiger in his den
And deal out slaughter in the dragon's pool.

A diet of dough and vegetables irks me.
I find the dull monastic table rude.

But I can still consume five thousand men
Whether they are roasted, baked or stewed.

Their hearts and entrails most regale my taste;
Blood from their throats most gratifies my thirst.
Thin soup, fat dough, sweet herbs, sour curds, pale leeks,
Such nauseating viands are accurst!

Give me a ton of flour, even if poor,
To stuff in dumplings with five thousand men
For mincemeat and if any of it's over
I'll salt it down and gorge it once again!
Do not stop me! I am all aglow!
I must be the messenger and go!

FA PÊN: Hui Ming, the scholar does not really wish you,
But you insist on going. Do you dare?

HUI MING: *Do not ask me if I dare or not!*
The question is whether you have the need.
You say that I am fearful as a tiger.
I am instead the son of lust and greed.

CHANG: You left your family for a pious life.
Why do you fail to study sober classics,
Say prayers and follow with the other monks
Going to worship in the sacred halls?
Do you really wish to take my letter?

HUI MING: *Classical discourses are a bore;*
Religious meditation I distrust!
My newly polished, sacrificial knife
I see has not a single speck of rust.

The other monks throughout this monastery,
Who are neither men nor women, idly rot
By daylight in their cells and never care
Whether the monastery burns or not!

If you really wish to send your word
For rescue and support to one who can
Exert all skill in letters and in arms,
Though many leagues away, I am your man!
I shall go boldly to that distant place
And never bring your mission to disgrace.

CHANG: Will you go alone or with assistance?

HUI MING: *Give me some younger monks to carry flags,*
And banners for my elegant array;
Also some weakling monks with tongs and pokers
To do me kitchen service on the way.
You here at home stand firm, giving the monks
At least some touch of confidence and cheer
While I stride boldly forward through the foe
Who circle us, defying sword and spear.

CHANG: But if they stop you, what will you do then?

HUI MING: *One glance of mine will make the ocean roar;*
One roar of mine will make the mountains quake;
One step of mine will make the whole earth tremble;
One lifted arm can make the heavens shake!

My iron poker fells my farthest foe;
My belt-knife stabs my foe when near at hand;
I toss my lesser enemies in air;
The larger foes I shatter where they stand.

CHANG: Well then, I shall give my letter to you.
Only tell me when you plan to start.

HUI MING: *I have been bold and headstrong all my life.*
The tireless heart within me never fails.
I am a mass of stubborn bravery;
Courage deep within me never quails.

Others bend to women's flowery wiles
While I bend iron bars and massive piles.

Whether an obstacle is slight or strong,
I face it without trace of hesitation.
Fearless of death, I rush against the foe,
Acting with absolute determination.

I am one to overthrow the strong
And bow before the weak. I much prefer
The bitter to the sweet. – You love this girl
But I shall not go forth because of her.

You must not send me on a love affair.
I do not go to win a bride for you.
The consequence of that is in your hands
If you are not relieved by General Tu.

Be careful in your letter what you say,
For though you speak good words to win a wife,
A single error that your brush has made
May bring about disgrace throughout your life.
Be careful, for unless you write your best
The scholar will be slain with all the rest.

Strike the drum three times to rouse my soul
And cry to Buddha with gaudy flags unfurled!
May my courage in going forth be clear,
Shouted and proclaimed throughout the world!
Five thousand bandits tremble as I come,
Terror-smitten, frozen, stiff and numb!
[*Exit.*]

CHANG: Lady, you may now assure your daughter,
Bidding her be calm. The General's army,
Once my letter reaches him, will come.

The letter flies by night. Then, like a gift
From Heaven, the White Horse General will be here!
[*They all go out.*]

TU [*entering, with soldiers*]: My name is Tu, my given name is Ch'üeh,
My courtesy name Chün-shih. My family home
Is eastward of Lo-yang. During my youth
I read Confucian classics with Chang Chün-jui.
Later I left my civic occupations
For military life. Winning first honors
In military science, I became
Commander of the armies of the West.
Now I am field-marshal of an army –
A hundred thousand soldiers at my call –
To guard the frontier passes of P'u Kuan.
A messenger has come from Ho Chung Fu
Reporting my sworn brother, Chün-jui,
As staying at the P'u Chiu Monastery.
I know well why he has not come to see me.
Recently General Ting Wên Ya has fallen
Aside from loyalty. He allows his troops
To plunder all the countryside. My duty
Is to march against him and restrain him,
But since I'm lacking all the evidence
I must not act impetuously. I now
Am going to my tent to hear more news.
[*He goes through the tent entrance and sits down.*]

HUI MING [*entering*]: I've left the P'u Chiu Temple far behind
And promptly enter at the P'u Kuan Pass.
The entrance to the General's tent is here.
I'll hurry in to see him.

SOLDIERS: Stop!

TU: No, no!
Let whomever he may be come in.
[HUI MING *enters the tent and bows before* GENERAL TU.]
Bold monk, why have you come to spy upon us?
HUI MING: I am not a spy. I am a monk
From P'u Ch'ui Temple to which the bandit Sun,
The Flying Tiger, has brought extreme vexation.
Five thousand of his robbers have besieged it.
He wishes to abduct the only daughter
Of the former Minister of State, Ts'ui.
A visitor is there, Chang Chün-jui.
He has given me a letter to your honor
Imploring you to save them from their peril.
TU: Soldiers, no more stand guard upon this priest!
Chang is my brother. Hand me his letter quickly.
[HUI MING *bows and hands* TU *the letter.* TU *reads it aloud.*]
'Your younger brother and your fellow-student,
Bowing and again saluting you,
Presents this letter to your Excellency,
The High Commander of the Imperial Arms.
During the two long years since I last saw you
All nights when the wind blew and the rain fell
My earnest thoughts have always been of you.
Leaving my home to reach the capital,
I passed Ho Chung. It then was my intention
To visit you and join in earnest talk
But, suddenly, the hardships of the highway
Sickened me. I now am somewhat better
And out of danger. I am resting briefly
Inside the quiet P'u Chiu monastery.
Suddenly rogues have threatened it with force.
The widow of the Minister Ts'ui,

Suffering many troubles since his death,
Had brought his coffin to the monastery,
Hoping that it there might rest in peace,
If only briefly, and might there receive
The customary ritual and prayers.
Unexpectedly, a brutal stranger,
Hearing of the great beauty of her daughter
And gathering five thousand men about him,
Placed the monastery under siege.
No sooner did I see their helplessness
Than fury seized me. I passionately longed
For prompt destruction of the criminals,
But yet I knew that during my whole life
I had lacked the strength to catch a chicken!
Even if I had sacrificed myself
It could have had no possible result.
Finally, I recalled that you, my brother,
Have powers to keep the province in control,
Holding the winds and clouds at your command.
It cannot be too daring to compare you
To the venerable hero, Shao-hu.
I am now in fearful peril. I depend
On you to save me. Words cannot express
My longing for your charitable aid.
Fall upon Ho Chung like a thunderbolt!
Starting at dawn, you will arrive by evening.
Fish on dry land are longing for a flood.
Even in the world below, the shade
Of the great Minister will be also grateful. –
Hoping you will give his word attention,
Your younger brother, Chang, again salutes you.
Written the second moon, the sixteenth day.' –
[*He ceases reading.*]

Since things stand so, I shall at once give orders. –
Monk, set out in haste ahead of us,
But I shall come tonight and probably
Even before you reach the monastery
The bandits will be prisoners in my hand.

HUI MING: The monastery is in desperation.
Your honor must arrive with utmost speed.
[*Exit.*]

TU: Officers and men of three divisions,
Listen to my commands! Choose from your troops
Five thousand of the most redoubted horsemen.
We leave tonight direct for Ho Chung Fu,
To P'u Chiu Temple, to save my younger brother.

OFFICERS: All of us hear your orders and obey.
[*All go out.*]

SUN [*entering, with some soldiers*]: The White Horse General suddenly has come.
What is there to be done? What's to be done?
We must all dismount, take off our armor,
Cast down our spears and kneel before the General.
Our destiny lies wholly in his hands.

TU [*entering, with some soldiers*]: Why have you dismounted, thrown your spears
And armor to the ground and basely knelt?
Do you suppose that you will be forgiven?
Well, I order Sun, the Flying Tiger,
To be beheaded. All you other men
Who may not wish to enter in my army
May return freely to your native farms.
All who desire again to join the forces
Should give their names and so may be enlisted.
[*Enter* MADAME TS'UI *and* FA PÊN.]

MADAME TS'UI: The letter was dispatched two days ago.

We have received no answer and no news.

CHANG: I hear outside the monastery gate
A sound of orders like the roar of thunder.
My elder brother probably has come.
[TU *and* CHANG *see each other and bow.*]
Since I last saw you, honorable brother,
I have been deprived of your instruction.
Today our meeting seems to me a dream!

TU: I have just learned that you were travelling
In the same general region as myself.
But since I have not come to you before
I truly beg of you a thousand pardons!
[TU *and* MADAME TS'UI *see each other and bow.*]

MADAME TS'UI: A widow and a newly orphaned daughter
Stood at the doors of death. But here today
You have brought us once again to life.

TU: Because I failed to take all due precautions
Against the lawless conduct of the bandits
You and your family have been alarmed.
For this I well deserve a thousand deaths.
[*To* CHANG.]
May I ask my honored younger brother
Why he failed to come to visit me?

CHANG: Your brother unexpectedly fell ill.
That is the reason for my negligence.
I should accompany you back today
Except that yesterday this lady promised
I should be married to her lovely daughter.
May I trouble you to be my sponsor?
My thought is that a month after the wedding
I shall visit you and thank you deeply.

TU: Congratulations and best wishes to you! –
Madame, I shall undertake this duty.

MADAME TS'UI: There are other projects that I have in mind. –
Meanwhile may I serve you tea and dinner?
TU: Five thousand men have just surrendered to me.
I must go and consummate this business
But I shall certainly return in time
To offer you my warm felicitations.
CHANG: I shall not venture to detain my brother
And so obstruct his military duties.
[TU *mounts his horse.*]

I see the horsemen leave the monastery
While clashing cymbals lift their brazen cry.
The soldiers follow to the P'u Kuan Pass,
Raising shouts of victory on high.

MADAME TS'UI [*to* CHANG]: We never shall forget your kindness, sir.
Now you must move out of your temple quarters
Into the quietness of my library.
Tomorrow I shall have a humble meal,
Giving my orders to Hung Niang, my servant,
To urge your presence. Do not fail to come!
[*Exit.*]
CHANG [*to* FA PÊN]: Well, I shall take my luggage and remove it
Into the library. The fires of war
Kindled by bandits happily have brought
A fairy lady to her faithful wooer.
Clouds and rain of passion come at last. –
Flying Tiger, I am grateful to you!
FA PÊN: When you are at leisure, Master Chang,
Come to my room, as ever, for a talk.
[*Exeunt.*]

SCENE SIX

CHANG [*entering*]: Last evening Madame Ts'ui declared that she
Would tell Hung Niang to bring an invitation
For me to come at leisure to her banquet.
I rose before the dawn in hope to see her
But still she has not come. Where can she be?

HUNG NIANG [*entering*]: My mistress orders me to summon Chang,
So I must hurry quickly as I can.

Five thousand bandits have been swept away
Swiftly as scudding clouds or passing rain
While the whole family, in the midst of death,
Has suddenly been brought to life again.

With carefree spirits we should thank the gods,
Worshipping them with sacrifice and prayer,
And no less voice our gratitude to Chang
Whose single letter saved us in despair.

Today the East Pavilion lies in cloud
And melancholy moonlight leaves the West.
Your lonely quilt and pillow no more need
Be cold. He'll warm them whom you love the best.

Ying Ying, you'll joy to burn your precious incense
While gentle breezes of the night-time fill
Your room, stirring your silk embroidered curtains
Though all inside the green-gauze screens lie still.

Here is the entrance to the library.

In this silent and secluded room
Do I hear footsteps pacing on the floor
While I am standing on the frost-chilled moss?
I shall cough once outside the scholar's door.

CHANG: Who's there? Who's there?
HUNG NIANG: It's only I, Hung Niang.

He opens the red door, speaks out in haste,
Joining his hands with bows of salutation
Before I have the time to wish him well.
My coming seems to warrant an ovation!

His brilliance dazzles me! He wears a hat
Of jet-black, shining silk. His scholar's gown
Is white and gleaming. From his buckled belt
Gold ornaments are hanging down.

Do not suppose that only Ying Ying's heart
Is captured! Though I commonly am cold,
His talents, character and charm of face
Leave me in love's harsh servitude enrolled. –

Sir, Madame Ts'ui has given me directions . . .
CHANG: I am immediately upon my way!
HUNG NIANG [*aside*]: *Just hear! Before I can pronounce a word*
He jumps to his reply! I scarcely bring
The message to him, when he shouts, 'I come,
Lady, I come,' and flies to meet Ying Ying.

Scholars, when they hear an invitation
To dinner, welcome it as soldiers take
A military order. They obey
Eagerly for their empty stomach's sake.

CHANG: May I dare to ask you, Hung Niang,
Why this feast is being celebrated?
Has Madame summoned other guests than me?

HUNG NIANG: *First, she celebrates our new-won safety,*
Second, she extends our thanks to you.
She wishes to keep all the monks away
And orders me to say no gifts are due. –
Betrothal to Ying Ying being the end,
I see that you are eager to attend. –

[*Aside.*]
Just look at him! He paces back and forth
Bowing to his shadow with high admiration.
These impoverished scholars are struck mad
With pride on passing their examination!

He has so groomed his head that not a fly
Dare light on it for fear of falling off.
He has stored some grains of ancient rice
And turnips at which common men would scoff.

But this man who has shown himself so wise
In one thing, surely must be wise in all!
So the habitual stumbler, falling once,
Is certain ever afterwards to fall.

Similarly, I have heard that plants
Grow in unison and harmony,
But, surely, no young scholar ever lived
Free from love's miserable malady!

Heaven has granted him a noble mind;
He shows extreme fastidiousness in dress;
His soul exhibits jade-like fortitude
While his heart melts in loving tenderness.

He passes nights brooding in solitude.
Genius, we hear, is ever passion's slave.
When a lovely girl rejects a scholar
Too often he is driven to his grave.

Well, tonight you shall be fortified
By Ying Ying's faith and absence of pretence,
But recollect the joy my little mistress
Must feel after her life of innocence.

You must be calm and gentle! Nevertheless,
When in the lamp-light two at length are one,
Her charm and beauty will inspire you so
All caution and restraint will be undone.

CHANG: May I inquire, Hung Niang, of what arrangements
Are made for the occasion, for I wish
To go there with becoming preparation?

YING YING: *Our floors are strewn with petals of red flowers.*
This is the hour of joy and revelry.
My mistress ordered me to hasten to you
Urging you to come immediately.

The bridal room contains embroidered hangings
With pairs of mandarin ducks in the moon's ray.
A screen of precious jade presents to view
Amorous peacocks in the spring at play.

For music there are ivory castanets
Pacing the rhythm of the swan-necked lute
Together with close harmony provided
By union of the male and female flute.

CHANG: Hung Niang, I have a question. I am travelling;
There's nothing I can offer as a gift.
What will your worthy mistress think of that?

HUNG NIANG: *Where marriages are promptly consummated*
No betrothal money need be given.
You are the male and female phoenixes
Whose starry union was decreed in heaven.

You must not fear to be as other stars,
The yearning Cowherd and his Weaving Maid,
Who, long dissevered, meet but once a year.
Not even the smallest trifle should be paid.

The merit that you gained in giving us,
As champion for our rescue, General Tu,
Makes every common gift or ceremony
Superfluous, for nothing more is due.

First of all, you conquered Ying Ying's heart,
A million soldiers harbor in your breast!
Moreover, men of literary talents
Have in love's contests always won the best.

Whoever heard of any man who gained
A girl who shines with jewels, pearl and jade,
Who failed to come from ranks of earnest scholars
Reading classics in the studious shade?

You have no companions on your travels
And Ying Ying only has her family.
The occasion is relieved of complications.
This will be a modest ceremony.

You are the only guest. Unworldly monks
Could only trouble such a gala day.
Please do as Madame Ts'ui beseeches you,
Follow me at once and come away.

CHANG: If this is so, Hung Niang, go on ahead,
I shall be with you very shortly after.

HUNG NIANG: *Do not stand too much on etiquette,*
Madame awaits you. Don't be over-nice!
'Better be compliant than obsequious,'
The sage has said. Don't make me ask you twice!
[*Exit.*]

CHANG: The maid has left, I'll shut my study door,
When I approach the Madame she will say,
'Ah, you have come, Ying Ying and you will make
A happy couple. Drink two cups of wine
Before you walk into the marriage chamber!'
[*He laughs.*]
Flying Tiger, what a benefactor
I found you! I am vastly in your debt,
Some time later, when I live at leisure,
I shall assign a thousand strings of cash,
Bidding Fa Pên to chant a requiem
For the repose of your immortal soul.
Then I myself shall pray the Heavenly Dragon
To send from heaven a rain of sacred law
On which the Flying Tiger may arise
With clouds of morning into Paradise.
[*Exit.*]

SCENE SEVEN

MADAME TS'UI [*entering*]: Hung Niang has gone to summon Master Chang.
I wonder why the girl has not returned?

HUNG NIANG [*entering*]: Chang has asked me to go on ahead.
He will follow me a little after.
[CHANG *enters*. MADAME TS'UI *sees him*.]

MADAME TS'UI: Good Master Chang, had it not been for you
The other day, how could it possibly be
That we should be alive and standing here?
My family owes its life solely to you.
I have therefore ordered a small meal.
It's not at all intended to repay you
But still I hope you will not think it worthless.

CHANG: Everybody's happiness depends
On the good fortune of a single person.
The victory enjoyed over the bandit
Was wholly owing to your own good fortune.
Please do not refer to that again!

MADAME TS'UI: Servant, bring the wine! – Drink from this cup.

CHANG: How can I decline to drink a cup
Afforded by my elder?

MADAME TS'UI: Please sit down.

CHANG: The rites prescribe that I should stand beside you.
How can I dare be seated in your presence?

MADAME TS'UI: Are you not acquainted with the precept, 'Obedience is better than politeness.'

[CHANG *whispers his thanks and sits down.* MADAME TS'UI *whispers to* HUNG NIANG *to summon* YING YING.]

YING YING [*entering*]: Now he has swept our enemies away
As winds blow off the stormclouds. Peace returns.
Sun and moon will bless our festival.

Scholar Chang well knew a host of men.
What rescue could another man have made? –
Instruments and song are now at hand,
The hall is readied, all the banquet laid.

An east wind wafts among the swaying curtains
Delicate fumes of incense softly blended
With faint flower-perfume. Blessed is the one
By whom the threat of our destruction ended!

HUNG NIANG: My mistress, you got up this morning early.

YING YING: *Just now before my green-gauze screen I painted*
My brows, wiped powder from my pure silk gown,
Then with frail finger-tips quickly arranged
Hair ornaments of gold to be my crown.
If not disturbed, I would be sleeping yet
Under my bright, embroidered coverlet.

HUNG NIANG: My little lady finished dressing promptly.
Have you already washed your face and hands?
Your fresh complexion seems to me so fragile
That touch or breathing on it would defile it.
You are a lucky lover, Master Chang!

YING YING: *Really, Hung Niang, you are talking madly*
To say that breath or touch could hurt me badly.

HUNG NIANG: The stars above created my young lady
To be the wife of some accomplished man.

YING YING: *Stop your foolish jabbering, I say!*
Though you have prattled wildly all your life.
How can you tell that he's a noble man
Or whether I could be a great man's wife?

HUNG NIANG: Well, once you two were sad but now you're gay.

YING YING: *All you can say is that we both were sick*
With love in common and now enjoy good health.
We both should hold a feast in gratefulness. –
My mother worries too much about wealth.

HUNG NIANG: But if you are to marry Master Chang
Why are not your family and friends
Invited to the banquet? Next, my mistress,
Why is such a meager meal prepared?

YING YING: You can't imagine her frugality!

My mother fears my dowry might make
My family poor and, being very loath
To spend too much, she makes one celebration
For two events do services for both!

She holds this banquet on my wedding day
By giving it to serve as victory feast.
Assuredly, the hero merits honor
But I should have a separate rite at least!
Also, this hero for his service merits
The total wealth my family inherits!

I shall use this curtain for a screen
Before I enter where my family sit.
With shy feet hidden underneath my dress
I'll hear their talk but take no part in it.

[CHANG *catches a glimpse of* YING YING *and pretends to have encountered her by accident.*]

CHANG: Pardon me, my lady, pardon me!

YING YING: *Who would have believed that he would see me here*
Half-hidden by curtains? I could almost say
This clever man possesses second sight!
It makes me for the moment shrink away.

MADAME TS'UI: Come nearer, daughter; do not shrink aside
Pay your honor to your elder brother!

CHANG [*aside*]: Ah, those words are a bad augury!

YING YING [*aside*]: My honored mother must have changed her mind!

HUNG NIANG [*aside*]: See how love has brought them to disaster!

YING YING: *He seems like one who stumbles among thorns.*
He neither lies nor sits, crouching in pain,
So bewildered that he cannot speak.
He faints and cannot be restored again!

Old woman, what is this that you have done?
Why should I, your daughter, call him brother?
Suddenly I now have lost my love,
Separated from him by my mother!

I am like the lover by the bridge
Waiting his darling till the rising tide
Overwhelmed him, or like him who fired
The temple of God when parted from his bride,

Or like the two inseparable fish
Having one eye together but forced apart,
Plunging on in darkness. – Why should I
At one word perish of a broken heart?

My mind grows dizzy; my head droops low; my neck
Is powerless; my jet-black hairs fall down undone.
How can we ever speak or meet again?
My very eyes seem alien to the sun.

My breath is utterly consumed in sighs.
The abyss of my despair no mortal knows.
This banquet that I believed my wedding feast
Is now consumed by scavengers and crows.

MADAME TS'UI: Hung Niang, fill up a cup of heated wine
So that Ying Ying may greet her elder brother!

YING YING: Hung Niang, take this cup of wine away!

This is a sorry cup of wine I hand you,
You who look as though you wished to die,
Bowing your head in silence. Is the cup
Too large, that you should wish to set it by?

Now you have drunk it, you look more at ease,
But as time passes then how will it be?
How I long to tell you what I feel
But cannot, sitting at my mother's knee.
Though you are close to me, you seem as far
As bright, unfeeling stars in heaven are.

[CHANG *finishes his wine;* YING YING *sits at the table.*]

MADAME TS'UI: Hung Niang, pour out more wine and you, good sir,
Must drink a second cup and drain it dry.

YING YING: *Although you have escaped from your impasse,*
Others have long detected your ill will.
Though you attempt to placate men with words,
You only leave them more unhappy still.

Beauties are always sad and scholars frail;
Fatherless children live without a guide.
My dowry weighed too much and now my fate
Is only for my mother to decide.

[CHANG *laughs bitterly.*]

You think that he is laughing happily
When his heart overflows with bitter tears.
Had not his letter saved us from the bandits
Fate would have realized our bleakest fears.

If Chang does not desire to marry me,
What other object can he hold in view?
You are inscrutable as Heaven's will
And yet my destiny must hang on you!

My powdered face must now remain as white
As palest blossoms of the early pear.
No longer will my lips be cherry-red
But sickened with the pallor of despair.

My sorrow will be deeper than the sea,
Blacker than a thundercloud on high,
Boundless as the amplitude of earth,
Interminable as the clearest sky!

You first implored his aid as you would pray
The sheltering spirit of the T'ai Hêng range
Or Guardian of the Eastern Sea; but now
How cruelly, how bitterly you change!

You crush twin blossoms of a single flower,
Tearing apart the lover's fragrant knot.
Age's ills receive a gracious balm
Whereas youth's sharper sorrows not a jot!

You have destroyed propitious years that smiled
For us with joy, felicity and fame.
You have betrayed him with you honeyed words,
Giving me to him with a sister's name!

MADAME TS'UI: Hung Niang, conduct your mistress to her room.

[YING YING *and* CHANG *exchange farewells. She goes out with* HUNG NIANG.]

CHANG: Your servant has been overpowered with wine
So begs your leave, my lady, to retire.
Nevertheless, with your most kind permission,
I earnestly desire to speak my mind.
Not long ago when bandits threatened us
You promised that whoever should succeed
In driving them away would take your daughter
To be his wife. Did you not give your word?

MADAME TS'UI: I did.

CHANG: Then who stepped forward to the rescue?

MADAME TS'UI: You did. We surely owe our lives to you.
But when my husband, the Prime Minister,
Was living . . .

CHANG: Stop a moment, Madame Ts'ui.
When I hastily dispatched a letter
To General Tu, did I anticipate
As my reward only this frugal banquet?
When Hung Niang came this morning to invite me
I confidently believed your former promise
That I should now be married to the girl.
I cannot tell why you should so abruptly
Call us 'elder brother,' 'younger sister.'
The proverb says, 'Never too late to mend.'
I beg you, Madame, for consideration!

MADAME TS'UI: When the last Prime Minister was living
He had formally betrothed his daughter
To Chêng Hêng, my dear nephew. I already
Have summoned him to come here to receive her.
What can I do? I offer you today
A generous money-gift to show our thanks.
Marry into another noble family
So that all persons may be satisfied.

CHANG: How can you believe it! But if General Tu
Had failed to come and kill the Flying Tiger,
Thwarting his insidious intent,
What might you then have said? I have no use
For pay. Madame, I say good-bye and leave.

MADAME TS'UI: Stop a moment! You have drunk too much.
Hung Niang, gently give our elder brother
Your arm and lead him quietly to his room.
Tomorrow we will speak of other matters.
[*Exit.*]

HUNG NIANG: Wouldn't it have been better, Master Chang,
If you had drunk a little less profusely?

CHANG: Ah, Hung Niang, you are too simple-minded!
What wine could I have drunk? Since I first saw
Ying Ying I have had neither wine nor food.
The pain that I have suffered till this moment
Surpasses words, yet I can speak to you;
It were useless thinking to deceive you.
Now it is wholly purposeless to mention
A letter that I wrote the other day.
But Madame, undeniably a person
Of eminence, whose every word should therefore
Have full integrity of gold or jade,
Solemnly promised me her child in marriage.
Not only both of us have heard the promise

But countless priests and laymen in the temple
And the great Lord Buddha overhead.
Now abruptly she has changed her mind,
Plunging me in absolute despair!
To me it seems the reasonable course
Must be to loose the girdle at my waist
And with it hang myself before your eyes,
But yet how sad it is that any stranger,
Lonely, in travel through a distant land,
Should shut his chamber door and hang himself
So that his ghost must wander far from home
Haunting the confines of a foreign earth.
[*He loosens his girdle.*]

HUNG NIANG: Don't be so desperate! I sympathize
With all your feelings for my little mistress.
It's all too true that until recently
I never knew you but we no sooner met
Than you had to pardon me for rudeness.
Do not be angry with me any longer!
Today the promise of the girl in marriage
Is known to all. It is the sage who said
That one good deed surely deserves another.

CHANG: I shall be truly grateful for your help
But what plans have you to achieve our end?

HUNG NIANG: Sir, I have seen that you possess a lute
On which you certainly must play with skill.
Ying Ying is passionate about such music.
Tonight the girl and I will surely go
Into the flower-garden to burn incense.
When I signal to you by a cough,
You must begin to play. I shall observe
Her thoughts and at a favorable moment
Report your feeling to her. If she speaks,

I shall repeat her words at dawn tomorrow. –
Now it is late. I fear at any minute
Her mother will be calling. I must go.
[*Exit.*]

CHANG: Once I passed many solitary nights
Inside the monastery halls and now
I lose all prospect of the bridal chamber.
[*Exit.*]

Part Two

SCENE EIGHT

CHANG [*entering*]: Hung Niang admonished me to wait awhile
Tonight inside the garden where Ying Ying
Burns sacrificial incense. She would have me
Play lute-tunes expressive of my heart
To test Ying Ying and hear what she will say.
Reflection tells me that the plan is good.
Twilight is falling. Why should not the moon
Rise just a little earlier for my sake?
Listen to the beating of the drums
And gentle ringing of the vesper bell!
[*He tunes his lute.*]
My lovely lute, good friend by lake and land,
I lean on you to grant me my success.
Heaven send me now a gentle breeze
To blow the lute-tones to my lady's ears,
Themselves jade-moulded, exquisitely powdered,
And most receptive to all lovely sounds.
[YING YING *and* HUNG NIANG *enter.*]
HUNG NIANG: Come, little mistress, let us burn the incense!
How bright the moonlight shines throughout the garden!
YING YING: I cannot find the heart to burn the incense.
Dear Moon, how can you find the heart to shine?

The moon has risen in a cloudless sky,
The wind sweeps crimson blossoms on the stair
Compressing them with fragrance. Separation
First pained me, later numbed me with despair.

My mother gave my love a good beginning
But brought it to a miserable end.
He is to me unreal as a mirage
And I to him a painting of a friend!

Yesterday in my room I dreamed of marriage,
Today I hold him only in my thought,
Speak of him with agonizing lips
Or meet him in sad dreams that come to nought.

When I was all elated, mother told me
To raise my green sleeves and hand Chang some wine.
The act I thought auspicious till she bade me
Greet him as some forgotten brother of mine!

HUNG NIANG: Tonight there is a ring around the moon.
Tomorrow there will certainly be storm!

YING YING: Yes, there is the ring around the moon!

They say a maid inside embroidered curtains
May be polluted merely by man's touch,
But when I see the moon alone in heaven
I feel no blame of Heaven can be too much.

The sky-god once forbade the Moon's warm lover
To follow her to her fairy house above,
Shrouding her within a veil of clouds,
So that she might not know the force of love.

[HUNG NIANG *coughs lightly.*]
CHANG: That's Hung Niang coughing. The dear girl is here!
[*He plays his lute.*]
YING YING: Listen, Hung Niang, what is that sound?
HUNG NIANG: Guess, mistress!

YING YING: *Is it a tinkling from head-ornaments*
Of someone walking; or, sounding much the same,

A wind-swept, decorated skirt; a hinge
Complaining in a breeze; a curtain-frame?

Is it some distant monastery bell
Or bamboo rustling in a shaded vale,
Scissors clinking, or a water-clock,
Or water dripping on a metal pail?

Now that I hide behind the Eastern wall,
I find at last from where the clear sounds come;
Someone well-versed in music plays a lute.
Its notes are floating from the Western Room.

Now it is strong, like clashing swords and spears,
Now it is soft, like flowers that fall on streams,
Now low, like lovers at casements whispering,
Now shrill, like cranes that cry to the moonbeams.

His mind is weary yet his sorrow endless,
His love lies utterly beyond his reach.
I know the sense before the song is over,
Music alone more eloquent than speech!

HUNG NIANG: Lady, stay here and listen. I am going
To see your mother but will soon return.
[*She pretends to go away.*]

YING YING: *It is not that I have a keener hearing*
Than others that the meaning becomes plain.
It is simply that we love each other
And know the true significance of pain.

CHANG: I hear a murmuring outside her window.
It must be she! Well, I shall play again.
I'll move a little nearer to the window.
Ah, my lute! At such an hour I think
Of Ssu Ma Hsiang-ju, the scholar, who in old time

Wooed Cho Wên-chün, playing the eloquent tune,
'The phoenix seeks its mate.' How can I call
Myself a second Hsiang-ju? But certainly
Wên-chün dared not be likened to Ying Ying!

To see her once means never to forget.
Madness on one day not to see her at all!
The phoenix flies through heaven to find his mate. –
My lady is not by the Eastern wall.

I play my lute to clarify my heart.
When will this cloud of severance pass by?
My only wish, to be with you for ever;
Not to fly forth with you, will mean to die!

YING YING: How movingly he plays! So sad a prayer
And such sad music flood my eyes with tears
Before I am myself aware of it!

From first to last, what vast variety!
What originality is here!
His song is neither the faint night-time bell
Nor like Hsin's purer music, loud and clear.

It is not like the song Confucius sang
Lauding the celestial unicorn,
Nor like the plaintive notes the phoenix sings
When exiled from his mistress and forlorn.

Word follows word, as drops in water-clocks
Record long melancholy hours of night.
Sound follows sound, as rustling in a gown
Of one who wastes away before our sight.
Numberless sorrows that his notes explore
Only make me love him more and more.

CHANG: Your mother was forgetful and unjust,
But you, dear girl, could never prove untrue.
[HUNG NIANG *approaches unnoticed.*]
YING YING: Your resentment is without cause:

That was my mother's cruel change of mind.
If I were only mistress of my fate
You could not think me ever false of heart.
I'd seek you as a phoenix seeks her mate.

But this I cannot do. Both day and night
She keeps me at my needlework. She tries
To thwart my entertainment of a lover,
Heedless of how I seem in others' eyes.

Here in my room the wind moans through my screen;
A scholar's lamp glows in his lonely room,
Between, thin red paper on a window
Yet strong enough to signalize our doom.

There is no mountain range rising between,
Still no hope of any message gleams;
Even though Wu Shan Mountain had twelve peaks,
Kao's goddess came to him in dreams.

HUNG NIANG: What's this of dreams, my mistress, that you speak?
What if your mother heard the words you say?

YING YING: *She came like a swift wind to startle me. –*
I haven't moved. Why should she waste her breath?
I will caress her, keeping her from mother
And so betray me to a brutal death.

HUNG NIANG: I have just heard that Chang is leaving us.
Mistress, whatsoever can we do?
YING YING: Go, and tell him to stay three days longer.

Tell him, my mother has new words for him.
Hearing that, he will not leave us now. –
Mother is cruel, holding us apart
And likewise faithless to her solemn vow.

HUNG NIANG: Mistress, you do not need to give me orders.
I know perfectly what I should do.
I shall go to see the man tomorrow.
[*Exeunt* YING YING *and* HUNG NIANG.]

CHANG: The lady now has gone. I wonder, too,
Why Hung Niang didn't stay a little longer.
Then she would have told me how Ying Ying
Received my playing and the songs I sang. –
Well, as things are, all I can do is sleep.
[*Exit.*]

SCENE NINE

[YING YING *and* HUNG NIANG *enter.*]

YING YING: Ever since I heard the lute last night
I have been wretched! Dear Hung Niang, since you
Have nothing now especially to do,
You might as well go to the library,
Hear what Chang may say to you and then
Return to me repeating all he said.

HUNG NIANG: I will not go, for if your mother knew
It would not be for me a laughing matter.

YING YING: Still, if you do not tell my mother of it,
How could she know? Go then immediately!

HUNG NIANG: Well, I must go. I will say to him only
That he has given you extreme vexation.
Not having drunk the marriage cup by day
You should not play the lute to her at night.

She loses heart for her embroidery.
She rubs no rouge nor powder on her face.
Grieving eyebrows show her misery.
Could two hearts meet, such grief would be displaced.
[*Exit.*]

YING YING: Hung Niang has gone. How long it is to wait!
My feelings baffle me, defeating speech.
All night I could not sleep. By day I drowse.
[*Exit.*]
[CHANG *enters from the opposite side of the stage.*]

CHANG: This grief will be my death! I asked the abbot
To tell the family I am really ill,
So why have they not come to visit me?
I'm sad and weary and will sleep a little.
[*He sleeps.*]

HUNG NIANG [*entering*]: I have been ordered by Ying Ying to go
To Chang's apartment, so I now shall do so.
If not for him, we should not be alive.

The coffin of our late Prime Minister
Is resting for the present in the hall
Of P'u Chiu's isolated monastery
Where death might suddenly have come to all.

My fatherless young mistress might have died
At hands of brutal bandits had there not
Been with us Master Chang, who brought in troops,
Saving us from our miserable lot.

His letter wiped five thousand bandits out.
Only by him miraculous aid was given.
That only saved a family from death,
Not the presumed benevolence of Heaven.

In recompense the widowed mother gave
Chang and Ying Ying, her daughter, to each other,
Later she revoked her promised word,
Pronouncing them as sister and as brother.

Now that the marriage rite has been renounced
The scholar's studies fall into decay,
The lady's rouge and powder blur with tears,
Her ornaments stand all in disarray.

He, who was once as handsome as P'an An,
Has now turned gray and she, who once was fair

As Tu Wei Niang, has shrunk into a ghost
Of what she was through longing and despair.

He, in his bleak condition, no more reads
Poetry or history's more weighty page,
While she, neglecting her embroidery,
Lingers in an absent-minded daze.

He with his lute sings songs of desolation;
She fumbles at her verse with stricken heart;
Expression through the music or the brush
Shows equal venom from love's poisoned dart.

A learned scholar and a lovely girl!
How strange our checkered human nature is!
Why is the course of true love never smooth?
Why must it fall to misery like this?
If I were they, I'd draw no further breath
But end existence with reposeful death! –

Well, here I am at last before Chang's window.
I'll wet it with my finger just a little
To see what's doing in the library.

Silently peeping in, I see it all.
He lies full-clothed upon a lonely bed
Having, no doubt, found sleep impossible.
How pale he is and how discomforted!

Ah, Master Chang, if you don't die of sickness
You positively will expire from grief!
Your face is sallow and sunk, your breath is weak. –
I'll knock with this gold hairpin and be brief.

CHANG: Who is there knocking at my chamber door?

HUNG NIANG: *I am the five-fold Pestilential God,*
Casting poisoned seeds of love abroad!

[CHANG *opens the door and sees* HUNG NIANG.]

CHANG: My thanks for the assistance that you gave
Last night! Such gratitude will live for ever. –
I long for what your mistress had to say.

HUNG NIANG [*laughing*]: O, I would rather tell you how she acted.

Last night the wind was soft, the moon was high.
My visit here is at her own demand.
She puts no rouge nor powder on her face.
She calls you the chief scholar in the land!

CHANG: Well, since your little mistress loves me so,
I have a letter that I wish to send.
May I trouble you to take it to her?

HUNG NIANG: *When your poetic letter comes in sight*
She will be in a frenzy of delight.

Nevertheless, she will control her face,
Archly inquiring where the letter came from.

'*You scamp,' she'll say, 'what do you take me for?'*
Your poem will fall in fragments to the floor!

CHANG: I know your mistress would not treat me so. –
You only say this since you do not wish
To take my letter. I shall give you money.

HUNG NIANG: *What a horrid, vulgar beast you are!*
Are you showing off your wealth to me?
Not all your gains from teaching could suffice!
Do you really believe I want a fee?

Are honest people swayed like flowers in wind,
Or purchased like some common prostitute?
Though a mere servant, I have dignity,
With strength of temper to be resolute.

If you only had the will to say,
'I am a poor, lonely bachelor,'
I should look with all respect upon you,
Carrying your letter to her door.

CHANG: Then I shall say precisely what you wish:
'Pity me, a poor, lonely bachelor!' –
Now will you take my poem, as I have asked?

HUNG NIANG: Yes, that will do. Now write and I shall take it.
[CHANG *writes the letter.*]
[*Aside.*]
How beautiful the scholar's writing is! –
Now read, so I may know what you have written.

CHANG [*reading*]: Chang salutes, bowing a hundred times,
Offering his message to Miss Shuang Wên.
Yesterday your honorable mother
Repaid my services with much unkindness,
So that I now am less alive than dead.
After the feast I could not sleep, so played
My lute to find expression for my heart.
Its music was my elegy, which meant
The player and his instrument would soon
Be silent, never to be heard again
Nevertheless, because of Hung Niang's visit,
I am dispatching you some trivial lines.
The ancient poet, Sung Yü, although his home
Lay by the Eastern Wall, still thirsted for
The holy waters of the mystic West.
Man's life is precious to him, so perhaps
I can persuade you to take pity on me?
I wait impatiently for your reply,
Adding a poem I hope that you may read:

'When sorrow in my heart increased
I took my lute and played a song.
Spring has come dispensing joy
Where gentle feelings rightly belong.
Though love's delights are hard to win,
We should not squander precious hours,
But take our pleasure where the moon
Casts silent shadows from the flowers.' –
Chang again salutes a hundred times!

HÙNG NIANG: *I thought that you would slowly smooth your paper,*
Making a careful outline with the brush;
Now you have answered in a single stroke,
Finishing all your message in a rush.

You commenced it with formality
But ended with a lyric of eight lines,
Folded it with an outline of a heart,
In the most gay and gallant of designs.
Though your behaviour may be empty show,
No common person could have acted so!

Your transfer in the characters for love-birds,
Female and male, shows genius at its best.
Whether your note brings joy or wrath, I'll watch.
On that, please set your learned mind at rest.

I am truly pleased to be of help.
I, also, have determined what to say.
I'll say, 'The one who played the lute last night
Sends you post-haste by me this note today.' –

I shall take this note for you, good sir.
But I must add that you had better mind
Your own career and scholarly ambition.

The hand that wishes to abduct this girl
Also seeks to pluck a high degree,
The laurels of the moon, and win at length.
The loftiest literary dignity.

Do not let the warbling of a bird
Deflect the phoenix-flight of your ambition!
No beauty hiding in a curtained bed
Should lure you from a scholar's high position
Like lovers of old times, you now are sick
With passion. May relief be sure and quick!

CHANG: Your words are wise, Hung Niang. I shall retain them
Strictly in mind through all my days to come. –
You must be very careful with my letter!

HUNG NIANG: Put your mind at rest, dear sir, for that.

Long before your lovers' eyes had met
I pondered on your union, night and day.
How could you think I should neglect a letter
Or linger lazily upon the way?
I promise that from all that I shall do
She will come once, at least, to visit you.
[*Exit.*]

CHANG: Well, she has my letter. I will say,
Without unseemly boasting, it's a charm
To bring the girl to me. So when Hung Niang
Returns the news will certainly be good.

Had I not caught a favorable wind
To waft my verses and advance my schemes,
How could I hope a fairy on the clouds
Would fly to visit me in joyful dreams?
[*Exit.*]

SCENE TEN

YING YING [*entering*]: I'm looking for Hung Niang's return here shortly.
Still, since I got up this morning earlier
Than I do usually, I shall now
Lie down again and hope that I may sleep.

HUNG NIANG [*entering*]: I went to Master Chang on urgent orders
From Ying Ying. Here I bring his letter back. –
I shall report to her. – But what is this?
I can't hear anywhere a single sound!
My mistress must have fallen asleep again!
The poet has painted all this scene precisely:
'A slowly rising sun lightens green blinds;
Swallows in pairs flit through a quiet sky.'

Curtains hang motionless where no breeze stirs,
Their green gauze fragrant with their orchid and musk,
I open the red doors. The brass rings clang.
A silver lamp still glows through morning's dusk.

I softly draw warm hangings at her bed.
I lift the silk embroidered counterpane.
Jade hairpins lie aslant, her hair undone,
Although the sun is high, her eyes remain
Shut fast. Profound sleep covers every feature.
She is, indeed, a very lazy creature!

After a while she rises in her bed,
Sits upright, several times scratches her ears,

Heaving a sigh. – Well, how shall I begin?
And how shall I deliver her this letter?
I shall put it on her dressing case
And wait until she spies it for herself.
[YING YING *prepares herself for the day.*]

HUNG NIANG: *The rouge and powder worn by her last night*
Have gone, hair masses fallen out of place.
She lightly powders, carelessly adjusts
Her locks; then lifts the letter from her case.

She breaks the envelope. She reads its message
Intently, yet again and yet again.
She shows no trace of any weariness.
Next, she knits her brows in sharpest pain.
Bends her head, reveals her snow-white shoulder,
And with hot rage amazes her beholder!

Good heavens, all is lost!
YING YING: Come here, Hung Niang!
HUNG NIANG: I'm here!
YING YING: Tell me, where does this thing come from?
I am the daughter of a Cabinet Minister.
Who dares put this letter in my hand?
Am I accustomed to allow such manners?
I am going to tell my mother all about it.
So that she may give a good spanking.
HUNG NIANG: It was you yourself who sent me to him
And he who merely sent a note by me.
If you had not dispatched me, how could I
Possibly have dared to take it from him?
Besides that, you know well I cannot read,
So how could I tell what the man had written?

Such evidence shows that the fault is yours.
And I become the victim in all this.
If you are not accustomed to such things,
Please tell me, mistress, who in heaven is?

Young lady, do not make so great a fuss!
Instead of telling Madame all about it,
Kindly let me go as an informer
And take this letter that you have myself.

YING YING: Going there, on whom will you inform?
HUNG NIANG: Why, against Master Chang. Who else, please tell me!
YING YING: Wait, Hung Niang. This one time I forgive him!
HUNG NIANG: But, Mistress, come to think of it, I fear
The scholar probably would get a thrashing.
YING YING: I didn't ask you of our scholar's health.
HUNG NIANG: I shall not speak of it.
YING YING: O do, please tell me!

HUNG NIANG: *Just recently his face has grown so pale*
It is a most distressing sight to see.
He shows no interest now in food or drink.
He even moves about reluctantly.

YING YING: A skilful doctor must be had at once!
HUNG NIANG: He is not really sick. He says himself:

'*I have abandoned sleep, forgotten food,*
Day and night I languish through frustration.
I look with yearning to the Eastern Wall,
Watching with tear-dimmed eyes the loved one's station.

The only remedy for my despair
Is some erotic, turbulent affair.'

YING YING: Luckily, Hung Niang, you always show
Discretion in your speech, for otherwise
If any second person knew of this
What of the honor of my family?
From henceforth, if you have another talk,
Be certain that you never speak of it!
All relations between Chang and me
Must be those of brother and of sister.

HUNG NIANG: Ah, little miss, what honorable terms!

If you think his gallantry will lead
To harm, how could your mother fail to know?
How could you or I escape the peril
That must accompany his overthrow?
You place a ladder to allure him out,
Snatch it from under, and then rudely flout!

YING YING: Though all our family is in his debt,
How can he be excused for acting so?
Give me my brush and paper, so that I
May tell him not to act this way again!

HUNG NIANG: My lady, can you write the scholar this?

YING YING [*mysteriously*]: No matter, for you do not understand. –
[*She writes.*]
Hung Niang, take this note to him and say
That when your mistress sent you to him last
The message was no more than courtesy
Exchanged between a brother and a sister.
It has no further meaning. If you dare
Repeat what you have done, I will report
All his actions to my lady mother
And you, Hung Niang, will surely suffer, too.
[YING YING *throws her letter on the floor.*]

HUNG NIANG: My mistress, there you go, threatening again! I will not take your letter. So why bother?

YING YING: How ignorant a fool this creature is! [*Exit.*]

HUNG NIANG: Ah, mistress, why must you be so temperamental?

Young girls affix no fetters on their tongues
But fling their mad abuse on every side.
If you persist in showing such bad temper
You must not think to be your scholar's bride,
You should set examples for the good
Of highborn families in our neighborhood.

Often in dreams I saw you as united
But, sadly waking, found you single still.
For your sake I forsook my food and sleep.
No robe could guard me from the morning's chill.
My grief was such as prudent men despise.
Silent tears kept streaming from my eyes.

As long deferred as planet Mercury
In rising is your union, hoped in vain.
Although I close the side-door when he leaves,
I wish him as your husband to remain,
Or you in bridal glory all your own,
My intermediary aid unknown.

One night not long ago, when in your room
You dreamed of splendor, you were in despair,
Fearing your brilliant garments were too thin
To keep from you the cold, keen midnight air.
You looked at them and quivered when you saw
How frail the silk, the breeze how sharp and raw.

Then why upon that chilly night in spring
On listening to the lute's entrancing tune,
When moonlight sparkled on the heavy dew,
Did you not shiver in the silver moon?
Was it because your passion kept you warm,
Your gallant lover shielding you from harm?

You were on that night by no means ashamed
When standing at your window to behold
That wretched creature strumming on his lute
There in the limpid moonrays, bright and cold.
Then you were like the woman whose flesh and bone.
While waiting for her lover turned to stone!

You plotted for the clouds and rain of love
And I have gladly been your messenger.
You never blame yourself but challenge others
Heedless of what ills for them you incur.
I suffer most from you, as there had been
An iron red hot imposed upon my skin.

Publicly all your flowery talk appears
Serene; at home, you scowl and burst in tears. –

If I refuse to take my mistress' letter
She will call me disobedient.
But Chang is waiting for a prompt reply
So I must go immediately to him.
[*She knocks at* CHANG*'s door.*]

CHANG: Ah, you have come at last! What of my letter?
HUNG NIANG: Sir, all is lost! But do not be dismayed!
CHANG: My letter held all hopes for a reunion.
Hung Niang, you showed too little eagerness!
This is, then, the miserable end!

HUNG NIANG: How can you say I wanted eagerness?
Heaven only knows, your letter was too weak!

The truth is, you contrived your own misfortune,
Not that I have failed to serve you here.
That letter is the fatal evidence
Of guilt which brings you summons to appear
For judgement. Furthermore, complicity
In your affair prejudges even me!

Had she not been my friend, the girl would surely
Have failed to pardon your impertinence
And also have convicted me as guilty
Of low connivance and high impudence.
Henceforth our visits will be rare. The moon
Will shine no longer on your Western Room!
The phoenix now will leave his bright pavilion,
The rain-clouds vanish from the mount of love;
You will go one way, I shall go another.
These things no longer shall be spoken of.
There is nothing further to be done.
The past is over. All the guests have gone. –

This ends it all! You need not speak again
Of any feelings that may vex your heart. –
My mistress will expect me. I must go.
CHANG: My dear Hung Niang!
[*He stops speaking awhile and sighs.*]
Hung Niang, if you should leave me,
Who would there ever be to take my part?
[*Kneels.*]
Hung Niang, Hung Niang! Find how to save my life!
HUNG NIANG: Honored sir, you are a learned scholar.
Can't you read what passes in my mind?

Do not destroy yourself with cunning schemes!
Merely your wishing to enjoy your lust
Will cause my flesh and bones to suffer pain
And prove yourself unspeakably unjust.
My mistress, brandishing a rod in hand,
Will beat me for fulfilling your command!

Your case is as impossible as putting
A massive cable through a needle's eye.
Do you wish me as your go-between
Afterwards to have me pine and die?
How shall I speak when I am stricken dumb
Or serve your cause when I am beaten numb?

CHANG [*still kneeling*]: Hung Niang, no other way is open to me.
My only hope for life depends on you!

HUNG NIANG: *Well, I cannot refuse your tragic plea,*
However great is my perplexity.

No words that I can find reveal my trouble. –
Here is the answer to your letter. Read it.
CHANG [*reads, rises and smiles*]: Ha ha, Hung Niang!
[*Reads again.*]
This is a glorious day!
[*Still reads.*]
If I had known before that such a letter
Was on the way, I should have been prepared
To greet it in a ceremonious fashion
But now that it's too late for such a welcome
I trust I may be honorably pardoned. –
I know that this will make you happy, too.
HUNG NIANG: What do you mean?

CHANG [*smiling*]: The anger of your mistress
Was all pretense. You just should see her letter!
Hum, hum, hum, hum!

HUNG NIANG: Can this be really true?

CHANG: Her letter makes an assignation for me
To meet her in the evening in the garden.

HUNG NIANG: A meeting in the garden! Well, what for?

CHANG: Why, just to meet each other in the garden.

HUNG NIANG: Well, meeting in the garden. – But for what?

CHANG [*smiling*]: For what do you suppose that lovers meet?

HUNG NIANG: I simply do not believe it!

CHANG: Believe it or not!

HUNG NIANG: Then let me hear you read my mistress' letter.

CHANG: It is a four-line poem with five-word lines,
Altogether wholly wonderful!
[*Reads.*]
'I wait by moonlight in the Western Room,
My door half-opened by the soft spring air.
When flower-shadows move along the wall
I'll know the one I dearly love is there.' –
Are you a disbeliever now, Hung Niang?

HUNG NIANG: How can this be possibly explained?

CHANG: But what is there that needs an explanation?

HUNG NIANG: Still, I cannot wholly comprehend.

CHANG: Then I really must explain it to you.
'I wait by moonlight in the Western Room'
Means that I must come to her at moonrise.
'My door half-opened by the soft spring breeze'
Means that she will leave the door ajar.
'When flower-shadows move along the wall'
Means that I myself must climb the wall.
'I'll know the one I dearly love is there'
Means no more than simply, I am coming.

HUNG NIANG: Can this really be the explanation?

CHANG: Well, if this not the explanation
Try to give another one yourself!
I should not dare to fool you, dear Hung Niang,
For the deciphering of allegories
I tell you, I'm a veritable Lu Chia!
And when it comes to dalliance with girls
I tell you I'm a regular Sui Ho!
And for more serious passion, a Lu Chia,
If this cannot explain it, what else does?

HUNG NIANG: You say she really sent you such a poem!

CHANG: Look, here it is.

[HUNG NIANG *stays motionless.* CHANG *reads the poem again.*]

HUNG NIANG: Can that be what it says?

CHANG: Miss Hung Niang, you are really laughable!

HUNG NIANG [*angrily*]: So my mistress made a fool of me!

Whoever saw a messenger so baited
As I have been, caught like a foolish fish?
Though my clever mistress still is young,
Too well she knows how to attain her wish!

You tell your secret lover when to jump
The Eastern Wall and come clandestinely
By moonlight to the private trysting-place,
How long your cunning ways have baffled me!

Plotting to consummate your love affair,
You find a quiet spot where none may spy,
Here inside the crowded monastery,
And, busy as I am, your scout am I!

The paper is as bright as clear, smooth jade,
Its writing breathes a scent of musk and flowers.

The page is moist not by her fragrant touch
But dewed with tears of blood profuse as showers.

The ink seems blended with warm springtime rain.
I can no longer doubt, I must declare
That you, great scholar, shall with ease attain
The young girl with a gold bird in her hair.

Ying Ying has shown her strongest love for you
But brought me weakly cringing to my knees.
Her words to him would make a snowstorm warm
While those to me would make midsummer freeze.

Today I see you as you really are,
Most artful lady, lurking under cover.
I'll keep a sleepless watch on wiles you take
To lure to you your ardent, handsome lover.

CHANG: How shall a scholar climb a garden wall?

HUNG NIANG: *Flowers that grow beside the wall are low.*
A swaying door beckons an invitation.
A fragrant beauty is the scholar's goal,
Her Dragon Gate, his first examination.

If a mere mass of blossoms frightens you,
How pluck the laurel of a high degree?
Her brows, like shaded hills in spring, are tense.
Her eyes, like autumn waves, sparkle with glee.
Truly, the goal of all desire is near.
Delay no more; hasten and have no fear!

CHANG: I have already seen the garden twice.

HUNG NIANG: Although you have already been there twice,
This visit, truly, cannot be the same.

You played at verses with a wall between.
True love is real and no poetic game.
Letters you exchanged were mere by-play.
You both shall find reality today.
[*Exit.*]

CHANG: Life goes by destiny! When Hung Niang came
A moment past, I was in agony.
Who would have dreamed the girl would give me joy?
Truly, when it comes to solving riddles
I am Sui Ho, and gallant as Lu Chia!
If her quatrain does not come to this
How can it possibly be explicated? –
Today this tedious sunlight never ends!
Oh Heaven, on whose bounty we rely,
Why should you cause this endless wait for night?
Make the sun promptly vanish out of heaven! –
A learned letter from a learned friend
Arrives and darkness hastens from the West;
But now, when union in the flowery garden
Lures me, the sun stands rooted at its zenith! –
Now it is noon. – Well, I shall wait awhile
And look a little later. – Today all nature
Conspires against the setting of the sun.
In all heaven's vault no slightest cold appears. –
I feel a fragrance float on a far breeze. –
Where is the art for speeding day's slow pace,
Cajoling this unfeeling orb to set? –
At last it enters on its western course!
But I must wait awhile, wait on in patience. –
Who put in heaven that odious three-legged bird,
That foul male-monster? Where can I fetch the bow
Of Hou I and bring down the sun's bright disc? –
Some fixed boundary is set for time.

Pale lamps commence to glow. At last I hear
Brisk drums of the first watch. I close my door,
Grasp the swaying branches of a willow;
In a mere instant leap the garden wall.
Already I seem to clasp you, my young girl!
With what a tenderness I dream of you! –
A braid of pearls lies hidden in this letter.
All the happiness that now foregathers
From three millennia of my incarnations
Hastens to blossom in this flower garden!
[*Exit.*]

SCENE ELEVEN

HUNG NIANG [*entering*]: When my young mistress ordered me today
To take her note to Chang she played a role
Utterly false, making an assignation.
Since nothing has been said to me about it,
I'll breathe no word of this. I'll only ask
That she shall come to burn the usual incense.
We'll see if she can hoodwink me again. –
[*Calls.*]
Mistress, let us go to burn the incense.

YING YING [*entering*]: How sweet the flowers are in the evening air!
The moon has risen early in full splendour,
Flooding the court where deepest silence reigns.

HUNG NIANG: *This springtime breeze is fresh. It penetrates*
The screen of gauze, loosening golden rings,
Dropping embroidered curtains to the floor.
Evening mist envelopes all and clings.
Finally frail sun-rays touch the tower and pass.
The girl adorns herself before her glass.

Far from the noise and friction of the world
Bright ducks sleep on the surface of their pond.
A flock of solemn, jet-black, indolent crows
Drowse upon the willow boughs beyond.

Her small feet crush the fallen flower petals.
The garden path is soft with moistened moss.

Pearls of dew dampen her silken shoes.
High on her head her jewelled hair-bells toss.

My tender mistress and the scholar Chang
Are both impatient for the night to come.

Ever since the rising of the sun
Both have been yearning for the lyric moon.
When they saw the sun sink past the trees
They felt that twilight could not fall too soon.
Each hour appears an age, day ending never.
They pray High God to quench the sun for ever!

Dressed bewitchingly, she comes intent
To meet him on the hills and vales of love.
She longs to clasp him as the orioles
Mate on branches and the boughs above.

No food or drink tonight has passed her lips.
Heretofore a bride of quietness,
She now is passionate and uncontained,
Reason displayed by stormy restlessness. –

Mistress, hide behind this garden-rock.
I shall shut the gate, lest someone hear.

CHANG [*entering*]: Finally my auspicious hour has come!
[*He looks through the gate.*]

HUNG NIANG: *I thought I saw a swaying shadow cast*
Over the garden from the japonica tree
On which dim crows are sleeping but I find
This is not the object that I see.

Here comes the scholar with his black silk cap
Archly askew. He stands behind the wall,
She behind the rock. This is no place
For common talk. They use no words at all!

CHANG [*clasping* HUNG NIANG *by mistake*]: My dearest girl
HUNG NIANG: Get off, poor fool! It's me! –
How lucky that your error was with me!
How would it be if I had been my mistress?

Perhaps from hunger you are seeing stars!
I'll teach you what a distance you should keep!
You are a sufferer from extreme excitement.
Really, you should look before you leap!

Have you actually been asked to come?
CHANG: I am a master of poetic riddles,
Keen as Sui Ho, gallant as Lu Chia.
I am certain I shall overwhelm her.
HUNG NIANG: Don't go through the gate! Someone might say
That I invited you. Just jump the wall.
Cannot you see how fortunate you are?
There is a magic in the air tonight
Assisting you to capture your delight.

Look where a film of clouds obscure the moon,
Like colored paper at a cradle's head.
Flowers and willows are the lover's curtains,
Green moss their spacious, cool, brocaded bed.

Night is beneficent and beautiful.
The canopy of branches here is hung
With delicate buds. You must be temperate
In love and recollect that she is young.

Speak gently to her with caressing words.
Remember that affection can be swayed
Only by love. She is no common woman
But soft and beautiful as flawless jade.

Look how her hair is ample as the clouds.
See how fair her face and what rich charms! –
Henceforth I need not drink cheap wine or tea
Or suffer these inordinate alarms.

I pity one who has so long lain down
Under a lonely coverlet to rest.
Take courage, brace yourself and banish fear,
Clasping your lady to a manly breast!

[CHANG *leaps over the wall.*]

YING YING: Who is it?

CHANG: It is I.

YING YING: Hung Niang! Hung Niang!
[*She does not reply.*]
[*With anger.*]
O Master Chang, what manner of man are you?
You come while I am burning holy incense.
What can be your apology for this?
[CHANG *is too surprised to speak.*]

HUNG NIANG: *What have I, a go-between, to fear*
From those who must be loving man and wife?
I must tiptoe secretly to hear,
Smiling at their love's ironic strife.

One is charged with anger, one with shame.
One of them speaks; one has no word to say.
The man is firm; the woman shifts her mind.
One chatters endlessly; one swoons away.

Where is your boasting, sir, behind her back?
Come, hurry! If this matter becomes known
You're not the only one to be disgraced!

Why is the valiant Sui Ho afraid?
Where is Lu Chia's gallantry now gone?

You stand there with hands clasped and body bowed
As if you were a figure carved in stone.

When no one was about your tongue would wag.
Your lofty words are now a faded bloom.
Who would have believed your conduct by the rock
Would be unlike that in the Western Room?

YING YING: Help me, dear Hung Niang! A thief is here!
HUNG NIANG: Who is it, mistress?
CHANG: Hung Niang, it is I.
HUNG NIANG: Who told you to come here? What business have you?
[CHANG *remains tongue-tied.*]
YING YING: Drag him off at once to see my mother!
HUNG NIANG: But if we drag him to your mother's judgement,
That would be ruinous to his good name.
I must solve the matter for you, mistress. –
Master Chang, come here and kneel before me.
Having read the ethics of Confucius,
You should understand all proper acts
And rites established by the Duke of Chou.
Why did you come here at this hour of night?

The one who sits in judgement holds the plum.
It is not that we seek to lay down law.
Your scholarship is boundless as the sea;
But then, your conduct here is rash and raw.

You are a late intruder on our house,
Abductor, robber, interloper, thief!
You who would pluck high learning from the moon
Plucking at honest women, come to grief!

Learning's Dragon Gate is yours, of course,
But now our garden gate makes you a horse! –

Mistress, for my sake, please forgive this man!

YING YING: We are indebted for our lives to you,
And so are bound to recompense that kindness;
But since we stand as sister and as brother
How can you yield to such a rash desire?
If my mother chanced to know of this
How could you possibly remain unhurt? –
For Hung Niang's sake this time I will forgive you,
But should your insolence appear again
You will be dragged before her to your judgement
And that will be the end of your affair.

HUNG NIANG: *Thanks to the prudence of my little mistress*
For my sake you are pardoned for your sin,
But should your case ever have come to court
You had been beaten on your dainty skin.

YING YING: Hung Niang, remove the incense. Come with me.

[*Exit.*]

HUNG NIANG: Shame on you, sir! Did you not call yourself
Master in solving all poetic riddles.
Keen as Sui Ho, as gallant as Lu Chia?
All such wit might just as well be dead!

No longer prattle of the night of love,
One moment worth a thousand coins of gold!
Resign yourself to lead a lonely life
Penned up in learning's chamber, bleak and cold!

The master in the art of solving riddles
Made his mistake by knocking at a door
Which swayed half-open in the evening breeze,
But what was all your resolution for?

Now an obstruction rises like a mountain;
Flower-shadows on the wall are deep in gloom;
The moon of love is hidden by its cloud;
Shadows darken in the Western Room.

Preen yourself as boldly as you will,
As once, you told us, did the scholar Ho,
But she can paint her brows without your aid,
Playing Chang Ch'ang, and much prefers it so.

You, sad victim of a false romance,
Are like a rain-cloud out to drought.
Your foolish labor to attain a lady,
To your extreme vexation, comes to nought.

Your gallant speeches spoken to your love
Must be forgot. Leave poetry to your betters!
Stop this scribbling of erotic verse!
Resort no more to amatory letters!

You're a mere novice in the realms of love;
But you, my mistress, leave your angry looks!
You are a Cho Wên-chün, he a Ssu-ma.
So let him now continue with his books!
[*Exeunt.*]

SCENE TWELVE

MADAME TS'UI [*entering*]: Early today the abbot sent a message
Telling me Master Chang was gravely ill.
Accordingly, I sent a doctor to him.
I also ordered Hung Niang to see him
To ask what medicine he needs, what illness
He has, what of his pulse, then tell me promptly.
[*Exit.*]

HUNG NIANG [*entering*]: Madame has ordered me to visit Chang.
She can't know what rebuff he met last night.
On that account I'm fearful for his life.

YING YING [*entering*]: Master Chang, I hear, is gravely ill.
I have a good prescription you must take him.

HUNG NIANG: Young lady, so you've changed your mind again!
O very well, since Madame orders me
To see him, I shall take him your prescription

YING YING: I must wait patiently for your return.
[*Exeunt.*]

CHANG [*entering*]: Last night when visiting the flower garden
I found myself so seriously hurt
That all my old-time malady returned.
I clearly see that I am lost for ever!
Madame has bade the abbot call a doctor
But no physician can provide a cure.

That only a benign prescription coming
From a young girl can ever bring about.

HUNG NIANG [*entering*]: My mistress, having made Chang gravely ill,
Has now provided him a new prescription,
Of what strange nature, heaven only knows!
I only dread that it may make him worse.
Still, I shall faithfully deliver it. –
Travellers when homesick lead a life apart;
No medicine can cure a broken heart.

It was you, Ying Ying, who first composed
Verses more fair than fine embroidery
Which laid the scholar prostrate on his bed,
Sleepless, fasting and in misery.

His figure fragile as ascetic Shên,
His hair as gray as that of grieving P'an,
Inordinately hurt by your rebuff,
Today he seems the shadow of a man!

Ah, once you stood beside your half-closed door,
Watching the moonrise, harkening to his suit,
Composed a love poem rhyming with his own
And rapturously listened to his lute!

Last night, however, you spoke stupidly,
Calling yourself his sister, him your brother,
Cruelly asking him what brought him there.

Now he lies hopeless, languishing, dismayed,
Caught in a trap you thoughtlessly have laid.

Well, you have the impudence to say
'Hung Niang, I have an admirable prescription
Which you must carry to this ailing man.'

You have made my life unbearable!
I am kept going like a needle and thread!
From now on, things may go which way they will
And I myself be less alive than dead.

Where now is 'love as lofty as the hills?'
Where now 'devotion deeper than the sea?'
I fear they now are faint as far blue peaks
And farthest streams in shimmering haze can be!
[*She sees* CHANG.]
I am sorry for you, Master Chang.
How is your health now?

CHANG: When I die, Hung Niang,
Please be my witness in the court of Hades!

HUNG NIANG: Many people in our sorry world
Grow mad through love but none is mad as you!

Your mind no longer dwells on learned books
Vast as the sea, dense as a forest glade.
You dream of nothing but of beds of flowers
With lovers sprawling in the willows' shade.

Your heart is bent on meetings with a girl.
Scholarly ambition now is doomed.
Your aim has only been for plucking flowers
Since the first spring bigonia have bloomed.

How could you ever fall to such a state?

CHANG: How could I dare be false in telling you?
My trouble is entirely with your mistress.
Last night when she dismissed me to my study
I truly lost my mind through grief and anger.
The savior had been wronged by those he saved.
The proverb says, 'girls dote and men betray,'
But between us the adage stands reversed.

HUNG NIANG: But really your distress is not her fault.

Look to yourself! Emotion now consumes you.
You are a skeleton of what you were!
You may object that scholar's always fall
In desperate love – but not as you love her!
Your scholarly ambition vanishes,
Your matrimonial prospect languishes.

Well then, my little mistress orders me
To learn what medicines you now are taking.
Besides, there is another remedy –
Heaven knows what – that I have brought to you.
The note I take has this prescription in it.

CHANG: Where is it?

HUNG NIANG: Here it is.

CHANG: I am delighted!
Her message is a poem. If I had known
You carried me these verses from your mistress
I should have welcomed them on bended knee.
Hung Niang, my health is suddenly restored!
Miraculously my sickness disappears!

HUNG NIANG: There you are again, good Master Chang!
But don't you make mistakes a second time!

CHANG: When did I make mistakes? Last night I made
No error. All things hang on chance or fate.

HUNG NIANG: I don't believe that! Please read her poem to me!

CHANG: If you wish to hear her lovely words
Step here and make your most respectful bow.

[*Reads.*]
'Never distress your soul with female trifles,
Nor waste a rich endowment sent from Heaven!

Little I thought my maiden modesty
Would ruin talents that the gods had given!
In order to reward your courtesy
Common proprieties cannot be kept,
So I present you with another poem.
I cannot with such verses prove inept.

I send this consolation to a lover
Who in responding to it must not write
For, without fail, I give my sacred promise
That I myself shall come to him tonight.'

Hung Niang, this poem can in no way compare
With that your mistress sent me yesterday.
[HUNG NIANG *bends her head, reflectively.*]

HUNG NIANG: No indeed! Ah, now I see it all!
My mistress has a magical prescription.

When the cassia moon-flower casts its shade
At midnight scholars should retire to rest.
You hide within the shadow of a rock,
Following the fortune that rewards you best.

You may take this potion more than once,
Again and yet again, yet should reflect
The all-seeing mother may be still awake
Or I play false. Therefore be circumspect.

You truly are a pedant if you pore
Over this note to cure your cold despair.
The secret of your health resides in you,
Not in the verses that you ponder there.

When yesterday you saw your heavenly girl
From sheer embarrassment you missed your cue.
How natural is it that my youthful mistress
Should show this base ingratitude to you!

You sleep beneath a flimsy coverlet
And for your pillow use your long-necked lute.
How can you find the room for her to sleep?
How keep her warm, if so irresolute?

Take courage! Recollect that in the garden
Beside the swing, when night was almost spent
And all was dark, you failed her! Had you not,
Her poem today need never have been sent.

We have silk pillows handsomely embroidered
With mandarin ducks affectionately paired.
We have rich coverlets of turquoise blue.
But to what end are gorgeous beds prepared?

If you do not undress, what does it matter?
Better then not to have come at all.
But if your love is joyfully fulfilled
Happiness will be yours, beyond recall.

Master Chang, I ask you to be frank
Concerning your relations with my mistress!

Her eyebrows are the lines of distant hills;
Her eyes are pure and dark as autumn ponds;
Her silken skin is whiter than whitest milk;
Her waist, like slim and pliant willow fronds.

Lovely her freshness, lovelier her heart.
She has no need for elegance of dress.
She has no need to give you magic potions.
Only herself must save you from distress.
She is your god of mercy, loved Kuan Yin.
With her your cure for sickness must begin.

And yet, however that is, I still have doubts.

Let me repeat her verses yet again,
Lovely as an ever-fresh refrain.

CHANG: *Hung Niang, the verses we have heard today*
Rise far beyond the poem of yesterday.
HUNG NIANG: Truly, as for that I cannot say:
Your past has gone for ever, its rhythm and rhyme.
I speak only for the present time.

I really doubt Ying Ying will come tonight.

Why should she come here at so late an hour
Like some night-blooming lotus late in flower?
CHANG: Do not consider if she come or not.
I only ask to have you as my helper.
HUNG NIANG: *When have I ever failed to do my best?*
I have no wish for gold or royal jade.
I only wish for flowers to dress my hair
And long, embroidered gowns, expertly made.

Even should my mistress lock her door
I would still labor for you and not tire
So that finally, either late or soon,
You shall gratify your heart's desire.
When she comes, how can you not pursue
Your goal? Success or failure rest with you.
[*Exeunt.*]

SCENE THIRTEEN

YING YING [*entering*]: I have ordered Hung Niang to take my letter
To Chang. I long to meet with him tonight.
I wait impatiently for her return
And further must determine how to act.

HUNG NIANG [*entering*]: My mistress ordered me to take her note
To Chang with plans for meeting him this evening.
But being fearful she would shift again
And bring him to despair, I must return
And learn still further of my mistress' thought.

YING YING: Hung Niang, prepare my bed. I wish to sleep.

HUNG NIANG: Yes, sleep is good. But what about the man?

YING YING: Which man?

HUNG NIANG: What man? There you go off again!
Will you fling this scholar in his grave?
This is no laughing matter, I can tell you!
If you break your promise, I shall tell
My mistress that you sent me with a note
For assignation between Chang and you

YING YING: What a malicious animal you are!

HUNG NIANG: I am not the artful one, but you
Who must on no account deceive him twice.

YING YING: But bashfulness is overpowering me!

HUNG NIANG: Who else will ever see you except myself?
Come, let's go; let's go! – Come, little mistress,
There is nothing else that we can do. –

Mistress, let's go, let's go! – My little lady,
Why do you stand motionless? – Let's go!
[YING YING *moves forward reluctantly.*]
Although my mistress still declines to speak,
Her slow-paced steps betray her. She is yielding.

My mistress is as pure and fair as flowers.
Her thoughts were on her love from dawn to night.
At last she settles in a firm resolve.
Now, no more vacillating, she goes forthright.

She leaves her room, she paces towards his study
Where, like the Prince of Ch'u, who left his land
To meet the Fairy Queen, he prepares for her,
Placing all things in order and at hand.
[*Exeunt.*]

CHANG [*enters*]: Ying dispatched her maid to bring a note
Of assignation for our love tonight.
The night's first watch is now a long time passed.
What can this mean? Why hasn't she arrived?
This recalls to me an ancient verse:
'Since earth lies ready and the sky is clear,
Why does not the Heavenly One appear?'

At dead of night I stand beside my door,
A travelling scholar in an alien place.
Sad and lonely is the library;
Fragrant vapor spreads through silvery space.

Where are there clouds to bring me word of her? –
Moonlight is snow on walls, diamonds on dew.
Monks slumber in their cells; crows fly from trees;
Light breezes rustle in the tall bamboo.

These remind me of gold ornaments
She wears about her girdle. Every shade

That moves among the flower beds calls to mind
Her coming and the promise she has made.

I find no rest in body or in thought.
All my spirits waver in agitation.
I lean against the door, reading the skies,
But glean no hope from any constellation.

My thoughts entangle. From utter weariness
My eyes keep barely open. At times I pity
Myself that even in dreams I met with one
Whose beauty well could overthrow a city.

Whoever errs should first correct himself,
But if I turned aside from her, relit
My lamp of learning and rebuked my heart,
How could I keep her from possessing it?

I still lean on my door, with hand on cheek.
How can I tell if she will come or no?
How can she scheme to leave her mother's side?
Now I face my final overthrow. –
While I suffer from such ills as these
Doubtless my tormenter lies at ease.

She does not come. Will she be false once more?

If she will come, she has already left
Her chamber to approach my library.
If she does not, my only hope is gone,
Plummeted into a boundless sea.

I count my footsteps, pacing back and forth.
Although you have refused me cruelly,
I never bore you malice in my heart
Inducing you to change your thoughts of me.

Why have you promised to arrive by night
And left me waiting till the break of dawn?
We have exchanged love-glances half a year,
During which all my thoughts have been forlorn.

I am prepared to suffer slights and wrong,
A scholar travelling in a foreign place
Forcing myself merely to eat and drink
Only to flourish in your love and grace.

It was my sincerity alone
Maintained this life I wretchedly endure.
Astrologers who probed my six-months' grief
Would find ten years were needed for its cure.

HUNG NIANG Mistress, I'll go ahead while you wait here.
[*She knocks on the door.*]
CHANG: The lady has arrived!
HUNG NIANG [*entering*]: Ying Ying has come!
Take her to your coverlet and pillow.
CHANG [*bowing*]: At times no words will serve to speak our feeling.
Only Heaven can reveal it truly.
HUNG NIANG: Don't speak so loud, or you will frighten her.
Await her here and I shall bring her to you.
[*She leads* YING YING *into the room.*]
Come in! I shall stand here outside your window.
[*Exit.*]
CHANG: Ah, how fortunate I am today!
Please consent to enter in my room!

One glimpse of you and I am almost cured!
Who could have hoped that you who one night past
Rebuffed me so, now proving such affection,
Would of yourself return to me at last?

Though I have not the grace of Sung Yü
Nor the great manly beaty of P'an An,
Nor talent of Tzu-chien, I pray, dear girl,
Show pity to a wandering fellow-man.

[CHANG *embraces her and leads her to a seat.*]

Her bright, embroidered sandals are minute;
A single hand enfolds her pliant waist;
Out of bashfulness she bows her head
Upon a pillow with two love-birds graced.

Her golden hairpins dangle from her locks;
Her cloud-like locks, now loosened, flutter down;
Since disarrangement makes her lovelier,
I'll loose her girdle and undo her gown.

Fragrance of the orchid and the musk
Fills my study. Ah, with every grace
You fetter me! Your are a clever one!
Why must you bow and turn aside your face?

I clasp a body that is smooth as jade
But fragrant, soft and warm. At last it's clear,
Like, Liu and Yüam, I am in Paradise
And all the opening flowers of spring are here!

The peony's heart at last is gently plucked,
It opens at the touch of spring-time dew.
I am enchanted at the long-wished sight
As more and more her beauty comes to view.

I am as happy as a darting fish
In water; like a butterfly in air
I gather sweetness from the dainty buds;
I kiss your fragrant mouth, your cheeks, your hair!

You half reject me and half welcome me;
I see your swelling breasts and, lost in bliss,
I furtively observe beneath the lamp
How exquisite your total figure is!

The pure and silken handkerchief is stained
With drops of delicate red. – I cannot tell
What is the source of all this loveliness
Wherein the spirit of beauty comes to dwell.

I am a lonely student traveller
Who from the very moment that we met
Has been enamored with you. Whether near
Or far, I've been unable to forget.

But now my love-sickness at last is cured,
My rudeness pardoned. Sleep will now return.
I am at rest now with a new flame,
Pure and steadfast, all my soul will burn.

Tonight I have achieved my happiness,
My soul ascending to the highest heaven.
Now to my wasted figure, my sick mind,
New vitality, new joy is given!

Dew is falling on the fragrant earth.
Out of the clouds beneficent rain has streamed.
Moonlight filters through my library.
Tell me, was I awake or have I dreamed?

I, who have waited upon you tonight,
Will love you always and be grateful to you.

HUNG NIANG [*entering*]: Young mistress, you had best be going home,
Or else your mother will observe your absence.
[YING YING *rises.*]

CHANG [*holding her hand*]: *How strange that sadness seems inevitable!*
Though one glimpse leads to love that none forgets,
When a moment comes for briefest parting
How unsupportable are our regrets!
Tonight we met, untroubled and unvexed.
When shall I loose your fragrant girdle next?

HUNG NIANG: My mistress, we must now return with speed,
Or else your mother will discover us.
[*Exeunt* YING YING *and* HUNG NIANG.]

CHANG: *Although the spring has pierced her milk-white breast,*
The truth of love is painted on her brow,
Making all other things beside her poor,
As all who glimpse her flower-like face avow.

She shows more beauty in her red and white
Than all the splendor of the star-filled skies.
Treading the green moss with embroidered shoes,
She leaves me, but her form still haunts my eyes.

The scholar is unworthy of her love,
Yet it's his chief desire to do her right.
I thank her for the kindness she has shown,
Hoping that she'll come earlier tonight.
[*Exit.*]

SCENE FOURTEEN

[*Enter* MADAME TS'UI *and* HUAN LANG, her adopted *son.*]

MADAME TS'UI: I have been watching Ying Ying for some time,
Noticing she's embarrassed in her speech.
She roams about continually dazed.
Her form and manner are not what they were.
I have my thoughts but have not yet decided.

HUAN LANG: Two nights ago, when you were all asleep,
I saw my sister going with Hung Niang
Into the garden-court to burn their incense.
I waited half the night. No one returned.

MADAME TS'UI: Call Hung Niang! Tell her to come at once!

[HUAN LANG *calls* HUNG NIANG.]

HUNG NIANG [*entering*]: Why do you call me loudly, little master?

HUAN LANG: My mother hears that you the other night
Accompanied my sister to the garden.
So now she wants to question you about it.

HUNG NIANG [*troubled*]: Ha, little miss, you've got me into trouble! –
Young master, you go first and I shall follow.
'The sacred pond stands full of limpid water
On which the loving mandarin ducks now sleep,
But wind has blown aside the pictured curtain;
The parrot speaks the secrets love should keep.'

If you had gone at dark and left by dawn
Your joys, like heaven and earth, would still endure.
But since you blindly seek for dangerous bliss
Your conduct leaves me anxious and unsure.

You should have gone by moonlight and returned
By earliest rising of the morning star.
Your mother always shows a jealous mind,
Warping our acts from what they truly are.

She must have been suspicious of your scholar,
Fearing my mistress had become his wife,
Doubtless she thinks myself your go-between,
So for your pleasures I have risked my life.

Besides, not speaking of your growing beauty,
Seeing what clothes you wear and what you wore,
The tension at your buttons and your girth,
She finds all these quite other than before.

I am concerned that when I meet the mother
She will scold me as a wretch and say:

'*I ordered you to guard my daughter well;*
Why, then, have you led the girl astray?
If she should so address me with her malice,
What in my defense have I to say?

Well, I will say that as her maid from childhood
I have never once dared to deceive her.

So I shall clear myself of this affair
And not incriminate the guilty pair.

What had I to gain from such a union?

Their heads were like two lilies on one stem.
They clung like love-birds in a paradise

While I, not even venturing to cough,
Stood by the window, both my feet like ice.

There on the dampened moss my feet would freeze,
My dainty slippers stiffen and contract.
Now my tender skin must smart from whips. –
What profit had I from the lover's acts? –

Well, my little mistress, I am going.
If I extract myself from this grave peril,
Do not be too elated. If I cannot,
Don't be too desperate! Wait and hear the news.

[HUNG NIANG *approaches* MADAME TS'UI.]

MADAME TS'UI: You wretch! Why don't you kneel? Confess your guilt!

HUNG NIANG: Madame, I have nothing to confess.

MADAME TS'UI: Don't you persist in contradicting me!
If you will speak the truth, I may excuse you.
If you do not, I'll thrash you till you die!
You went at midnight with her to the garden.

HUNG NIANG: I did not go. Who saw us?

MADAME TS'UI: Huan Lang,
My son, he saw you. Can you still deny it?
[*She beats her.*]

HUNG NIANG: My mistress, take your noble hand away!
I beg you, calm yourself and hear me speak.

As we were sitting in our room one night,
Our sewing finished and our hands at ease,
Some one mentioned that our elder brother
Had, sad to say, contracted a disease.
Then we decided that we both would go
To see him and inquire if this was so.

MADAME TS'UI: 'Inquire,' you say! And what did he inform you?

HUNG NIANG: *He said that you had recently returned*
Evil for good, plunging his heart in pain.
He insisted I go home the first
And Ying Ying should a little while remain.

MADAME TS'UI: You little wretch! She, an unmarried girl,
To stay behind! How can I pardon that?

HUNG NIANG: *Why not? To treat him with the healing needle*
And never failing cone! It happened there.
Now for a month the two have been together,
Mating as orioles, a happy pair.

Surely, there is nothing more to say!
The two enjoy each other now completely.
Please overlook our trespass, if you can,
Or else desist from probing it too deeply.

MADAME TS'UI: You, you rascal, are the root of this!
HUNG NIANG: The fault is not with me, nor him, nor her.
No one is at fault except yourself.
MADAME TS'UI: Scoundrel, how can you be blaming me?
It is impossible that I am guilty.
HUNG NIANG: Good faith is basic to all human dealing.
A faithless man is of no human worth.
When, not long ago, a band of brigands
Besieged the P'u Chiu Temple, you declared
Your daughter would be married to the man
Who drove the bandit company away.
If Master Chang had not been deeply stirred
By the superior beauty of my mistress
Would he have devised the plan that saved us?
But once the robbers had been driven off

And we restored to peace, you broke your word.
Wasn't that breach of faith? – Even at that,
If you decided not to keep your word,
You should have offered him a gift of money,
Asking him to go off to distant regions.
You did a wrong to keep him in a study
Only a hand's breadth from your daughter's chamber,
So encouraging the eager girl
And longing student! Now the thing is done.
If you, Madame, do not scrupulously
Maintain the strictest secrecy about it.
Three results will follow in its wake.
First, the family of the Minister
Will be subject to extreme disgrace;
Second, Chang, who once has been our savior,
Will be grievously humiliated;
Third, if you drag this matter into court,
You'll be condemned as negligent in watching
Over the children of your family.
If you accept the counsel I have given
You will pardon this light trespassing,
Bring the matter to a happy ending,
And so procure much benefit to all.

The proverb says, when a girl comes of age,
Keeping her in her home is seldom wise.
One of these is a literary genius,
The other among all women wins the prize.

One knows the nine schools and the three religions,
The other, to embroider, paint and sew.
That elsewhere such perfection may be found
Is more than you or I shall ever know.

Therefore do not strive to thwart their union.
Is one who saved your life become your foe?
He prayed the White Horse General to come,
Who then achieved the Tiger's overthrow.

You should observe the lovers' horoscopes,
Seeing them not as people but as stars,
And so perceive how reckless is a plan
That such auspicious destiny debars.

Besides, you should consider the disgrace
Your family must feel should you explore
The matter further. Wisely drop the case
And for the future think of it no more.

MADAME TS'UI: Well, all the little wretch has said is wise.
I am the parent of a worthless girl,
Yet, even so, it is my bounden duty
To keep our honored family from disgrace.
No male in it has ever broken laws,
No female ever dared to marry twice. –
I must give my daughter to this beast.
Go, Hung Niang, and bring that bad girl here!

HUNG NIANG [*calling to* YING YING]: Young mistress, I have suffered from the rod
Again and still again. At last I spoke
And finally have been spared. Your mother orders
That I should tell you to come promptly to her.

YING YING: How can I see her when shame overwhelms me?

HUNG NIANG: Ah, little mistress, you are wrong again!
Why should you be ashamed before your mother?
If so, why did you act the way you did?

When the bright moon arose above the willows
And you fulfilled your passion in the night,

I was ashamed. I turned my face away,
Biting my servant's dress with all my might.

How could I dare to fix my eyes on you?
I only saw your tiny shoes. The flame
Of ardor burnt in one while one was silent.
Then you showed no slightest trace of shame.

[YING YING *and* MADAME TS'UI *see each other. They are in tears.*]

MADAME TS'UI: My little girl, you have been hurt and wronged.
You have acted basely in a way
Only accountable for crimes that I
Committed in an earlier existence.
How can I blame anybody else?
If I dragged your trouble into court,
Disgrace would fall upon your father's name.
Nothing of this vile nature should occur
In the household of a high Prime Minister!
[YING YING *continues to weep.*]
Comfort your little mistress, Hung Niang.
Unhappily this trouble came about
Because my daughter proved herself unworthy
Of the high decorum of our household manners. –
Go to his study and tell that wretch to come!
[HUNG NIANG *calls* CHANG.]

CHANG [*entering at the side*]: Who calls me?

HUNG NIANG: Master Chang, your guarded secret
Is now found out. My mistress calls for you.

CHANG: The only way to clear my difficulty
Is now for you to help me. Do you know
Who told the Madame this? I shake with fear!
How, then, can I dare to stand before her?

HUNG NIANG: Don't lose your courage! Put a brave foot forward
By going immediately into her presence.

The truth was out. What could I ever do?
So I confessed at length, reluctantly.
The man no longer makes the first approach,
So now she offers you some wine and tea.

Why are you gloomy? There is no more need
For me to serve you as a go-between.
Though I was not a perfect chaperon
What is the sense of making such a scene?

You are as useless as a withered stalk
That bears no grain, whose head is hanging lax,
Whose spear-point looks as though composed of silver
Yet in reality is only wax.

[MADAME TS'UI *sees* CHANG.]

MADAME TS'UI: What a fine sort of scholar you have been!
Do you not know that conduct which the sages
Deplore, no honest person should engage in?
I could hand you to the magistrate
But that would bring dishonor on my family.
Accordingly no other choice remains
Than marriage with my daughter as your wife.
Not for three generations has my family
Ever had a son-in-law who lacked
Official rank. Therefore you must proceed
Tomorrow to the capital to pass
The highest of the State Examinations.
In the meanwhile I myself shall take
Good care of Ying Ying as your future wife. –
But if you fail, do not come here again!
[CHANG *kneels before her.*]

HUNG NIANG: Thanks to heaven, to earth and to my mistress!

The burden of your fault is now forgiven.
Relax all frowns, since you are free from harms.
Incredibly, passion has come to bliss,
So hasten to enjoy your true love's charms.

MADAME TS'UI: Hung Niang, give word to see his luggage packed.
Prepare the wines, the viands and the sweets.
Tomorrow we'll attend on Master Chang
As far as the Pavilion of Farewell.
There we shall offer him a final feast. –
Inform the willows by the river bank
To wave auspiciously on his departure.
[MADAME TS'UI *and* YING YING *go out.*]

HUNG NIANG: Master Chang, do you feel glad or sad?

We must wait till you return again
When drums and flutes will sound throughout the hall
As love-birds mate in joyful matrimony
In peace and happiness beyond recall.

Then only will I have my due reward
For service rendered as a go-between,
Drink the wine of your true gratitude
And once again be cordial and serene.
[*Exeunt.*]

SCENE FIFTEEN

MADAME TS'UI [*entering*]: Today we bid farewell to Master
Chang
Who starts his journey to the capital.
[*To* HUANG NIANG, *offstage.*]
Go at once, Hung Niang, and tell your mistress
That she should come with us, for we must start
To visit the Pavilion of Farewell.
I have already sent sufficient orders
For preparation of the farewell feast
And also have invited Master Chang,
Who, I am sure, has finished packing now.
[YING YING *and* HUNG NIANG *enter.*]
YING YING: Today we bid our traveller good-bye.
Saying farewell at any time is sad
But how much more with autumn coming on,
Most melancholy season of the year.
CHANG [*entering*]: Last night her ladyship sternly demanded
That I must travel to the capital
To take the final high examination,
Offering to me that, if I succeeded,
She will give Ying Ying to me in marriage.
Now there is nothing else for me to do
So I am going to the final feast
Held in the Pavilion of Farewell
Where I must meet my little lady mistress,
Bidding her a sad and last good-bye.
[*Exit.*]

YING YING: At joyful meetings or at tragic partings
A glass of wine is drunk as sign of love.
In all four quarters of this busy world
Man mounted on his horse is on the move.

Faded leaves are falling to the earth;
Overhead the clouds are dark and gray.
Chilly winds blow fiercely from the west;
Southward wild geese take their heavy way.

At dawn the trees though silvered with the hoarfrost
Are dyed with crimson like a shame-flushed face.
They must feel pathetic sympathy
For separations through bleak, empty space.

My regret is that we met too late;
My sorrow is that we must part too soon.
O autumn wood, delay the westering sun!
Forestall the rising of the autumn moon!

Though hanging branches of the weeping willow
Are long, it is impossible to bind
His white horse with them so that a short while
He may delay, easing my soul and mind.

O forest, make his riding-horse move slowly
While baggage carts progress without delay;
Now, though we scarcely have declared our love,
He must be on his melancholy way.

When suddenly I heard the words, 'I'm going,'
Grief made my golden bracelets dangle loose.
At thought of the Pavilion of Farewell
Each limb shrinks, as of no future use.

HUNG NIANG: My little miss, you have not finished dressing!

YING YING: Hung Niang, you do not know my heart today!

Who is there who can comprehend my grief
As horse and carriage are prepared to start?
I have no strength to decorate myself
When boundless anguish overwhelms my heart.

I only wish to draw my coverlet
And pillows about me, falling back to sleep.
Who cares if my rich robe is soaked with tears
While one I so much love I cannot keep?

Today I am too sad to talk or move,
Suffering a hurt no medicine can heal.
Later I will write my love a letter,
However ill and wretched I shall feel.

[*All arrive at the Pavilion.* CHANG *bows to* MADAME TS'UI. YING YING *turns her face away.*]

MADAME TS'UI: Come closer, Master Chang! Now that you both
Are my own flesh and blood, you do not need
To shun each other. Come, my dearest child,
Turn yourself about to greet this man! –
Chang, be seated there, – I shall sit here. –
You, my child, sit there. – And now, Hung Niang,
Pour out the wine and you, sir, drink this cup
Down to its bottom. – Since I have firmly promised
My daughter's hand in marriage, you must now
Go to the capital to prove yourself
Worthy of her. You must exert all efforts
To win first place in your examination.

CHANG: I, as a man of poor accomplishments,
Rely entirely on the influence

Descending from the late Prime Minister,
And upon you yourself, most gracious lady!
I am confident of my return
With highest place and most distinguished honors,
Winning those laurels solely for your daughter.
[*They all sit down.*]

YING YING: *Faded leaves are scattered by the storm.*
Over the ground mist pours its chilly breath.
He sits uneasily at the banquet table,
His features knitted in a look of death.

I dare not let the warm tears fill my eyes
Lest others should perceive my wretchedness.
When people look, I quickly bow my head,
Pretending to arrange my silken dress.

Even though we may be one at last,
How can I fail to feel this pain today?
I am so utterly distraught by love
That all my slender figure faints away.

Before our joy in union is completed
This culminating sorrow is our fate.
We love in secret. Yesterday our love
Was known. And now today we separate!

Though I have undergone the bitterness
Of days when fierce love-longing wrought our curse,
Who ever would suppose that separation
Such as we suffer now is vastly worse!

MADAME TS'UI: Hung Niang, help your mistress pour the wine.

[YING YING *rises and pours some wine.*]

YING YING: Please drink this cup I reach you with my hand.

You trifle with me, treating a long farewell
As if forgetting times when we were blessed,
Holding each other firmly, hand in hand,
With cheek to cheek together closely pressed.

As son-in-law of the late Minister Ts'ui,
You join a family with a noble name.
Is not this match, like two flowers on one stem,
Better than lofty literary fame?

[*She sits down again.*]

The feast moves far too fast. For just this moment
We are sitting face to face and eye to eye.
Were not my mother here, I should have courage
To lift my plate to Chang and hold it high!

As man and wife we should be close together
But here are placed at tables opposite,
So that we merely steal some furtive glances
From these far-distant stations where we sit.

Repeatedly I speak my own devotion
Through timid glances of the eyes alone,
Until I feel like her who for her husband
Yearned so she came transfigured into stone.

MADAME TS'UI: Hung Niang, pour out some festive wine again.

HUNG NIANG: Mistress, you have not breakfasted today. So you must now consent to drink a little.

YING YING: *All wines and foods that you have handed me*
Have tasted more like common mud and earth.
No rarest drink or viand pleases one
Whose spirit famishes, then dies of dearth.

All water that you serve seems merely dregs,
Tea and rice are flat, dull, savorless.
My cup is more than half filled up with tears,
All things come salted with my own distress.

Why are we two lovers separated?
Fame is trivial as a small snail's horn.
Profit trifling as a house-fly's head.
Why should we sit apart and live forlorn?

The cups and platters soon will be removed.
My carriage travels east, his horse goes west.
Both will linger sadly on the way
While past green hills the sun sinks down to rest.
How can I know where he will sleep tonight?
Even in dreams he vanishes from sight.

MADAME TS'UI: Hung Niang, order the carts to be made ready
And ask the scholar Chang to mount his pony.
I myself return with your young mistress.
[*They rise and prepare themselves.* CHANG *bows to* MADAME TS'UI.]
I have nothing more to say to you.
Only remember the extreme importance
Of winning rank and station. Come back soon!
CHANG: I shall be careful to obey you, Madame.
[CHANG *and* YING YING *exchange bows.*]
YING YING: Since you must go, be sure that you return
Whether you win official rank or not!
CHANG: My lady, set yourself at ease for that!
If members of your family cannot gain
The highest rank in scholarship, who can? –
The time has come for me to bid farewell.
YING YING: Stay just one moment longer! I can offer

No other parting gift than to present you
With this impromptu poem that I have made:
'You loved me dearly once, but leave me now
Lost and abandoned. What am I dreaming of?
Only that all the ardor granted me
May now be given to your second love!'

CHANG: Lady, you have failed to understand me!
How could I ever love another woman?
Your poem dismays me! – Well, you do not believe me.
So we must wait till I return at last
After I win the highest rank in learning.
Then a poem of mine will answer yours.

YING YING: *My crimson sleeves are wet with tears of love;*
Your scholar's gown of blue more deeply soaked.
The oriole flies east, the swallow west.
When will your exile ever be revoked?

Before you go I only ask of fate
To drink this cup of wine to honor you,
But well before its rim has touched my lips
I swoon to think of perils to ensue!

I pray that when you reach the capital
You guard against the heat. In travelling please
Be moderate in all you eat and drink.
Be careful of your health and take your ease.

In sad, deserted villages, when rain
And dew have fallen, rise early; do not wait.
In country inns where wind and frost are keen
And dawn comes dim, be careful to sleep late.

When riding through a blustery autumn gale
And I am not beside you on the way,

You must take all precautions for your warmth,
Guarding yourself discreetly, night and day.

From no one in the world can I have help
And Heaven itself is known a niggard giver.
My grief would crush the mountains of Hua Shan;
My weeping overflow the Yellow River!

I shall stand high upon the Western Tower
At evening as the weary day is done
To watch the fading willows by the dike
And mark the old road in the sinking sun.

One night ago and we clung close together.
Now I return to find my empty bed.
The warmth last night under green coverlets
Seems ages past, leaving me dreams instead. –

I can devise no plot to hold you here.
Already you have mounted on your horse.
With tear-filled eyes, with agony in our looks,
Each of us goes upon a separate course.

I hardly care whether your scholarship
Wins you high place and honor for your life
But only dread that you will give me up,
Choosing for yourself another wife!

The wild goose and the azure-tinted phoenix
Will bear my frequent messages, but come –
Whether or not you gain the highest honor –
Speedily back to me, as to your home!
Song-girls at court arouse my keenest fear.
You must not linger there as you did here!

CHANG: Lady, your words to me are gold and jade,
Inscribed indelibly upon my heart.
We shall meet soon. Do not be sad! I am going. –

I bow my head, as impotent to check
Warm tears, and, though in deepest misery.
Attempt to simulate a look of pleasure.
[*Exit.*]

YING YING: My soul already leaves me. How can I
Follow you, even in my fondest dreams?

The green hills intervene. I cannot see him.
An envious forest shields him from my sight.
Evening mists and vapors hide me from him.
Twilight descends, fading too soon to night.

On the old road no human voice is heard.
Faintly I hear the neighing of his horse.
Reluctantly I climb into my carriage,
Sadly to ride upon my homeward course.
How hurried was I on the outward way!
How, going back, I seek a long delay!

MADAME TS'UI: Hung Niang, assist your mistress in her carriage.
Already it is late. Return with haste. –
Though I have seemingly indulged my daughter,
I may have done what a stern mother should.
[*Exit.*]

HUNG NIANG: Your mother's carriage hastens far ahead.
Come, my little mistress, we must follow.

YING YING: Hung Niang, where do you think that Chang is now?

He must by now be in the midst of mountains.
His whip glints through the twilight down the road.
The whole world's sorrow now seems pressing on me!
How can my carriage carry such a load!
[*Exeunt.*]

The West Chamber

PRODUCTION COMMENTS

An Interview with John H. J. Hu

BECAUSE of numerous practical difficulties in producing a play the length and complexity of *The West Chamber*, it is, unfortunately, a play which is rarely seen by Western audiences. But it need not be one which is enjoyed only as an outstanding example of the dramatic literature of China. Many of the problems of producing this play with Western actors can be successfully overcome with careful study and analysis, without loss of any of the play's poetic beauty and charm.

With this in mind, and after careful study of the play, I drastically revised the script for the experimental production presented at Indiana University. In the revision the first scenes, in which Chang Chün-jui visits the temple and falls in love with Ying Ying at first sight, are eliminated. It was also possible to remove the scenes in which Madame Ts'ui promises to marry her daughter Ying Ying to whoever can save them from the bandits who have surrounded the temple and demand that Ying Ying be married to their leader. It was found that the acting version can effectively start with the scene in which Madame Ts'ui tries to deny Chang Chün-jui his promised reward even though he has engineered the bandit's defeat. During the ensuing fierce argument, past events are recalled to witness whether there is a breach of faith on the part of the matriarch. In a later scene Chang Chün-jui, in order to enlist Ying Ying's maid as a go-between, confides in her how he has fallen in love with her mistress in a spontaneous and irresistible way. From this point onwards, the action unfolds in the chronological order of the original events.

This revision enables the director to reduce the characters from the large number in the original script to four; Madame Ts'ui, Ying Ying, Chang Chün-jui and Hung Niang.

In the study of these characters the director finds that, while Madame Ts'ui is essentially calculating and domineering, her daughter's motivation is extremely subtle and complex. Ying Ying's aristocratic education, her sense of filial piety, self-respect, and fear of exposure all tend to bind her to rectitude; on the other hand, the natural yearning for mutual love, her resentment over her mother's breach of promise, her gratitude to Chang and her fear of his dying of a broken heart all induce her to return his love. Her inner conflict, then, is not simply one between love and honor, or reason and emotion; it is one kind of love or reason in conflict with another.

Collateral with the shifting attitude of Madame Ts'ui and Ying Ying towards him, Chang Chün-jui's mood fluctuates from anger and frustration to hope and blissfulness. In the meandering course of his romance, the maid occupies the pivotal position. Quick-witted and earthy in her humor, she carries messages for the lovers and thus rekindles the suppressed affection; she urges her mistress toward the initial tryst with Chang, after the latter has twice tantalized the heroine; finally, when the affair is exposed, she persuades Madame to let the lovers marry. Behind Hung Niang's action is her sympathy for the lovers, her honesty in recognizing the force of the flesh, and her bravery in pointing out the mistakes of her superior. Thus we find every character in this acting revision of major importance.

To identify and differentiate the *dramatis personae*, Yüan

theatre is known to have followed six principles aimed at distinguishing the Chinese characters from the non-Chinese, the moral from the immoral, the civilian from the military, the old from the young, the rich from the poor, and the nobility from the common people. Aside from these principles, little attention was paid to historical authenticity and total accuracy, as wardrobes from different periods and locales might be freely intermingled in one play. Furthermore, a story set in the T'ang Dynasty (618–907) could use a wardrobe of the Sung Dynasty (960–1279), into which period most of the extant Yüan plays fell. Beyond this general knowledge, scholars have not been able to go past and provide sufficient guidance for specific costume designs. Thus, after a strenuous but futile effort to reconstruct a lost heritage with the aid of archaeological discoveries of pre-Yüan and Yüan theatre made in the last two decades in mainland China, the director decided to let the characters appear in costumes that their counterparts in the Peking theatre normally wear. Consequently, the following description of major costumes and accessories in *The West Chamber* is merely suggestive:

Chang Chün-jui: scholar's cap (*Wen Sheng Chin*), light yellow gown (*Tieh-tzu*), high-soled boots, a fan.

Ying Ying: pale blue robe (*P'ei*) with 'water sleeves' and pleated skirt.

Madame Ts'ui: gray wig, purple three-fourths robe and skirt, with a heavy walking staff.

Hung Niang: pink jacket and wide trousers (*K'u Ao*) with a handkerchief. All the female roles wear flat-soled shoes.

Scholars agree that black and white were the only colors used in facial make-up in the Yüan theatre; the multi-colored and complex make-up characteristic of the Peking Opera theatre gradually developed only after the Ming Dynasty. In the production of *The West Chamber*, actors wear the make-up that their corresponding roles in Peking theatre normally wear. This was done partly for lack of sufficient information about Yüan make-up, and partly in order to be consistent with the acting style and costuming.

After an analysis of the script, characters, and costumes, it is important to turn to the type of staging to be used. Though we find many changes in Chinese drama from the beginnings of the ritual dance to the well-known Peking Opera, it is interesting to find little change in the basic conventions of the playing area. With the exception of the recent Chinese Communist theatre with its realistic scenery and lighting, the Chinese stage is still an almost square platform with a rug, two chairs and a silk-draped table. This simplicity allows for a rapid change of locale which is indicated through speech, movement, and properties.

In the traditional Chinese theatre the stage was a raised platform supported by four lacquered columns, two doors at the rear of the stage, the one on stage right for entrances, the one on stage left for exits. Between the two doors hung a large embroidered curtain or banner. The stage projected out into the audience which allowed the audience to sit on three sides of the playing area. As in all theatres this particular design and simplicity of decor influenced and still influences the techniques of production.

In the experimental production at Indiana University it was found that, without violating the traditional setting, one door could be used for the exits and entrances of Chang Chün-jui and the other for the remaining characters with great effectiveness. Another effective innovation was the addition of a large square window on the back wall in place of the embroidered panel or banner. Thus lighting, designed to filter through the window, suggested the time of day, as well as creating the appropriate atmosphere.

Properties in this play are simple; two chairs plus a few items such as a fan and an incense burner practically exhaust the property list. However, the frequent scene changes necessitate the help of the traditional stage hand, the so-called property man. Though such a role is often said to be theoretically invisible to the audience, his presence can nevertheless be distracting to a Western audience. Therefore, great care should be taken in planning his movements so that he can function with the least interference in the flow of action.

Though the traditional Chinese acting is often described as symbolic or stylistic in the West, these epithets need rarely be used in rehearsal. A more useful motto is one given by Ch'i Ju-shen, one of Mei Lan-fang's teachers: 'In the traditional Chinese theatre, every sound is as rhythmic as music, every movement is as graceful as dance.' In pantomiming the crossing of a door sill or the climbing of a wall, the actor is urged to exert his imagination and visualize the things which are actually missing from the stage. Once he is thus mentally prepared, the actor can start practicing his specific movements and pantomime.

Convention and his particular characterization require that Chang Chün-jui must be simultaneously vigorous and yet feminine; his robustness tinged with the softness of a *tan* or female role. To meet with this seemingly self-contradictory demand, it is helpful to practice repeatedly walking in small steps, with heel down first and with the right hand holding the fan to the height of the shoulders. The fan being a constant accessory, the actor must learn how to open or fold it with his thumb at one jerk; the action lasts only about a quarter of a second. Ying Ying should be demure and graceful throughout the play, even though her reserved manner is conspicuously relaxed after the consummation of their love. Accordingly, her acting is largely marked by mincing gait, and elegantly folded hands when sitting down. The most exacting technique for her impersonation is perhaps the various uses of the water sleeves: flapping them to display her displeasure, raising them near her lips to conceal a smile, or moving them back and forth before her eyes to simulate wiping away some imaginary tears. In sharp contrast, her maid Hung Niang is lively and brisk, with her action punctuated by coquettish glances, mincing but sprightly steps, and the fluttering of her handkerchief. Madame Ts'ui, a lady of eminent social position, walks always in sedate but faltering steps while leaning heavily on her staff.

In addition to these individual techniques, the actors must learn how to act in ensemble. For example, in the scene in which Madame Ts'ui beats Hung Niang to force her to confess Ying Ying's tryst with Chang Chün-jui, the beating should become a coordinated dance: when Madame Ts'ui's staff falls on one side, Hung Niang, with handkerchief in hand, dodges to the other. When these movements are repeated several times with increasing speed, the staff, the handkerchief, and the human figures (remember the colorful costumes) are intermingled into a most picturesque tableau.

Although a large portion of a Yüan play such as *The West Chamber* was originally sung to the accompaniment of an orchestra, the production can rely upon the beauty of the spoken word accompanied by music. In this particular production Chinese music of remote origin, recorded on tapes, was effectively used during the performance and for the introduction and intermission. Since Chang Chün-jui is versed in flute playing, with which he succeeds in arousing Ying Ying's emotions, a lingering flute tone was used as a fixed motif which appeared whenever Ying Ying thought of him or mused over their love affair.

Though the director might feel uneasy about the freedom in which he deals with the original play and the resulting directional approach, he will find the acting style, the conventions of Chinese theatre, and the beauty of the verse, with the rich sentiments generated by the story, all of universal appeal for an audience. It is inevitable that the imagination of the audience is stimulated in the presentation of this play which demands a combination of the elements of speech, movement, music and song so characteristic of all Chinese theatre.

IKKAKU SENNIN

An Introduction to

THE JAPANESE NOH PLAY

By Roy E. Teele

IT has been six hundred years since Kan-ami (1333–84) created the Noh play as we think of it – a magnificent theatrical art combining music, dance, poetry, costume and setting. If any of these elements is lacking we have, so to speak, a headless or a legless man. Yet it is unfortunately true that for most Westerners only the poetic texts are available. They are well worth reading and study, but we should not forget that they give us less than 'half a man.' We can supplement with pictures and verbal descriptions, but only supplement, never replace the real performance.

In Japan the Noh play has had a fairly continuous history for six centuries, but for the past four centuries it has been primarily a performing art, for scarcely any new plays entered the current 240-play repertory during that time. Other plays were written, perhaps thousands, but even those which were performed at all were soon dropped from the repertory. As a result we have a relatively fixed and limited number of plays.

To some extent origins determine the nature of an art; therefore we must briefly consider the sources of the Noh play. Three major sources are Japanese popular entertainment, religious 'performances,' and Chinese entertainments. The first must be divided into two aspects, the folk and the aristocratic. 'Field plays' were popular celebrations related to rice planting; and the *kuse* (a song-and-dance form) was so enjoyed among aristocrats that it was taken into the Noh play as its climax. Buddhist temples and Shinto shrines had dances of various kinds, as well as chanting, such as the Buddhist *shomyo*, which sometimes had semi-theatrical aspects. At the court Chinese dances were loved, and acrobatics and farces from China were widely known, at least in adapted forms. Borrowings and adaptations from all these sources, not all in any one play of course, made up Kan-ami's theatrical form, later to be refined by his son Zeami (1363–1443). As accomplished poets, musicians and actor-dancers, Kan-ami and Zeami were constantly aware of their audiences. At precisely what time or place, or with the help of what unknown predecessors and collaborators, we cannot know, but we can say that by the second half of the fourteenth century Kan-ami had created a non-representational (symbolic, conventional) drama widely popular under the name *sarugaku*. From the point of view of origins, then, the Noh play is a popular theatrical form, not hieratic drama.

In discussing the plot and ideas of Noh plays we may start at a rather conventional point, the five-fold program division: god, warrior, woman, madwoman, and demon plays. There are thirty-nine plays in the first group, best exemplified by *Takasago*. For the most part these plays are based on temple or shrine legends, sometimes more folk than sacerdotal, and certainly never 'scriptural' to the extent of medieval European miracle plays. In the second group there are sixteen plays, almost all related to the twelfth century Genji-Heike struggle. Their burden is the suffering of warriors in Asura, the Buddhist hell for warriors, not at all the glories of war. Even a play which does not use this theme, *Yashima*, rather than glorifying battle tells of the reckless act by which Yoshitsune retrieves his bow so that no one will accuse him of weakness because of its size. *Hachi no Ki* and *Funa Benkei* reveal greater admiration for certain military qualities, but they are classified as fourth- and fifth-group plays because of the structure of the first and the kind of characters in the second.

There are thirty-eight plays in the third group, the women or 'wig' plays. Some critics refer to this group as the 'heart' of the Noh, partly because it is central in the program, chiefly because these plays best exemplify *yugen*, that subtle elegance and grace which Zeami and later critics so greatly admired. God and warrior plays have their own *yugen*, and Zeami insisted that even 'demons' should be played with *yugen* rather than pure terror or horror. Still it is the women plays which seem best to show this quality, the quintessence of the Noh. Most famous of the women plays is *Hagoromo*, or 'The Feather Robe'. Like *Carmen* or *Aida* on our opera stage, it is frequently performed by all 'schools,' and seems almost omnipresent and inevitable on programs. It is the favorite of amateurs when they appear in special performances. The beauty and pathos of the heavenly maiden who cannot return to the moon until the fisherman returns her feather robe are matched by the lyrical beauty of the text – one of the most often translated.

The fourth group, the so-called 'madwoman' plays, is most numerous of all, ninety-four in number. The group is subdivided so that it contains not only the stories of women driven mad by love and loss, but also people who become so 'attached' to this world by hate or love that after death they are forced to linger. But the most important subgroup is the 'real life' play. In it there is no return of a spirit from the dead, as in somewhat over half the two hundred and forty plays currently performed. Instead a set of 'living' characters is involved in action with a beginning, middle and end. In short. it is relatively close to our Western concept of drama. *Hachi no Ki* is an example of this kind; an old warrior is brought back from semi-exile after he demonstrates to his disguised master the hospitality and loyalty proper to a true warrior. *Ikkaku Sennin* likewise occurs entirely in 'the present.'

The plays of the fifth group have a supernatural being as their *shitê* or protagonist. Although the usual name for this group would suggest that the supernatural being must be a malignant demon, in fact a great many plays have helpful spirits. One brilliant example is *Kokaji* in which a fox spirit helps Munechika forge a sword. Melodramatic situations, fantastic characters, varied mimetic dances, unusual and gorgeous costumes, all make the plays of this group – fifty-three in number – very popular.

Another approach to the content of the plays has already been suggested: to examine the literary or historical sources of their plots. Over forty plays were taken from the epic-romances which narrate the Genji-Heike struggle. The 'Lancelot' of these tales, Minamoto Yoshitsune, is the subject of a number of plays: as a youngster in *Kurama Tengu* and *Eboshi Ori*, as a young lord served by Benkei in *Hashi Benkei* and *Funa Benkei*, and as the object of his brother's jealous fury in *Shozon* and *Ataka*. Others of the forty treat other heroes and special episodes. The *Tale of Genji* provides the plots for a dozen plays, and other Heian works like the *Tales of Ise* are also used. Ono no Komachi, the Sappho of Japan, is the subject of five plays, and other poets, even individual poems, are the basic material for plays.

Associations with place are of great importance, not only from the point of view of historical events which have occurred there, but also because of their natural beauty. Temples and shrines have both personal and religious significance; they have also natural settings with special characteristics. A whole nation, such as China, may provide the physical and cultural background for a number of plays. Over twenty involve China: the poet Po Chu-i appears under his Japanese name,

Haku Rakuten; *Choryo* tells of the Chinese general Chang Liang; *Shojo* has a Chinese wine spirit as its *shitê*; *Kantan* is a tale of a magic pillow which causes a sleeper to dream he is emperor of China; and *Yokihi* recounts the tragic story of the love of Yang Kuei-fei and the emperor Hsuan Tsung. China was as close to fourteenth-century Japan as Rome to early medieval European states, and as important culturally.

India was distant and shadowy; the one play set in India is Zempo's *Ikkaku Sennin*. Like the four other extant plays by Zempo it is romantic in tone and esoteric in subject. This is not surprising since Zempo was of the third generation of Noh-writers, one of the last in that opening two-hundred-year creative period, not unnaturally seeking new subject matter. He could not possibly have known that forms of this story had appeared in the Indian epics, the *Ramayana* and the *Mahabharata*, but he could have found it in any of at least five versions in the late fifteenth century, all modified by their transmission from India to Japan through China (where the water-associated dragons were added). The date of composition is not known, but the first specific reference to the play is a record of a performance in 1524, when Zempo would have been seventy.

More than half of the current repertory of plays have two scenes, the first starting with a travelling priest's visit to a site famous in Japanese history or literature. Arrived at the place after a beautifully descriptive *michi yuki*, or travel song, he meets a local man or woman, and discusses with him the event which has made the place famous. Suddenly this person disappears. There is an *ai kyogen*, or interlude, during which a special actor called the *kyogen* actor retells the story in popular language, while the 'local' man or woman (the *shitê*) changes mask and costume. He returns to the stage transformed into the hero or heroine and proceeds to retell the event, or to re-enact it while the chorus retells it. Not the total action, only some quintessential aspect of it. Thus, in *Yashima*, it is not the Genji victory at Yashima, which everyone in the audience would already know quite well, but the historically trivial detail of Yoshitsune's recklessness in retrieving his bow. Psychologically and poetically it is of great importance, and it gains a subtle beauty when the audience realizes that the whole is seen through the eyes of the returned spirit of Yoshitsune. Poetry, music, dance, all reflect this.

In the same play the structure of the second half may be briefly indicated as a series of songs which reach their climax in the *kuse*, sung by the chorus and danced by the *shitê* (Yoshitsune). It opens with a *machi uta*, or waiting song, sung by the priests, then a *sashi* in which Yoshitsune laments the need to return from the warriors' hell to this scene of warfare. After a series of exchanges with the priests, Yoshitsune states explicitly in the *age uta*, or high song, which the chorus sings for him, that it is 'terrible hatred' which has drawn him back to this scene. However, he immediately then begins another *sashi* describing the serene night of the battle, leading up to the *kuse* in which he expresses his inmost emotions as he retrieved his bow:

> My fighting name is still just half achieved.
> Suppose my bow
> Were to be captured by the enemy. 'Yoshitsune,
> That weakling!' they'd say.

Then in a final song the chorus explains that the enemy portrayed in song and dance was in fact only the sea gulls, and the sounds of battle were but the breeze storming through the tall pines.

The song forms of the Noh play are named in various ways.

The *machi uta*, or waiting song, is simply a song sung by the *waki*, or secondary actor, as he waits for the *shitê* to appear (for example, after making the 'between acts' costume change). The *age uta*, or high song, is so named because it starts on a relatively high pitch. In neither case is the meter of the 'song' defined. It varies so much, indeed, that exact definition is not possible. In most cases it is a group of six or eight twelve-syllable lines. These twelve-syllable lines, even more than our once popular English iambic pentameter, were *the* preferred metrical form. The combination of seven- and five-syllable units, from the eighth century on, seemed to fit the Japanese language as smoothly and naturally as iambic fits English. Therefore, most poetic forms in Japanese are made up of combinations of these groups of seven and five syllables. In their musical setting they are sung to an eight-beat measure.

Sashi is an untranslatable term for a short introductory or transition passage, usually made up of seven- and five-syllable rhythmic units. The *kuse*, the most important form, is the climatic song-and-dance of the play, a form very popular such as Shizuka Gozen who became Yoshitsune's favorite. Like the *uta*, the *kuse* is made up of a series of twelve-syllable lines. In number they range from ten to fifty. Often the *kuse* is marked by the repetition of a line at the beginning and a part of a line at the end, but even where there is no formal sign the *kuse* is defined by its lyrical unity.

It was Ezra Pound who discovered that a Noh play as a whole may have a lyric unity beyond that of plot and character, a unity of imagery which reminds one of the image clusters in Shakespeare's plays. The moon images in *Miidera*, the moonlight in *Matsukaze* joined with the pine images, the lute in *Tsunemasa*, poetry in *Kayoi Komachi* – in every case, one or two images serve to give a lyric intensity to the plays such that they are clearly lyric dramas or dramatic lyrics of the highest order.

In rhetoric or poetic devices the Noh text is as sophisticated and complex as any Elizabethan play. It builds on the rhetoric of the *tanka* (31-syllable 'short poem') in the *Kokin* and *Shin Kokin* anthologies, and has added something of the art of 'extensive' writing through the influence of the *renga* or linked verse tradition, already in its formative stages in the fourteenth century. The favorite device known as the *kakekotoba*, or pivot word, may be seen in these lines from *Sekidera Komachi*:

> Bejewelled like the carriages of the Emperor
>   and his nobles were our robes bright colored
> Gorgeous pillows were spread in great ladies' chambers ...

where 'bright colored' refers back to 'robes' and forward to 'pillows.' The frequent use of the pun as a serious poetic device is complicated to double punning in these lines from the same play:

> She moistens the writing brush for the *Book of*
>   *Burnt Seaweeds*
> Rakes among the withered leaves of words,

in which the Japanese words *moshugaki* mean both 'seaweeds' and 'poetic anthology,' and the word *kaku* means both 'to rake' and 'to write.'

It is little wonder that the members of the Noh audience often follow the words in their text as the actors sing, for the text is not only very complex, it is also in a language no longer spoken. It is almost as difficult for a modern Japanese as Chaucer for a modern American. But there is another reason for following the text: many Japanese practise singing Noh as a hobby or avocation. They know the two major forms of vocal performance, the heightened speech which is like recitative, and the singing or chanting of verse. The latter takes two forms, the *tsuyogin* or strong style, and the *yowagin* or soft style. The soft is the older style, based in part on Buddhist *shomyo*, or chanting. It is flowing and highly decorated, with a sort of melancholy lyricism in its melodies, so that it might be called the minor mode. The strong style is like the major, straightforward and direct, with relatively little decoration, and therefore suitable for chanting a description of battle or the words of a warrior. Malm analyzes the tone system of Noh singing as one based on the interval of the minor seventh, its melodic passages constructed on three principal tones: A, the pitch center; E, next in importance; and B, an alternate final tone. Since the melody may move from one of these tones to the next only by fixed progressions, a song may be seen to be made up of a series of such formal progressions, arranged to fit the emotional or dramatic intent of a given set of words. The total melodic effect is that of a late Wagnerian opera rather than the set pieces of early Verdi.

The dance likewise is made up of a series of fixed movements. There are twenty-six, and the manner of progression from one to another is fixed so absolutely that on the stage motion seems to flow with a natural inevitability. Teaching is usually done by rote memory and constant drill from a very early age; at the same time, however, there are now manuals for the learner where diagrams show the fixed relationship between word and movement. The same movements serve for pure or abstract dance as for miming, so it must be supposed that the trained observer can follow some pantomime. When some obviously military personal property like a spear is used, or a religious object such as a Buddhist rosary, meaning is of course immediately clear.

Like virtually every phase of the Noh play, the dance has been thoroughly analyzed by Japanese scholars, with a resulting extensive terminology. The *jo no mai*, *shin no mai*, and *chu no mai* are of central importance as the three dances displaying the elegant grace of *yugen* in its quintessential form, being most often associated with the third group of plays, the women plays. They are slow and formal and to an inexperienced Westerner usually do not have the appeal of the striking *rambyoshi* in *Dojoji*, the story of a dancer turned to a snake under a great temple bell, or the *midare* of *Shojo*, which shows a wine spirit dancing on the river waves. All have an elegant precision which is possible only when actors spend years in exacting training and devote themselves completely to their art. To this day actors of all roles are male.

Costume and mask are immediately striking to any visitor in the Noh theatre. The gorgeous fabrics and magnificent styling suggest aristocratic life from the fourteenth through the seventeenth centuries without conforming precisely to any particular period. However, for particular roles the costume is fixed within rather definite limits. The feather robe in *Hagoromo*, for example, may vary in color, but the conventionalized feather pattern is always the same. The heads of the five major 'schools' or traditions of Noh acting all have collections of robes and masks handed down for centuries, repaired as long as possible and replaced when absolutely necessary with a close copy. Change or originality here, as elsewhere in the Noh theatre, is avoided. Greatness lies in fulfilling the traditions, not in changing them.

Only the *shitê* or one of his companions playing a woman's role wears a mask. Women's masks are numerous, but the *waka-onna* or young woman's mask is most widely known. The old woman, the jealous woman, the young man, the young warrior, the old man, the blind man, the old warrior, and the various supernatural beings all have their own special masks, either as types or as the characters of particular plays. All are remarkable as sculpture, many are masterpieces. In investigating some of the major schools' collections of masks, Professor Konishi has reached the conclusion that through the years there has been a process of selection whereby the individual (perhaps coarse, even grotesque) masks have fallen out of use in favor of more elegant, more generalized or abstract masks. This process of refinement may well have occurred in other aspects of Noh performance as well, even a certain refinement of the texts themselves. Since older programs show that more plays were performed in a day, it is suggested that the present tempo may be somewhat slower than in Zeami's day.

The ideal program, as Zeami describes it, is made up of five lyric Noh plays and three *kyogen* or comic Noh plays. The lyric Noh plays were performed in the order given in the discussion of the five-fold program; the *kyogen* interspersed between these may well have been related in theme. For example, a god play might well be followed by a farce making fun of priests or some episode in a shrine. Warrior plays might be followed by a play in which a peasant pretends to be about to commit ritual suicide. The plays move forward with an acceleration of tempo and excitement from the austere and dignified god plays to the moving women plays, and on to the swift-moving excitement of the 'demon' plays. Like the individual Noh play, the program may be considered in terms of the analysis of dance into *jo*, *ha* and *kyu*, or introduction, development and climax. The god plays were in the *jo*; warriors, women, and madwomen (to continue to use the traditional short names) were the three parts of the development; and the fifth group – like the *kuse* and its attached songs in the individual play – made up the *kyu* section.

One who has enjoyed the seven- or eight-hour theatrical experience of such a program probably will not speak of catharsis – Zeami never did – but he must have a sense of an all-encompassing human experience, moments of great lyrical intensity, in music, poetry, dance, and of laughter at the absurdity of life.

IKKAKU SENNIN

A Japanese Noh Play by
KOMPARU ZEMPO MOTOYASO

Adapted by William Packard
from the translation of Frank Hoff

IKKAKU SENNIN

CAST OF CHARACTERS

IKKAKU SENNIN (*shitê*), a holy hermit monk with extraordinary magic power. He has a horn on his forehead and therefore he is called 'Holy Hermit Unicorn'. He wears a mask

LADY SENDA BUNIN (*shitê-tsure*), a beautiful lady with irresistible charm who has been sent to seduce Ikkaku Sennin in order to make him lose his magic power. She wears a mask

TWO DRAGON GODS (*ryujin*) (Kogata), gods who are responsible for the rainfall. Because of Ikkaku Sennin's curse, they are trapped in a cave, which has caused a disastrous drought in the country. They wear masks

SHINKA (*waki*), a servant to the emperor of Barana, a kingdom in India

TWO KOUSHOU (*waki-tsure*), carriers of the palanquin in which Lady Senda Bunin rides

TWO ON-STAGE ASSISTANTS (*kuroko*)

CHORUS of six or eight

The play takes place in the Kingdom of Barana, India. The season is autumn.

First produced in this adaptation by IASTA, New York, in October 1964.

3. *Ikkaku Sennin:* from a performance at Indiana University.

The DRAGON Gods are depicted
by small children

Also w. Emperior as
1 it make's it less realistic
One can't depict the Emperor

2. Charm

3. Oportunity to train

Stage assistants bring out two props. One is a 'construct' (tsukuri-mono) *suggesting the hut in which the* shitê (IKKAKU SENNIN) *is concealed. The second 'construct' represents a rock pile in which the* DRAGON GODS *are hidden. Placing them is handled as part of the performance proper.*

A procession enters: the waki, SHINKA, *costumed as a court official, accompanied by two* waki-tsure (*his companions*), *who are the 'carriers' of a litter on which the* shitê-tsure, LADY SENDA BUNIN, *is imagined to be carried. Actually she is not carried at all, but walks on as the* waki-tsure *holds something like a baldaquin over her head to suggest the litter.*

They take some time getting to the center of the stage before SHINKA, *the* waki, *speaks.*

SHINKA: The prince I serve is a great prince, he is the emperor of Barana
who rules a kingdom of India, with many lands
along the Ganges.
Now in the country of this prince there lives a hermit
and he is a wizard.
He was born from the womb of a deer, and he has a horn,
one single long horn,
a horn that sprouts out of his forehead,
sprouts out of his forehead,
and therefore we have named this wizard
Ikkaku Sennin, holy hermit unicorn.
Once Ikkaku Sennin and the great dragon gods

had an affair of honor.
and the wizard won out, the holy hermit unicorn used
his magic
to undo the great dragon gods,
he drove them into a cave and made them stay inside.
Away in that cave, they could not cause rain to fall.
Since then my prince has come to grieve,
he sees that his whole countryside is dry, and so now he
knows
he has to free those dragon gods.
Listen, this is the prince's plan, this is the beautiful
young girl
who is going to go up into the mountains,
there where the wizard lives, the holy hermit unicorn,
and he may make a mistake and think she's lost her way.
Then he may fall in love,
he may say this young girl is so beautiful, he has lost
his heart and art
and all the magic that he used to use.
It may work out that way, that's what the prince is
hoping for,
and so we're going to carry her up to the unicorn.

[*The two* KOUSHOU *join* SHINKA*'s travel song.*]
Mountains and mountains and mountains,
mists that cover over all the weary travellers,
cold winds that blow through the open woods, as we
keep going,
no sleep on the mountain side,
no sweet dreams for us.
Mists and autumn rain,
autumn rains and mist fall down
on the deep ravine

so that even the lowest leaves receive water,
change to strange autumn colors.
We are kept so cold
as we keep climbing, climbing, climbing on our way.
The road goes through so much mist,
through clouds on high hills.
How do we know where we are?
Up in the mountains
we do not know where we are,
we wander around
wondering where does this road go, this road we're on,
does anyone know anything about this road?

SHINKA: Day after day, we've hurried on our way,
travelling on this old road that no one knows about,
now we are lost, we are all worn out.
Look, there are lots of rocks, they are lying on the ground and piled up in a mound, I wonder why?
– how sweet the breezes as they blow over the rock pile, I can tell the smell of pine.
Perhaps this is where the wizard lives, the holy hermit unicorn, perhaps this is the place.
Let's keep quiet and get close to it,
slowly, slowly, get up close so we can see if the wizard is hiding inside.

IKKAKU SENNIN [*speaking from within his hut*]: I scoop water from deep streams with my magic gourd,
I call forth all my art,
I lift up clouds that have folded over forests and I make them boil swiftly,
then I play music.
But I play alone.
The mountains rise up high above the river banks.
Green leaves suddenly become the color of blood.

I play music and I play alone in autumn.

SHINKA: Listen to me, listen, this is a traveller, we have lost our way and we want to speak to you.

IKKAKU SENNIN: Who's there? – I thought I would be free in these mountains,
I thought I would be able to escape from the human race,
and now someone comes –
O go away, go, go away, go!! Go!!

SHINKA: No, listen to me, listen, we are travellers and we are lost,
and the sun is setting,
and the road is dark,
so won't you let us spend the night right here?

IKKAKU SENNIN: No, no, I told you to go, this is no place for you to stay, not if you know what's good for you,
so go, I say this is no place for you to stay!!

SHINKA: You say this is no place for us to stay, and is that because the holy hermit unicorn lives here?
Ikkaku Sennin!! – show yourself because we know you now!!

IKKAKU SENNIN: I am getting up, I am coming out of here,
I am going to show myself to all these travellers!!

CHORUS: He takes the great grass gate and swings it to one side,
he takes the great grass gate and swings it to one side,
now he is aroused –
look, look at his face!!
Black hair snarled on his proud brow,
a single long horn sprouting out of his forehead.
See how he stands here – if he disappeared
we would still see him stand here,
strange and wonderful!

SHINKA: Are you the hermit we have heard about, which they call the holy hermit unicorn?

IKKAKU SENNIN: I am ashamed to say it,
but I am he, Ikkaku Sennin.
Tell me, who is this beautiful young girl, and tell me, why is one so fair on this rough road?
She should be found at court, some sort of princess – O the grace
that gazes from her smiling eyes,
she is like the silent sky,
or like the sweet peace of the deep sea,
she is not like the people of this world.
Travellers, you must tell me, who are you and why have you come here?

SHINKA: O now, we are no one you would ever notice,
we are only strangers who got lost.
Here is some *sake* which we brought along with us,
to cheer us up on our long journey.
Here, why don't you try some wine? – Here, have some *sake*!

IKKAKU SENNIN: We hermits prefer to eat the needles of pine trees,
the clothes we wear are made of moss,
and we do not drink anything but dew.
Year after year, we do not age, we do not change, we do not even die.
And that is why I say I do not want your *sake*.

SHINKA: All right, that's that, you do not want our *sake*.
Although if we asked it as a special favor, would you take just a little?

LADY SENDA BUNIN: The beautiful girl rises to pour out some wine, she urges the hermit to try some *sake*.

IKKAKU SENNIN: When travellers ask a favor, how can anyone refuse? – impossible, only the devil would say no.

CHORUS: A cup of wine is like the moon in the night sky,
a cup of wine is like the moon in the night sky.
The hermit reaches out and takes the cup of wine,
just as a hermit once plucked a chrysanthemum,
the dew dropped down to the ground.
That was one moment long ago, long ago,
but I will love you for that long.

IKKAKU SENNIN: O blessed ecstasy, the cup of wine!

CHORUS: O blessed ecstasy, the cup of wine!
– it is like the moon that circles in the night sky.
Red leaves on the autumn hills.
So many silk sleeves.
Two leaves move,
like two sleeves that are dancing together,
dancing in a great court dance,
blessed ecstasy.
Dance to the music of flutes, the music of strings.
Dance to the music of flutes, the music of strings.
Pass the cup around, pass the cup around, pass the cup around.
The hermit has fallen in love, he has fallen in love.
See how his feet have grown weak, and see
how the hermit's beginning to falter and fall,
he keeps turning in circles,
now he wraps his sleeve around him
and he sleeps.
The beautiful young girl is pleased,
she tells everyone to come away
and they all go down the mountain, down the rough mountain road,
until they are already at the court of the prince.

[SHINKA, LADY SENDA BUNIN *and the attendants leave the stage.* IKKAKU SENNIN *is asleep on the floor.*]

CHORUS: Rumble rumble rumble, where is it coming from?
Rumbles thunder from deep inside the cave,
rumbles cause earthquakes and make all creation shake.

IKKAKU SENNIN: Why have I been sleeping, sleeping all this while?
– it was the wine, it was the beautiful young girl,
it was the need for some sleep.
Rumble rumble rumble, something's wrong,
there's a thunder coming from inside the cave,
there where the dragon gods are kept captive.
Rumble rumble rumble, something's wrong, what is it?

DRAGON GODS [*from within the cave*]: Holy hermit unicorn,
you were dancing with humans,
and you let yourself get lost in lust,
and you confused your mind with wine.
No wonder now you do not know you are undone,
no wonder now you have no power.
Unicorn, you are about to lose the magic that you used to use.

CHORUS: Listen, listen to the whistle of the wind.
Listen, listen to the whistle of the wind.
See the darkness of the sky.
Feel the earthquake as the cave breaks open and the boulder stones are thrown down to the ground.
Tremble now at the landslide, as the rocks that blocked the entrance have been cast aside.
Behold, O holy hermit, here are the great dragon gods!!

[*The rock pile breaks up and the* DRAGON GODS *appear.*]

IKKAKU SENNIN: Now the holy hermit unicorn does not know what to do.

CHORUS: Now the holy hermit unicorn does not know what to do.
He takes a sword and he goes toward the great dragon gods.
The dragon gods have on the armor of their own real rage.
They create a few naked blades to use on the unicorn.
They hit and they hit and they hit, and it is all over.
Ikkaku Sennin has exhausted all his magic powers.
He goes round and round until he drops down on the ground.
The great dragon gods call together all the clouds,
there is thunder and brightness of lightning,
and it rains and rains and rains,
the great dragon gods make it rain.
Then they fly through the sky and over the ocean,
then they fly through the sky and over the ocean.
The great dragon gods return to their great dragon home.

Ikkaku Sennin

PRODUCTION COMMENTS

An Interview with William Packard and Vera R. Irwin

Noh, the ancient stage art of Japan, has drawn the interest of Western scholars and artists by its grace, by its formal qualities of precision and discipline and by its power to evoke the most poignant and sublime of emotions. This power, difficult to define, is a dark and obscure happening that animates the way the actor moves, the way he feels, and the way he is – a mysterious quality called *Yugen*. This theatre, which reached its perfection in the seventeenth century, drew its substance from Buddhist scriptures, the legends, myths and poetry of India, China and Japan, and from the folk dances and ritual dances of the temple. We also find that the plays fall thematically into five categories, *Ikkaku Sennin* belonging to the fifth, which traditionally has a supernatural being as its protagonist.

Each category or type of play has its own particular conventions and style of presentation, which was commented upon by Sadayo Kita, while directing *Ikkaku Sennin* with American actors. In an early rehearsal Mr Kita, a sixteenth-generation Noh performer from the Kita troupe of Tokyo, remarked:

Though this play has comparatively little *yugen*, the undefinable spirit of beauty, it has a great degree of dramatic quality that is lacking in other types of Noh. To perform this fairy-tale with its excessive elements of entertainment, to project the naive dramatic quality of the Noh Theatre, as found in this play, is to challenge the actor's skill and concentration.

What is the challenge in the Noh? For one thing, the tradition of the Noh is over 600 years old, and there is much ritual and tradition behind each gesture and each inflection of the voice. Noh is known as the 'immeasurable scripture' because it is the synthesis of all the arts, including song, dance, poetry, drama and religion. 'We work in pure spirit,' said Umewaka Minoru, the nineteenth-century Noh actor. And this pure spirit is shown through retraint and containment, so each performance of a Noh play, whatever category, is a manifestation of ultimate control.

The production of this play as of any Noh play is therefore not only a psychological and philosophical challenge to a Western actor, but is also a severe physical challenge. The actor is called upon to develop the disposition to endure, the stoic patience of waiting long periods of time on stage, and the silence of sitting alone, knowing that no one in the audience is going to get restless if there is not a great flurry of distracting action or instant 'entertainment.' As rehearsals progress, the stage movement, like that in all Noh plays, must be carefully re-created as it has come down through the ages. Observers from the Dance Notation Bureau, after a rehearsal of *Ikkaku Sennin*, at the Institute of Advanced Studies in the Theatre Arts, explained.

The movement is controlled, as if moving against resistance, such as a heavily weighted atmosphere pressing in against one. The whole being is involved in the movement. It requires great concentration. The actor is totally involved throughout the drama. The focus never wanders. The moments of stillness are as important as those of movement. In effort terms the movement is generally very bound, direct and slow. The shaping of the arms helps contain the energy. Most variations seem to come in the slight increases and decreases in speed and the variations in flow.

This analysis can provide the Western director and actor with an understanding of the formalized movement in Noh. An example of the technique necessary for this movement is found in the simple act of walking as described by the observers who stated:

> The style of the walk is very important. Contact with the floor must be maintained at all times. After standing still for a long time or even after a short pause it would not be in keeping to lift the foot to step, except before stamping or in order to step over something. Note that only in walking forward the front part of the foot is released from the floor. Note also that most of the travelling in space in this drama is confined to the forward and backward directions of the performer. The legs never straighten in the sense that the Western dancers think of a stretched leg. Their maximum straightening is a normal standing leg. The knees have an elastic quality, the flexion signs indicating enough give to produce a smooth, gliding movement rather than a change to a low level, resulting only in a dip.

This explanation is an indication of how an American actor must unlearn before he can begin to learn the elements of Noh movement.

The movement is always accompanied by the music of the *fue* (flute), the *kotsuzmi* (shoulder drum), the *otsuzmi* (knee drum) and the *taiko* (flat drum). And in accompaniment to the music the roles are chanted by the actors while the descriptive sections are chanted by the Narrator or Chorus.

Aware of the rhythmic and poetic quality of the dialogue and its synthesis with music and movement, the adaptation of *Ikkaku Sennin* was made to correspond syllable for syllable with the Japanese text. In addition, certain sounds in Japanese have to have the exact equivalent in English, and finally the very pronounced rhythms of the Noh Theatre require a great many distinct monosyllables in English. And yet, in adapting this play to the traditional rhythms and inflections of the Noh, the autumn imagery of *Ikkaku Sennin* is so subtle and poignant that it survives the adaptation, rehearsals, and performance. It is still there, in the text, and perhaps it is almost as haunting as it is in the original.

In *Ikkaku Sennin*, as in other Noh plays, the costumes are adaptations of the style of the elegant fifteenth-century robes worn by court nobles, warriors, civilians, monks and women of these ancient times. Costumes are elaborate and formal, the shape and heaviness having an effect upon the physical movement of the actor. The movement is also controlled by the amount of stage area the actor can see through the mask. The masked players in this play are the *shitê*, Ikkaku Sennin; the *shitê-tsure*, Lady Senda; and the *kogata*, the Dragon Gods when they are played by adult males, not by girls or children. The costumes and masks not only control the movement and pace of the movement but assist in deepening the mood and create a sense of artistic tranquillity.

The director will find in producing this play that the stylization is found in the technique of visual movement and poses, which, though simple, contain an amazing degree of feeling. The rigidly traditional patterns of the dance and the formal quality of the verse still allow the actor artistic freedom in interpretation and expression.

Many American actors find to their amazement that they are able to interpret more within the constraints of this art form than within the naturalistic form with which they are familiar. Peter Blaxill, an actor in the New York production of *Ikkaku Sennin*, when asked said:

> Noh acting is extremely stylistic, disciplined, and unrealistic. I wear a mask, and still I must emote. I've learned to use nuances of acting on which I never depended. It is extremely fascinating and I

think already my brief acquaintance with Noh has heightened my acting power and given me new tools with which to work.

With this discovery of an acting style which is both poetic and controlled, the actor creates an atmosphere which led Jerome Robbins, after observing rehearsals of the New York production, to say:

It is like turning on a light that illuminates another terrain of the theatre. Through extreme disciplines and limitations of space, costume, voice, action, expression, gestures, music and pitch; through the distillations of the essence of drama; and through an awesome, tender and religious love of the theatre, its props, costumes and the very surface of the stage itself, a final poetic release of beauty is achieved.

NARUKAMI

An Introduction to

NARUKAMI

By Leonard C. Pronko

IF the aristocratic and austere Noh drama corresponded to the needs and tastes of the warrior and princely classes of the fifteenth and sixteenth centuries, the popular and flamboyant Kabuki catered to an entirely different audience. By the seventeenth century, the merchant class in Japan was beginning to assume great economic importance. Before long it would become the mainstay of the country, despite its lowly status in the Confucian hierarchy imposed by the military rules of the Tokugawa period (1600–1867) in an effort to stabilize every aspect of Japanese life, and along with it their own rule. By the eighteenth century the average merchant disposed of sufficient money and leisure to afford the luxury of entertainment. Yet the Noh drama had become the almost exclusive property of the ruling classes. It was, at least in part, to satisfy the popular desire for performances that the Kabuki developed. The dates of its origin and rise correspond to those of the Tokugawa period, years of great stability and peace during which Japan was all but closed off to foreign influence. Kabuki's early heyday during the Genroku era (1688–1704) is contemporary with a renaissance in other Japanese arts and literature, which are marked by the color and tastes of a vivacious and pleasure-bent populace.

At its start, in the last years of the sixteenth century or the early seventeenth, Kabuki has been almost entirely a form of dance. Okuni, a dancing attendant from the Izumo Shrine, had come down to Kyoto – so the legend goes – and danced in the dry bed of the Kamo river; danced so well and with such originality and character that she soon attracted not only large audiences, but other performers as well. While most of the dancers were women, there were men in the troupe too. From the beginning, Kabuki made no effort to be illusionistic or representational. Indeed, part of the pleasure seemed to lie in the very difficulty of vanquishing the obstacles imposed by nature: men played women's parts, and women men's.

By 1629 it had become quite clear to the Japanese government (the Shogunate) that the dancing women of the Kabuki were in reality most practiced in a different profession, and the dancing was merely an enticement to attract customers for the real business after the performance. To terminate the corruption of the samurai – not by sexual play, but by social intercourse with those below them – the Shogunate outlawed women's Kabuki, and the popular theatre (or dance) passed into a second phase: young men's Kabuki, When women were no longer available, the pretty young actors playing women's roles apparently became efficient not only at the on-stage presentation, but in the after-theatre parties as well, with the result that they too were outlawed (1652). Only then did Kabuki begin to mature as an art, for it could no longer count on a pretty face, and had to develop more substantial offerings if it were to continue.

With the coming of *Yaro* (mature men's) Kabuki, the form slowly took on the characteristics which we associate with it today. The simple and often erotic anecdotes which had formed the basis of earlier productions were developed, made more complex. Dialogue came to play an important role, new kinds of music, new instruments, new forms of dance were added.

In the latter part of the seventeenth century the forms of

Kabuki became more or less fixed thanks to the genius of two actors, one in each of the major regions of Japan. In western Japan, cultural life centered about the mercantile center of Osaka and the cultural center of Kyoto, and it was here that Sakata Tojuro developed the kind of Kabuki which most satisfied the audiences of that area: refined, somewhat realistic, and dealing above all with courtesans and amorous young men. In the hands of Chikamatsu Monzaemon, these characteristics took shape in masterpieces which are considered to be the finest literary works of Japan's popular theatre. Chikamatsu, turning from the temperamental and wilful actors to the more obedient puppets, introduced to the theatre themes of contemporary life dealing with the tragic fates of the townsmen of Kyoto and Osaka. These works, and others originally intended for the puppets, were soon taken over by the living actors, thus beginning a period of interinfluence which was profitable for both theatres, and can be discerned today in repertoire and performance techniques.

The theatrical character of Kabuki in eastern Japan was determined by the first Ichikawa Danjuro. Living in the raw young city of Edo – today called Tokyo – which was the headquarters of the military rulers, Danjuro saw the people's admiration for the swagger and dash of the samurai, and he developed a dramatic manner geared to this taste. Highly stylized, bigger than life, Edo Kabuki favored tales of great military prowess, heroic feats and supernatural occurrences, spiced with humor. The superman who was most often the hero of such plays performed in an exaggerated and forceful style known as *aragoto*, wore colorful, grotesquely huge costumes, make-up to match, and spoke in a deep-voiced bombastic manner.

With the advent of these artists, Kabuki had come of age. For the next two hundred years or so it was to make no radical departures, but to develop instead the potential allowed by the various facets of a complex art. Essentially faithful to its non-representational, highly theatricalized form, it remained always a popular theatre, adapting to changing fashions and tastes, and taking advantage of new developments in theatre architecture, to enhance its esthetic principles of intimacy, surprise, picturesque beauty and total appeal. Now, rather than writing its name with the character first used, and which bore the derogatory meaning of 'slanted, inclined, off-balance, or eccentric,' the actors chose three Chinese characters meaning song (*ka*), dance (*bu*) and performance or art (*ki*), thereby stressing the composite character of Kabuki which has never forgotten its dance origins, and which is buttressed from one end to the other with songs and music integrated with the performance in a way which we in the West have yet to learn.

Kabuki theatre buildings today, no doubt for financial reasons, are much larger than those of the past. The stage opening is about ninety feet wide, and within it is a wealth of machinery (revolving stages, elevators) which helps in creating the wonders of a performance. Tricks of wig and costume permit the actor to change shape before the audience, thanks to a system of ingeniously contrived threads which are pulled at the proper moment by stage assistants. The assistants, ever-present in Kabuki, are dressed in black and considered to be non-existent. They are there to hand the actor a prop at the correct moment, to adjust his costume into attractive folds, give him a stool for sitting, manipulate stage animals (mice, butterflies, etc.), or even to prompt should that be necessary.

It is clear from such techniques of presentation that Kabuki does not attempt to convince the spectator that he is actually witnessing the event depicted. One is almost constantly aware of the actor's presence, for he is a virtuoso much as an opera singer or a ballerina is, and he usually plays directly to the audience. The structure of the theatre helps to bring the actor into intimate contact with his public, for there is a runway which connects the stage with the rear of the auditorium. Important entrances and exits are made on this *hanamichi*, so that the actor must cross right through the midst of the spectators where they may almost reach out and touch him. There, he may dance for some time, pose, or speak. And particularly at a point seven tenths from the rear of the auditorium and three tenths from the stage (the *shichi-san* or seven-three) he may strike those impressive poses called *mie*.

Unlike Western plays, which usually progress in a logical way, and which lead from exposition to development to climax to dénouement, Kabuki plays, existing for the eyes and the senses as well as for the heart, build to ever new climaxes. One must often attempt to appreciate each act of a play as a separate entity, and each scene of that act as a moment in itself. The climaxes of these moments are usually expressed, in the more heroic plays at any rate, in the *mie*: accompanied by the sharp sound of the clappers, the actor momentarily freezes into a pose using torso, legs, arms and head, and generally ending with a fierce sneer and a crossing of one or both eyes.

The theatricality of Kabuki cannot be too strongly stressed, nor can its great range of variety. In earlier times an entire play would be performed at one sitting, beginning at daybreak and ending at sundown; but today, with the impatience of modern spectators, there are usually two five-hour sessions, each different from the other and each incorporating scenes from longer plays as well as shorter dance or comic pieces of several kinds. A typical program includes a pure dance play (*shosagoto*), a tragedy of domestic life among the merchants (*sewamono*), and a heroic play of historical or pseudo-historical events (*jidaimono*). It is to this last group that *Narukami* belongs, or rather to a special collection within that group.

In the first half of the nineteenth century Danjuro VII (the great names of Kabuki actors are hereditary) set aside eighteen favorite plays which his family had performed over the years. These he called the *Juhachiban* (literally, number eighteen), and among them are several of the most impressive plays in the Kabuki repertoire: *Kanjincho*, *Sukeroku* and *Narukami*.

Narukami was written and first performed by Danjuro I in 1684 as one act of a much longer play, *Kodamatsu Shitenno* (*Four Generals at New Years*). His success in two roles of this play, including that of the priest seduced, marks the beginning of his great popularity. Until his tragic death in 1703, when he was murdered onstage by a jealous actor, Danjuro continued to write and perform in many of the works which were later to become part of the *Juhachiban*. During the first half of the eighteenth century his son, Danjuro II, carried on the family traditions, enhancing the family name by his broader talents, and reviving frequently the *Narukami* act within the framework of other plays. In 1742, when he was appearing for the first time in Osaka, after several months of poor audience reaction, he decided to obtain a sure success by reviving *Narukami*, and with his producer a play was arranged containing no less than three of the present *Eighteen Favorites*, *Narukami Fudo Kitayama-zakura* (*Narukami, Fudo, and the Cherry Trees of Kita-yama*). It is the text of this play and the traditional movement set by Danjuro II which, with various additions and deletions, serve as the basis for present-day productions of *Narukami*.

By the middle of the nineteenth century, when Danjuro VIII performed the play for the first time under the name of

Narukami (*Thunder God*), the text had become overlaid with many elements which made it more exciting to the audiences of that period, notably a very explicit eroticism, a more complex musical accompaniment, and the addition of two more acolytes at the beginning of the play.

When the play was revived in 1910, after an absence of more than fifty years, it was performed by Ichikawa Sadanji in a version which attempted to reproduce that of Danjuro II, rather than utilizing the traditions as they had developed by mid nineteenth century. This Sadanji script, which is used today, exists, of course, in a number of versions, and the present translation is an amalgamation of the most theatrically appealing aspects of three of these.

Narukami, derived from an old Buddhist legend, particularly as it is treated in the Noh play *Ikkaku Sennin*, presents a number of striking characteristics of a Kabuki text. At the same time it will afford the reader of this volume an opportunity to see how different is the spirit of Kabuki from that of Noh, even when both are treating a similar story. One notes immediately the flamboyant theatricality of the Kabuki version, its greater complexity, more developed psychology, rationalization of the situation, sense of the comic, and frank eroticism. The language, compared to that of the Noh text, is extremely simple and colloquial, with little that strikes one as 'poetic.'

There is perhaps no clearer indication of the difference between the aristocratic spirit of fifteenth- and sixteenth-century Japan and the emerging popular spirit of Genroku than the remarkable contrasts between Noh and Kabuki. In the former, all is understatement, refinement, a kind of naked austerity very different from the rich theatricality, joyous sexuality and comic verve of the latter. Both are stylized, but the earlier form is elegant and symbolic, the later one somewhat more realistic and outspoken, although Kabuki too has moments of great restraint, depth and elegance.

In *Ikkaku Sennin* no suggestion of indecency is allowed to obtrude; Lady Senda is never alone with the priest – indeed, she only accompanies the official messenger, for her role is a small one. The downfall of the unhappy priest arises not from lusty thoughts (much less, lusty actions), but from his reticence in refusing a proffered politeness – in this case, wine. Rather than the explicit tale of love recounted by Taema in *Narukami* and the graphic depiction of seduction, *Ikkaku Sennin* suggests only obliquely in a very sedate dance that the priest is drawn to the woman.

Narukami is perhaps easier to read than many Kabuki texts, for it resembles a Western play at least in its structure, which is unilinear and fairly logical, and in its characters who are treated with a modicum of psychological realism. Its blending of comedy, eroticism, religion and the supernatural is certainly appealing and readily comprehensible. But in reading any play, it is necessary to try to imagine the movement of the actors on the stage, the sounds of their voices; and in forms which are so patently theatricalized as the traditional theatres of the East, such an effort of the imagination is absolutely essential.

Before the curtain opens on *Narukami*, our senses are first assaulted by the beating of wooden clappers. As curtain time approaches, the crisp beats gradually accelerate. The music and the drums announce a mountain scene, and a soft rapid drumbeat suggests the presence of water. We first hear Hakuun and Kokuun speaking to each other offstage, then the grating sound of metal on metal as the curtain at the rear of the auditorium is thrown open and they enter on the *hanamichi*. Dressed chiefly in white, their shaven heads represented by close-fitting blue caps, the two comic acolytes relate the background of the story. While their behavior is not so highly stylized as that of Narukami and Taema, they are quite clearly actors who are dancers as well.

When the bamboo curtain is raised on the hermitage, we see Narukami's back, for he is kneeling in prayer. He soon rises and turns to face the audience. His actions are slow and dignified, his voice deep and strong, and his delivery somewhat exaggerated to Western ears, for the Kabuki actor uses the entire gamut of the human voice to achieve the maximum in expressiveness. His face is painted white without lines to suggest refinement, purity, but also so that his expression may be clearly seen – this was particularly important when plays were performed without artificial lighting. His hair style is that of a mountain priest, simply pulled back and tied at the nape of the neck in a kind of pony tail.

Taema is, of course, played by a man, for there are no actresses in Kabuki. Centuries of elaborating the techniques of the *onnagata* (actor of female roles) has resulted in a style which portrays the absolute essence of femininity. Taema is a young princess and speaks in a high falsetto. Her movements are gentle, delicate and graceful. Elbows held in, knees together, feet pigeon-toed, and head held at angles, the ultimate in Kabuki femininity contrasts with the masculine characters whose elbows are thrust out, knees separated, feet pointed out and head held straight with chin in.

Taema wears the usual red kimono of the Kabuki princess, decorated with gold and vari-colored flowers and water patterns. Across the front of her wig is a high, glittering, silver *kanzashi*, a kind of tiara, and inserted in the loop at the back of the wig is a gold drum-shaped decoration. Her make-up is refined and white, like Narukami's, but her bright costume contrasts with the basic white of the Priests and harmonizes with the colorful greens, blues and browns of the stage setting.

While Taema tells the story of her meeting with her lord and how she fell in love, she sits near the center of the stage facing front, an acolyte on either side of her following the story animatedly and excitedly. Taema mimes her tale, using sometimes her fan, sometimes her sleeves or simply her hands to represent objects. Narukami, sitting serenely on his platform behind them, listens at first quite calmly. But little by little he becomes intrigued by the amorous story. When Taema cannot remember the line of a poem written to her by her lover, Narukami supplies the last line, and cries out, tensely, 'And then what happened?' As he begins to speak he picks up an armrest which is at his left, places it energetically before him (the thud is part of the rhythm of the pose), frames his face with both hands, and with eyes open wide, eyebrows raised slightly, he leans toward the young woman as he asks her to go on – his voice first rising to the top of his range and at the end dropping to his lowest register.

The seduction scene is one of the highlights of the play and is handled subtly for such a subject. When Narukami massages Taema's breast, the princess holds her sleeves up shielding her right shoulder, and the Priest inserts his hand in such a way that the audience never sees any physical contact. In Kabuki there is rarely physical contact between actors, for the proximity is sufficient to suggest what is meant.

When Narukami has sunk into his cups, Taema performs what amounts to a dance, as she circles the stage and mounts the little hill from which she hopes to cut the sacred rope to release the rain god. When she succeeds, we see the rain dragon slither up the waterfall, and from overhead a delightfully stylized border depicting rain and lightning is lowered.

During all this, Narukami, hidden by a red cloth carried by stage assistants, has been changing to a long-haired bristling demon wig and putting bright red lines on his face to depict his drunkenness and his demon nature wakened by lust. The ensuing scene, requiring only a page or two of text, actually lasts ten or fifteen minutes, for it is a carefully choreographed battle between the priest-turned-demon and his restraining acolytes. It is here we witness the *aragoto* which is so notable an element of the *Juhachiban* pieces. The scene contains a number of impressive *mie*, and a *bukkaeri* or costume change to depict a change in character. Stage assistants pull threads in the shoulders and sleeves of the Priest's kimono and as he rises into a fierce pose the top falls down revealing a new costume underneath, white with great red and gold flames surrounded by a smoky black, to suggest the identity of the Thunder God.

Seizing the sutras on his altar, Narukami throws them at his acolytes. Then, taking one sutra, he tears it in half, throws one end of each half to acolytes whom he pushes off the platform. They perform backflips to the main stage floor (such acrobatics are often found in Kabuki fight scenes) and sit back holding one end of the sutra as Narukami holds the other ends in his hands at the center stair of the platform and performs an energetic *mie*. The sutra, sweeping up towards the center from either side, is supposed to resemble the shape of Mount Fuji; and for this reason the pose is known as the Fuji *mie*.

Later Narukami performs a famous *mie* embracing the right pillar of his hermitage, and another on the small hill holding in one hand a sacred rope and in the other a sword or Buddhist sceptre. His stance resembles that of the god Fudo and hence the pose is called the Fudo *mie*. After throwing a huge boulder at his acolytes, and accomplishing a number of other superhuman feats, Narukami strides to the *hanamichi*, and the curtain is pulled closed behind him.

At the seven-three he strikes yet another pose and begins a

spectacular dance exit (*roppo*) typical of many *Juhachiban* plays. Thrusting his arms out before and behind him in forceful patterns, he hops, now on one foot now on the other, flying at an accelerating speed down the *hanamichi*, the enraged Thunder God in vengeful pursuit of the seductive princess.

NARUKAMI
THE THUNDER GOD

From the Juhachiban

English translation by
MIYOKO WATANABE

A Kabuki play based on the
Noh drama *Ikkaku Sennin.*
First staged by Ichikawa Danjuro I in 1684.

4. *Narukami:* from a performance at Indiana University.

NARUKAMI

CHARACTERS

Priest NARUKAMI (Thunder God)
KUMO NO TAEMA (Rift of the Clouds), an Imperial Court Lady
Bonze HAKUUN (White Cloud), an Acolyte, pupil of Narukami
Bonze KOKUUN (Black Cloud), an Acolyte, pupil of Narukami
Other ACOLYTES
CHORUS
KŌKEN, a stage assistant
KYOGEN SAKUSHA, a man who counts rhythm with hyōshigi (wood clappers)

The action takes place at a secluded mountain retreat by a waterfall.
First produced in English by IASTA, New York, in October 1960.

SCENE ONE

[HAKUUN *and* KOKUUN *enter from* hanamichi.*]

HAKUUN: Have you heard? Have you heard?

KOKUUN: Yes, I heard! Yes, I heard!

HAKUUN: Here, here. From a while back you have been saying 'I have heard, I have heard,' but what in the world did you hear?

KOKUUN: Behind the main temple I heard a nightingale.

HAKUUN: You fool, that's far fetched from the subject matter. I'm asking if you have heard the reasons for our master, Priest Narukami, performing these esoteric religious austerities?

KOKUUN: No, I haven't heard the reason.

HAKUUN: Fool, how can one be so ignorant of this matter? If you don't know, I shall humbly deign to tell you. Our master, Priest Narukami, is performing these austerities because it seems that he made a request to the Imperial Household, but Imperial sanction was not granted. Thus he has shut in the Dragon God who controls the rain, and is performing the religious austerities to prevent even a drop of rain from falling. As you can see, for these thirty days not even one drop of rain has fallen. That's really something, is it not?

KOKUUN: Well, this drought will be enjoyed by the children for flying kites, but, with the coming rice-planting season, the farmers will encounter great hardship.

---

*See introduction, p. 277.

HAKUUN: To bring misery upon the farmers is a means to plague the Emperor.

KOKUUN: Now, I understand. So that his austerities will not be disturbed he has ordered you and me to act as guards here.

HAKUUN: So, just as you say. Ah, I feel melancholy; I feel dull.

KOKUUN: Well, I have some good medicine to cure your melancholy. Would you like to drink of it?

HAKUUN: What? You have medicine to cure melancholia? Then let me have a little.

KOKUUN: You shall, you shall. It's a medicine called a 'cure-all.' [*He reveals a hidden bottle.*]

HAKUUN: Why you insolent fellow! You subversive priest!

KOKUUN: What do you mean, subversive priest?

HAKUUN: Here from within you are breaking Master Priest's commandment of abstinence. You scoundrel! This matter cannot be ignored. I'm warning you; I'm going to report the matter to our master . . . but, if I did, that would make the *sake* go to shameful waste. All right. I'll have a drink too.

KOKUUN: Is it all right to drink?

HAKUUN: Sure, one must learn to adapt oneself to circumstances.

KOKUUN: But there is no appetizer to be had with the *sake*. Oh, I should have brought some tangerines or chestnuts.

HAKUUN: Don't worry! Don't worry! I have something here. Something called a 'helmet-hood.' [*He reveals an octopus.*]

KOKUUN: You pulpiteer! What do you mean by eating a forbidden octopus! I'll report this to our Master Priest.

HAKUUN: Here, here. I can't have you blabbing this.

KOKUUN: No, I won't listen. I won't listen.

HAKUUN: If you won't listen to me, I won't listen to you. Master Priest, Kokuumbo is drinking *sake*.

KOKUUN: Hakuumbo is eating octopus.

[*On the dais behind a bamboo screen is heard a bell.*]

HAKUUN *and* KOKUUN: That is the bell of our Master Priest.

[HAKUUN *and* KOKUUN *remove the screen.*]

CHORUS: For some time the Master Priest Narukami has shut in the Dragon God and this has cut off the rain from the land. In the depth of the mountains among the massive rocks sits Narukami before the altar. The waterfall falls from the sky and the sound of the water and the wind break against the rocks. On the dais of virtue he is entreating Buddha for mercy in answering his prayers. 'Ah the great deity Fudo Myoo, the great Fudo Myoo.'

[KUMO NO TAEMA, *striking a bell, enters on the* hanamichi.]

TAEMA [*chanting*]: Namu ami da Butsu. . . . Namu ami da Butsu . . .*

NARUKAMI: Indeed, how strange. In the depth of the mountains where not a bird is heard, where man rarely treads, I hear the voice of one chanting prayers far off in the distance beyond the basin of the waterfall. Here, Hakuun and Kokuun.

[*They do not answer.*]

Do you not realize that I am calling both of you?

HAKUUN *and* KOKUUN: Ai-i . . .

NARUKAMI: You indolent fellows. Why do you sleep?

HAKUUN: Oh no, no, how impious that would be. I am not sleeping.

NARUKAMI: You certainly were fast asleep.

HAKUUN: Oh no, I did not fall asleep; it was that bonze over there.

---

*Buddha, rest his soul in peace.

KOKUUN: Here, here, don't accuse others. Master Priest I was standing guard with my eyes wide open. It was my senior Hakuun who was sleeping.

HAKUUN: It was you who were sleeping.

KOKUUN: What do you mean, it was I?

HAKUUN: What do you mean by 'you'?

NARUKAMI: Is that a Buddhist priest's way of behavior? If you contend that you were not asleep, did you hear what I heard?

HAKUUN *and* KOKUUN: Eh-h?

NARUKAMI: Far off beyond the basin of the waterfall a sad voice chanting Buddhist prayers can be heard.

HAKUUN *and* KOKUUN: Eh-h?

NARUKAMI: Both of you, go to the waterfall and investigate.

HAKUUN *and* KOKUUN: Eh-h?

NARUKAMI: Go, I say.

HAKUUN *and* KOKUUN: Ai-i-i.

HAKUUN: Kokuumbo, it is the will of our master. Go and see.

KOKUUN: You go and see.

HAKUUN: You go and see.

KOKUUN: You go and see.

HAKUUN *and* KOKUUN: Confound you! [*Both raise their fists.*]

NARUKAMI: What is that?

HAKUUN: I was thinking that if there were a potato about this size, I could put it into your soup for you.

NARUKAMI: Fools!

HAKUUN *and* KOKUUN: Ai-i . . .

NARUKAMI: I said go.

HAKUUN *and* KOKUUN: Ai-i . . .

[*They go.*]

SCENE TWO

HAKUUN: Oh, how exquisitely beautiful!

KOKUUN: This is most extraordinary!

HAKUUN: That is a celestial being. Since there is no water in the universe, the celestial has come to wash her feathered robe.

KOKUUN: No, you're wrong, you're wrong. That is the Dragon Goddess. The Dragon Goddess has come to see the Dragon God who has been trapped in the basin of the waterfall.

HAKUUN: No, without doubt, her beauty bespeaks that she is a celestial.

KOKUUN: She is a dragon goddess.

HAKUUN: She is a celestial.

KOKUUN: Confound you!

NARUKAMI: What is that?

HAKUUN *and* KOKUUN [*to dissemble*]: O praise great Buddha, praise great Buddha.

NARUKAMI: With you, nothing can be settled. I shall have to see for myself. [*He calls out.*] Here!

TAEMA: E-eh?

HAKUUN *and* KOKUUN [*imitating*]: E-eh?

NARUKAMI: Silence!

HAKUUN *and* KOKUUN: Hai.

NARUKAMI: How suspicious that an exalted maiden should come through the mountain paths where even birds and animals dare not frequent. Tell me, what are you?

TAEMA: Do you mean me?

HAKUUN *and* KOKUUN [*imitating*]: Do you mean me?

NARUKAMI: Yes, I mean you.

TAEMA: I live at the foot of these steep mountains and daily I pine for my beloved husband, from whom I have recently been parted.

NARUKAMI: Did you part from your husband in life or death?

TAEMA: Today is exactly the forty-ninth day since his death.

NARUKAMI: The day for mass, isn't it?

TAEMA: Yes.

NARUKAMI [*prays*]: May Buddha's blessing rest upon his soul.

TAEMA: This keepsake only tortures me. [*She has his robe.*] If I did not have this, perhaps I might be able to forget him. From his new, light robe, I wanted to wash away the filth of this mundane world, but, for what reason I do not know, the drought has caused all wells to dry up and there is no water to be had. I have heard that at the waterfall in these mountain depths, the famed and precious waters never cease to run despite the drought. So I have dared to climb the hazardous mountain paths to wash the robe of my dear husband. Sweet and loving is a husband. Please understand how I feel in my heart.

NARUKAMI: Indeed, that is a pitiful tale, If you still think of him so dearly, you must have been passionately in love when you were together in life.

TAEMA: Inadequate is the word passionate. In the sky we would be likened to the inseparable lover birds; on earth to the entwined branches. The more I think back on it, how heavenly was our life.

NARUKAMI [*prays*]: Wordly passions eventually lead to holy passions. That I should converse with a woman is probably some turn of fate. To rest your husband's soul in peace in the next world, I should like to hear your story.

TAEMA: To divert my mind from sorrow, I wish to tell it to you. May I relate to you our past?

NARUKAMI: That would be best. Do go ahead and begin.

TAEMA: I wish to tell you my story, but it's such a distance from here to there. I want to draw closer to you and tell you my tale, but I suppose I would not be allowed to go nearer your side.

NARUKAMI: You need not hesitate. Come over here and tell me.

TAEMA: Then may I be permitted to draw nearer.

NARUKAMI: It's all right, it's all right.

TAEMA: Then I shall draw close to your side.

HAKUUN *and* KOKUUN: Here, here. You may not pass.

TAEMA: But the Master Priest has given me his permission.

HAKUUN: During the ascetic exercises admittance to women is forbidden.

KOKUUN: This is a restricted area, a restricted area!

TAEMA: Listen to the way they are speaking, Master Priest.

NARUKAMI: It is only natural that they speak so. No women are allowed near the dais. Sit between the priests and relate your story.

TAEMA: Very well. Then I shall tell my story here. Both of you, you too must listen to my story.

HAKUUN *and* KOKUUN: Go ahead. Go ahead.

TAEMA: Then I shall begin.

NARUKAMI: And I shall listen.

TAEMA: It is not long ago since I became intimate with my lord. I went flower-viewing at Kiyomizu in the middle of March during the spring of last year. Mount Otowa was covered with willowy cherry trees; it was truly a glorious spring personified. There were many private areas enclosed within curtains where the flower-viewing multitude assembled. Here you could hear the strings of the koto; there the tones of the shamisen and drums; everywhere people were singing and dancing. The atmosphere was irresistible. I, too, received permission from my mother and father to go flower-viewing. Outside our enclosure there was a slender, handsome young gentleman, about twenty years old, peering in at me. His noble bearing, his charm, his eyes, his lips. . . . O, I cannot describe him in words. I fell deeply and completely in love with him.

HAKUUN: Although you did not know him?

TAEMA: So magnetic was his charm that from the nape of my neck . . .

KOKUUN: Did you feel a chill creep over you?

TAEMA: Chill is not the word.

HAKUUN: Did you shake?

TAEMA: Shake is not the word. Sometimes I would become cold; then sometimes I would become hot. I was conquered by my lord's handsomeness.

HAKUUN: Fascinating!

KOKUUN: Irresistible!

TAEMA: And the lord was flirtatious too. He was staring at me steadfastly; yet pretended not to be looking at all.

HAKUUN: Mm. . . . How honey sweet!

KOKUUN: It's like eating rice cakes with dropping jelly.

TAEMA: Then the handsome lord took from the inner bosom of his kimono, a narrow strip of paper, and on it with his brush he readily wrote a poem and gave it to me. And his hands were so refined that words cannot describe their beauty.

HAKUUN *and* KOKUUN: And was his writing elegant?

TAEMA: Extremely elegant; moreover, he had written a very entertaining old poem.

HAKUUN *and* KOKUUN: And it said?

TAEMA: 'A lady whom I cannot say I have not seen and yet

whom I have not positively seen has conquered my heart.'

HAKUUN: 'A lady whom I cannot say I have not seen.'

KOKUUN: 'And yet whom I have not positively seen.'

HAKUUN *and* KOKUUN: 'Has conquered my heart.'

TAEMA: O dear, what was the complementary line?

HAKUUN: How could you forget such an important line?

KOKUUN: You should have written it on a tablet and tied it to your sash.

NARUKAMI: 'And today I have idly passed the day futilely gazing.' Was that not the complementary line?

TAEMA: Indeed, that is the very line!

NARUKAMI: And then what happened?

TAEMA: After that matters began to grow livelier.

HAKUUN *and* KOKUUN: That is only natural; that is only natural.

TAEMA: So I beckoned my lady-in-waiting, and had her ask him his name.

HAKUUN *and* KOKUUN: And did he tell you?

TAEMA: No, he did not tell me his name.

HAKUUN *and* KOKUUN: Oh Glory to the Holy Sutra of the Lotus of the Supreme Law!

TAEMA: Amazing is the benevolence of the Goddess of Mercy. I prayed fervently for guidance and in my dream an oracle answered me.

HAKUUN *and* KOKUUN: Very strange, very strange.

TAEMA: I was so happy . . . so thankful. That night after everyone had fallen asleep, all alone I ventured to the dwelling of the lord in the inner regions of Saga as directed by the oracle.

HAKUUN *and* KOKUUN: How brave, how brave!

TAEMA: There was a large river.

HAKUUN: Yes, there are the Oi and Katsura rivers.

KOKUUN: They are famous rivers.

TAEMA: Even though I wanted to cross the river there was neither a boat nor bridge. How I wished it were daytime, but there was only the pitch of darkness to rely upon. And though a woman I boldly pulled up the hem of my kimono. [*She demonstrates and* NARUKAMI *is amazed*.]

HAKUUN *and* KOKUUN: Did you roll it up?

TAEMA: I certainly did. I lifted my hem up very high and stepped into the water.

HAKUUN *and* KOKUUN: Oh, it's icy cold.

TAEMA: Disregarding the cold, I headed for the other shore and . . . splash . . .

HAKUUN *and* KOKUUN: Splash . . .

TAEMA: Zomburiko . . .

HAKUUN *and* KOKUUN: Zomburiko . . .

[*They all walk around, lifting hem.*]

Zomburiko . . . zomburiko . . . zomburiko . . .

HAKUUN: Oh, it's deep; it's fathomless.

KOKUUN: It's getting out of our depth.

TAEMA: Finally I reached the other shore.

HAKUUN *and* KOKUUN: Wring it, wring it. [*They wring their hems.*]

TAEMA: My hem was dripping wet, but to me it no longer mattered. I pushed aside the bamboo grass and treaded wildly on the reeds. I finally groped my way to my lord's hermitage.

HAKUUN *and* KOKUUN: You reached your destination.

TAEMA: I pushed open the garden gate and went far inside. There my lord was waiting for me, and extending his hand to me he said, 'Darling, did you come?' and pulled me in.

HAKUUN *and* KOKUUN: It's fascinating; I feel as if I'm melting.

TAEMA: We had many things to talk about. We enjoyed

burning incense. We drank *sake*. We were so happy but our flirtations soon turned to lovers' quarrels.

HAKUUN: Oh, I can't resist this.

KOKUUN: When two become madly in love, they become discordant.

TAEMA: I said, 'Oh, please stop it.' 'Of course, I'll stop,' he said. 'I'm going to pinch you; I'm going to strike you,' I continued. 'Go ahead and strike me,' he said. 'I really will strike you' and I slapped his head.

[*She slaps* KOKUUN*'s head.*]

KOKUUN: Please forgive me, please forgive me.

TAEMA: 'I'm bored: I'm going home,' I said. 'No, I won't let you go,' he said. 'No, I must go home.' I quickly and smoothly stood and was about to leave when he pulled me back by the sleeve and recited another old poem to me.

HAKUUN *and* KOKUUN: And what was that poem?

TAEMA: 'In this world where tomorrow's friends are unknown,' Oh dear, I have forgot the last line again.

NARUKAMI: 'How I regret to part with my companion of today.' Was that not the ending?

TAEMA: Indeed, that was the very way in which it ended.

NARUKAMI: And then what happened?

TAEMA: I said, 'I'm going to leave.' So saying I made him let go of my sleeve, but he again firmly seized my sleeve and drew me back saying, 'I cannot let you go.' Insisting that I must go, I freed myself from his hold and quickly . . .

[*As if pursuing her,* NARUKAMI *falls down the steps and faints.*]

HAKUUN *and* KOKUUN: Oh, our master has fainted. [*They call.*] Master!

TAEMA: Dear priest!

[*She looks around, notices the waterfall, goes to it, and from mouth to mouth gives him water.*]

HAKUUN: How happy we are, he has . . .

HAKUUN *and* KOKUUN: Come to life again.

TAEMA: Dear priest, have you awakened?

NARUKAMI: Priests!

HAKUUN *and* KOKUUN: Sir?

NARUKAMI: Indeed, unbecoming to a Buddhist priest, I became enraptured by a woman's tale and fell down from the dais. My reason left me, and suddenly I felt a cold drop of water in my mouth which made me feel refreshed.

TAEMA: That is only natural. The water from the waterfall was given to you directly from my mouth to yours.

NARUKAMI: Hm-m? You mean to say that it was you who gave me the water?

TAEMI: Ai-i.

NARUKAMI: And the one who caressed my chest, was you also? [*He glares at her.*] Priests, on your guard.

[*He pushes her away, climbs the steps of the dais and strikes a pose.*]

TAEMA: What are you doing?

NARUKAMI: You, suspicious woman. Following the example of the priest Ikkaku Sennin of India who was ruined by a beauty, you have come to break my supernatural power. Now, confess. You are the daughter of what court noble in the Imperial Palace? If you do not confess, I'll tear you apart this very moment. Woman, what is your answer?

TAEMA: How impious that would be of me, dear priest! Never would I degrade myself to such a being. In order to wash the keepsake of my beloved husband, I have with great difficulty climbed the mountain to this waterfall though I am but a woman. Never did I suppose that I would be suspected by your highness, the priest. I have no choice; I shall throw myself into the basin of the waterfall and join my husband in death. To all of you I bid farewell. [*Prays.*] May the blessings of Buddha be upon me.

NARUKAMI: Here, stop her.

HAKUUN *and* KOKUUN: Hai.

NARUKAMI: My, how impetuous you are. I no longer doubt you. I did reproach you, but I can now see that your heart is true. You need not die a futile death. Death does not bring salvation.

TAEMA: Being thus suspected, how can I live any longer?

NARUKAMI: Become a nun; become a priestess.

TAEMA: What? Then you will shave off my hair and make me your disciple?

NARUKAMI: Yes, indeed.

TAEMA: Do you really mean so?

NARUKAMI: Would I, Narukami, lie?

TAEMA: Oh, then I thank you very much.

HAKUUN *and* KOKUUN: Now we are finally relieved.

NARUKAMI: Both of you, go to the foot of the mountains and fetch the razor, the implements necessary for taking the tonsure, and the holy vestment.

HAKUUN *and* KOKUUN: Do you mean now?

NARUKAMI: Do so immediately.

HAKUUN: But my dear master, the sun has gone down.

KOKUUN: It's getting darker and darker.

NARUKAMI: Whether night is closing in or whether it be break of day, do you mean to disobey your master?

HAKUUN: Oh no, to disobey . . .

HAKUUN *and* KOKUUN: We have no intention.

NARUKAMI: Then be gone!

HAKUUN *and* KOKUUN: Hai-i . . .

HAKUUN: Hey, Kokuumbo. He is sending us off to the foot of the mountains.

KOKUUN: And later he and the beautiful maiden will be left all alone.

NARUKAMI: What did you say?

HAKUUN *and* KOKUUN: Oh nothing, it was just a thought, just a lustful thought.

[*Exeunt via* hanamichi.]

SCENE THREE

NARUKAMI: They are certainly stupid fellows.

TAEMA [*changes subject*]: My dear teacher.

NARUKAMI: That's right. I am your teacher and you are my pupil. Soon you shall be initiated and become a disciple of Buddha. You must keep your mind pure.

TAEMA: Then when the razor is brought, are you going to shave off my hair?

NARUKAMI: Yes, I'm going to make you a beautiful bald bonze.

TAEMA [*cries*]: Ha-a-a-a –

NARUKAMI: Here, why are you crying?

TAEMA: To think that I should have to shave off these thousand strands of hair.

NARUKAMI: Does it disturb your heart? Is that why you are crying?

TAEMA: Ai-i.

NARUKAMI: A poem reads:

> My parents have not caressed my raven hair
> For treatment thus to cause me such despair.

I well understand that you should be reluctant to part from your hair.

TAEMA [*feigns*]: Oh how painful, how painful.

NARUKAMI: What is the matter? What is the matter? [*Comes down steps.*]

TAEMA: The thought has upset me and my spasm grows more violent. Oh, it pains!

NARUKAMI: How pitiful, and yet there is no medicine to be had here. Here, let me massage you a little.

TAEMA: That would be more than I deserve. How could I ask a priest to . . .

NARUKAMI: Lady, you are ill; you need not be modest. Now are you ready? [*He rubs.*] There, it seems that the source of the illness has been suppressed.

TAEMA: It is pleasurably soothing.

[*As he is rubbing her breast, he suddenly pulls out his hand and looks surprised.*]

What is the matter?

NARUKAMI: I touched something very extraordinary.

TAEMA: What did you touch?

NARUKAMI: It is the first time since my birth that I have put my hand into a woman's breast. On your breast I felt something very soft like a pillow with a little tip.

TAEMA: Dear priest, how silly. That is a nipple.

NARUKAMI: A nipple? How sinful of me. I have forgot the gratitude I owe to my mother's nipple which reared me from a suckling. Truly, priests have no more human feelings than an offshoot from a tree.

TAEMA: Your words are laudable.

NARUKAMI: Come, let me massage you more. Below the nipple is the center of breath; and below the breath, the center of health, where the pain originates; below the pit, there is Paradise . . .

TAEMA: My dear master, what are you doing?

NARUKAMI: I beg of you; the temptation is too great.

TAEMA: Dear Narukami, what has happened to you?

NARUKAMI: Do you mean I have gone mad?

TAEMA: You are not in your right mind. Listen please.

NARUKAMI: You accuse me of sinning against Buddha?

TAEMA: The word sinning is mild. You, a priest . . .

NARUKAMI: I am corrupt. I am corrupt. I have fallen from grace. Do not deny me. Unless you submit, I shall transform into a fearful demon and bite into your beautiful throat and drag you with me to Hell. Woman, what is your answer?

TAEMA: Dear priest.

NARUKAMI: Is the answer no?

TAEMA: Oh, how could you?

NARUKAMI: Is the answer no?

TAEMA: Yes, I will submit.

NARUKAMI: Oh! [*Loudly grunts, for this is an unexpected answer.*]

TAEMA: My, what a ferocious look! Is that the way to make love?

NARUKAMI: Answer me. Again!

TAEMA: The answer is yes.

NARUKAMI: Oh bliss, an easy and peaceful death. Let's go to the Elysian fields. [*Referring to her body.*]

[*He begins to pull her over to the dais.*]

TAEMA: Be not so impatient. I have answered yes and you need not rush me so. Dear Narukami, do you really wish to marry me?

NARUKAMI: Yes, we'll fall headlong into the hellish pond of man and wife.

TAEMA: Then I'll marry you; but I don't want to marry a bonze.

NARUKAMI: It is said that men with hairless legs are not afflicted with beriberi. A bonze is only a cure for beriberi.

TAEMA: Then will you renounce the priesthood?

NARUKAMI: Even now.

TAEMA: Will you become a layman?

NARUKAMI: I will dress my hair in today's fashion.

TAEMA: Do you promise?

NARUKAMI: I vow to the founder of Buddhism.

TAEMA: That oath smells of the temple. And your name is Priest Narukami.

NARUKAMI: I'll change my name.

TAEMA: To what?

NARUKAMI: Mm . . . I'll change my name to [*the performer's real name.*]

TAEMA: Oh, you are a dear husband.

NARUKAMI: Now hurry, come with me.

TAEMA: Are you rushing me again? To prove that we are man and wife, I want to exchange nuptial cups.

NARUKAMI: All right, we'll have our nuptial cups. Here's sake and a sake cup. Are you surprised? I watched the stealthy movements of my acolytes, and I knew these were here.

TAEMA: How wonderful! They are just what we were wishing for. Here, you drink first.

NARUKAMI: In a secular home I heard somewhere that the woman should drink first and then she should pour for her husband.

TAEMA: My, how clever you are. All right, then in celebration I shall drink first.

NARUKAMI: Let me pour for you.

TAEMA: I cannot drink much. This is a cup uniting us in this world and in the next. [*She drinks and begins to pour for him.*]

NARUKAMI: Oh no, a thousand pardons.

TAEMA: What do you mean?

NARUKAMI: I can't drink a drop of sake; I even hate pickles.

TAEMA: You might have abstained until now, but now that you have taken a wife, it would be best for you to change your ways.

NARUKAMI: But I can't drink the stuff.

TAEMA: Are you not going to drink, even though I ask you to?

NARUKAMI: Oh, I apologize, and as I apologize you may pour all you wish. [*He makes a distasteful expression.*]

TAEMA: What's the matter?

NARUKAMI: It's the first time that I have ever drunk sake and my poor insides are churning. Ah-h, I'm cold.

TAEMA: Soon you'll become hot.

NARUKAMI: Now I'll return it to you.

TAEMA: It's bad luck to say the word 'return' at a marriage ceremony; you would not want the bride to return home.

NARUKAMI: Then the cup goes back to you.

TAEMA: You are not supposed to say 'go back' either.

NARUKAMI: Then finish the cup.

TAEMA: With a toast to ourselves I'll take another drink. [*Then she offers him more.*]

NARUKAMI: Oh no, I can't stand a drop more.

TAEMA [*pouting*]: Are you not going to listen to me?

NARUKAMI: Go ahead, pour! See, it's filled to the brim.

TAEMA: Admirable!

[*She looks into the cup and sees a reflection.*]

[*Frightened.*]

Oh!

NARUKAMI: What's the matter? What are you afraid of?

TAEMA: There's a snake in the cup.

NARUKAMI: You're stupid. There's nothing.

TAEMA: Look, there is.

NARUKAMI: No, that's not a snake; that's the sacred rope.

TAEMA: Oh yes, it is a sacred rope.

NARUKAMI: That's a precious rope. It prevents the fall of rain.

TAEMA: Oh . . . how?

NARUKAMI: This is a very important matter. Do not divulge the secret. I have a bitter grievance against the Imperial Court and have shut in the world's Dragon God in that cavern. Furthermore, I have pulled across it the sacred rope sanctified by esoteric prayers. To let the rain fall, all one has to do is to cut the rope in the center. The Dragon God will escape and it will rain in torrents. This is a grave matter.

TAEMA: If that sacred rope is cut in the center the Dragon God will escape and rain will fall? Indeed, it is a very strange thing. Here, go ahead and drink more.

NARUKAMI: Now I'll give you a drink.

TAEMA: Not yet, the conventional rule is three cups. If you're unwilling, do as you please.

NARUKAMI: I didn't say I was not willing.

[*She pours.*]

O, I can't drink any more.

[*He drinks.*]

TAEMA: O, wonderful, you have drained the cup completely. Now I can consider you my darling husband.

[*He falls asleep.*]

Here, wake up, wake up! My, is there such a thing to fall asleep before the marriage ceremony. If you don't wake up, I'll tickle you. Here, wake up, wake up! [*Changes, now apologetically.*] It is most impious, most dreadful of me, dear Narukami, but please do forgive me. It was not my desire to ruin you. But it was the august Imperial Order to demoralize you through seduction of lust and wine. I fear even myself to think that I have thrust you down into such a disgraceful state. As you informed me in your drunken state, if I cut the center of that sacred rope, the Dragon God will escape and jump into the bottom of the sea and there will be a torrential downpour to provide water necessary for the growth of crops.

In the cavern of profound depth at which I now gaze, in it. . . . Ah yes! I shall perform my task.

[*She climbs the rock.*]

[*She prays.*] O great Buddha! Great deities! King of the sea dragons, I pray let it pour with rain. I implore you, great Buddha; I will promise to dedicate my life to you.

[TAEMA *rushes down from rock, and leaves via* hanamichi.]

[*Symbolic rain and lightning.*]

SCENE FOUR

[HAKUUN *and* KOKUUN *with numerous* ACOLYTES *enter from* hanamichi.]

ALL: Master Priest, Master Priest.

HAKUUN: O, here he is, here he is!

KOKUUN: O, it stinks, it stinks.

HAKUUN: It smells like a wine cellar.

ALL: Master Priest, Master Priest!

HAKUUN: Dear Narukami, your divine spell has been broken.

KOKUUN: The sacred rope has been cut and the Dragon God has escaped to heaven.

HAKUUN: And consequently rain –

ALL: Pours.

KOKUUN: Thunder –

ALL: Roars.

NARUKAMI: What, does it rain?

ALL: It pours.

NARUKAMI: What, does it thunder?

ALL: It roars.

NARUKAMI: Why does it rain? Why does it thunder?

HAKUUN: Dear master, you've been ruined by that lovely woman. Did you think that she was an ordinary woman? As she was fleeing, I asked about herself.

KOKUUN: Her name is Kumo no Taema and she is the Imperial Palace's peerless court lady. By Imperial Order she had come . . .

ALL: To cause your destruction.

NARUKAMI: Mm – [*low, in anger*]. Then she came purposely

to break my religious vows. Good is short-lived, evil prolongs. As long as I am to be punished by Buddha and my austerities have been violated, I shall become living thunder and pursue that woman. How great is the challenge I face.

CHORUS: With malicious spite Priest Narukami, the Thunder God, sails the clouds and rides the wind.

NARUKAMI: In the east there is the land of Oshu and Sotogahama.

CHORUS: In the west there is Kumano and the Nachi waterfall.

CHORUS: In the north are the rough waters of Echigo.

NARUKAMI: Where humans do not tread.

CHORUS: A thousand miles I stride,

NARUKAMI: And speed over millions more.

CHORUS: Wherever she shall hide,

NARUKAMI: I'll seek her evermore.

CHORUS: Determined to overtake her, Narukami follows in great pursuit.

CURTAIN
(HIKIMAKU)

PRODUCTION COMMENTS

An interview with Miyoko Watanabe

THE play *Narukami* remains one of the perennial favorites of the *Juhachiban* group of plays performed by the great acting family Ichikawa Danjuro, for its theme is the universal problem of human weakness. Its appeal is also found in its mixture of comedy, bawdiness and Buddhism which is beautifully illustrated in the seduction scene, a scene both lascivious and profound. The change in the character of Narukami as he arises from his stupor and the subsequent change in the mood of the play combine to make this an interesting play of contrasts. These particular characteristics and the smallness of the cast, with only two major roles, make this play an excellent choice for Western actors.

When Onoe Baiko VII directed the play with American actors he first introduced them to the customs of Japan and to the background of Kabuki. This was done in the belief that drama is a reflection of the culture of a people; an awareness and knowledge which Baiko felt the actor must have in approaching the play. He next explained and illustrated the traditional style or patterns of Kabuki acting known as *Kata*, a style in which dance movement, song and dialogue combine to create a performance which is neither accidental nor exotic.

The major influence upon Kabuki dance movement are the Noh drama, the folk dance of Japan and the puppet theatre. The characteristics of movement derived from the puppet theatre, with its abrupt doll-like movements and patterned poses, were borrowed by the Kabuki troupes during the eighteenth century. Kabuki, in order to survive the great popularity achieved by the Bunraku at that time, absorbed not only many successful plays from its repertory but also the histrionic characteristics of these magnificent dolls.

Being not only the basis of Kabuki acting, but also of supreme importance following the climactic movement in *Narukami*, dance movement is concentrated upon in the first phase of rehearsal. The basic walk, which is in itself a form of dance, is found to be difficult for the Western actor as the posture is unlike that used in ballet. In Noh, the actor leans slightly forward from the hips and in Kabuki he assumes a squatting or 'sitting-in' position. The actor quickly comes to realize why Japanese women walked with toes inward and knees together which is a movement necessary when playing the female role. Legend has it that in practice sessions the actor (*onnagata* or female impersonator) tied his knees together or placed a piece of paper between the knees which he had to hold in place while dancing or walking female style. He must also be trained to develop the subtle and fluid movement of the shoulders, neck and head to express femininity. Movement is also influenced by the weight and lines of the costume, the heaviness of the wig and the manipulation of hand props. The costume, designed to accentuate the height and bulk of the actor, also requires exaggerated, liberal and broad movements which otherwise would be lost, particularly in *aragoto* roles.

Though emphasis must first be placed upon movement the beauty of the dialogue in Kabuki must not be neglected. It is more or less a singsong dialogue, and therefore many times Kabuki is referred to as an opera, although singing as we know it in America is not done by the actor. As I translated the play

I tried to keep in mind not only the meaning but the rhythm of the original dialogue. I tried to synchronize the English with the Japanese. In order that the actor get the right rhythms and intonations, the lines can be said in Japanese and then the actor may repeat the dialogue in English with the same rhythm and inflections. Sometimes this will be found very difficult because the Japanese use many vowels; in fact nearly every other letter in the language is a vowel, whereas in English there are many more consonants than vowels. In Japanese when a word ends in a vowel, you can put a rhythm, a melody, an elongation to it. But when this same word is translated with a consonant ending, this is almost impossible; you must elongate a vowel *before* the consonant. The voice must be tuned to the musical instrument, and the pattern of speech based upon the movement, character and feeling.

The greatest challenge to the actor is to coordinate his dialogue with his physical movements, each line and gesture to be choreographed as in dance.

Unlike Western theatre, it is the leading actor who establishes the timing of the play for the supporting actors and who cues the musicians through his movement and song.

Psychologically, Kabuki is realistic, but one must always remember that Kabuki is *theatre*. The American actors and actresses, who are accustomed more to the realistic theatre, have a tendency to face each other or come close to each other. But Kabuki is a dream world; beauty is the prime object. In the scene of the drinking of the *sake*, persons drinking ordinarily would face each other, but not in Kabuki. Both face front and yet must give the feeling of talking and drinking with each other. It must be made a picture, and when two come too close together, the picture as a whole is destroyed. For example, in drinking a cup of *sake*, if Narukami in his big heavy costume picked up a cup and drank in an ordinary manner, it would appear as if he were drinking a teardrop out of a bucket. This would look foolish; it would not balance with his costume. So he gives a better effect by arching his elbows and bringing his head forward and drinking in a big movement. This balances very well with the costume. Of course, this seems very unnatural at first to the American actor, but after he has become accustomed to the movement, he finds it to be natural to the moment. In the fighting scenes, when Narukami brings his hand around in a large counter-clockwise movement, to push off the acolytes who had been trying to hold him back, the movement at first seemed unnatural. But as each actor accustoms himself to it, it becomes very logical.

It is important for the actor to become aware of the psychological background of the physical movement. Originally it was a natural movement of expression, then it was made theatrical, polished and improved by the generations following. It has finally reached its state of perfection after many years, a movement that is virile, graceful, delicately controlled and at times subtle. The line, the posture, and the muscular control of the body must convey to the audience the actor's attitude towards the incidents in the play.

Music, an integral part of the art of Kabuki, is utilized to underscore the exaggerated and deliberate measured movements and gestures of the actor. The sound pulsates and moves ultimately to a series of crescendos paralleling the climax and denouement of the story. The wide range of percussion sound effects are used independently or to accompany chanting. The most unique of these is the sounding of wooden clappers which are used both to enhance the dramatic poses (*mie*) of the actor and as the signal for the opening and closing of the play. Clappers for the opening and closing of curtain are shaped slightly different from the ones pounded on a board to enhance the pose of an actor. Curtain clappers are called *hyoshigi*, or *ki* for short, and are oblong shaped, slightly curved at ends for easier clapping by hands; the other is called *tsuke* and is shorter and flat on all sides.

As movement in Kabuki is unlike ballet, Japanese music differs from Western music in its rhythmic patterns, which is a challenge to the Western actor.

SELECTED BIBLIOGRAPHY

GENERAL

1. Anderson, G. L., ed. *Masterpieces of the Orient*. New York: W. W. Norton and Co., 1961.
2. Anderson, G. L., ed. *The Genius of the Oriental Theatre*. New York: New American Library, 1966.
3. Bowers, Faubion. *Theatre in the East*. New York: Grove Press, 1969.
4. Brandon, James R. *Theatre in Southeast Asia*. Cambridge, Mass.: Harvard University Press, 1967.
5. Ceadel, Eric, ed. *Literature of the East: an Appreciation*. London: John Murray, 1953.
6. Clark, Barrett H., ed. *World Theatre, Volume I*. New York: Dover Publications, Inc., 1933.
7. De Bary, William, ed. *Approaches to the Oriental Classics: Asian Literature and Thought in General Education*. New York: Columbia University Press, 1959.
8. De Bary, William and A. Embree, ed. *Guide to Oriental Classics*. New York: Columbia University Press, 1964.
9. Gassner, John. *A Treasury of the Theatre from Aeschylus to Ostrovsky*. New York: Simon and Schuster, 1967.
10. Wells, Henry W., ed. *Asian Drama: A Collection of Festival Papers*. Vermillion, South Dakota: University of South Dakota, 1966.
11. Wells, Henry W. *The Classical Drama of the Orient*. London and New York: Asia Publishing House, 1965.
12. Yohannan, John D. *A Treasury of Asian Literature*. New York: New American Library, 1958.

INDIAN

13. Anand, Mulk Raj. *The Indian Theatre*. New York: Roy, 1951.
14. Ayyar, A. S. P. *Bhasa*. Madras: V. Ramaswamy Sastrulu and Sons, 1957.
15. Bhasa. *Thirteen Trivandrum Plays Attributed to Bhasa*, trans. A. C. Woolner and Sarup Lakshman, 2 Vols. London: Oxford University Press, 1931.
16. Bhasa. *Two Plays of Bhasa*, trans. A. S. P. Ayyar. Madras: V. Ramaswamy Sastrulu, 1959.
17. Buitenen, J. A. B. van, trans. *Two Plays of Ancient India: The Little Clay Cart and the Minister's Seal*. New York: Columbia University Press, 1968.
18. Gargi, Balwant. *Folk Theatre of India*. Seattle, Washington: University of Washington Press, 1966.
19. Gargi, Balwant. *Theatre in India*. New York: Theatre Arts Books, 1962.
20. Gupta, Chandra B. *The Indian Theatre*. Benares: Motilal Benarsidas, 1954.
21. Horrwitz, Ernest P. *The Indian Theatre: a Brief Survey of the Sanskrit Drama*. New York: Benjamin Blom, 1967.
22. Kalidasa. *Shakuntala*, trans. Arthur W. Ryder. New York: Dutton Ltd, 1959.
23. Kalidasa. *Works of Kalidasa*, ed. M. R. Kale, B.A. Delhi: Motilal Benarsidas, 1967.
24. Keith, Arthur B. *The Sanskrit Drama in Its Origin, Development, Theory and Practice*. London: Oxford University Press, 1964.
25. King Shudraka. *The Little Clay Cart*, trans. Revilo P. Oliver. Urbana: University of Illinois Press, 1938
26. King Shudraka. *The Little Clay Cart*, trans. Arthur W. Ryder. New York: Theatre Arts Books, 1934.
27. Lal, O., trans. *Great Sanskrit Plays in Modern Translation*. Norwalk: New Directions, 1964.
28. MacDonell, Arthur A. *A History of Sanskrit Literature*. London: William Heinmann, 1913.

29. Mathur, Jagdesh. *Drama in Rural India*. New York: Asia Library, 1964.
30. Rangacharya Adya. *Drama in Sanskrit Literature*. Bombay: Popular Pradashan, 1967.
31. Renou, Louis. *Indian Literature*, trans. Patrick Evans. New York: Wather and Co., 1964.
32. Shekhar, Indu. *Sanskrit Drama: Its Origin and Decline*. Leiden: E. J. Brill, 1960.
33. Wells, Henry W. *The Classical Drama of India*. Bombay: Asia Publishing House, 1963.
34. Wells, Henry W., ed. *Six Sanskrit Plays in English Translation*. Bombay and New York: Asia Publishing House, 1964.
35. Wilson, H. H., V. Raghavan, K. P. Pisharoti, and Amylya Charan Vigyabhusan. *The Theatre of the Hindus*. London: Luzac, 1955.
36. Yajnik R. K. *The Indian Theatre: Its Origins and Its Later Development under European Influence*. London and New York: Allen and Unwin, 1933.

CHINESE

37. Arlington, Lewis C. *The Chinese Drama from Earliest Time Until Today*. New York: Banjamin Blom, 1966.
38. Arlington, Lewis C. and Harold Acton, ed. and trans. *Famous Chinese Plays*. New York: Russell and Russell, Inc., 1963.
39. Buss, Kate. *Studies in Chinese Drama*. New York: J. Cape and H. Smith, 1930.
40. Chai, Ch'u and Winberg Chai, ed. and trans. *A Treasury of Chinese Literature*. New York: Appleton-Century, 1965.
41. Chen, Jack. *The Chinese Theatre*. London: Dennis Dobson Ltd, 1949.
42. Crump, J. J. *Anthology of Chinese Literature*. New York: Grove Press, 1967.
43. Giles, Herbert A. *A History of Chinese Literature*. New York: D. Appleton and Co., 1931.
44. Hung, Josephine Huang, trans. *Children of the Pear Garden*. Taipei: Heritage Press, 1961.

45. Kalvodova, Sis Vanis. *Chinese Theatre*, trans. Iris Urwin. London: Spring Books Ltd, 1960.
46. *Lady Precious Stream*, trans. and adapt. S. I. Hsiung. Harmondsworth, Middlesex: Penguin Books, 1958.
47. Li Hsing-tao. *The Circle of Chalk*. London: Heinemann Ltd, 1929.
48. Liu Wu-chih. *An Introduction to the Chinese Theatre*. Bloomington: Indiana University Press, 1966.
49. Scott, A. C. *The Classical Theatre of China*. New York: Macmillan, 1957.
50. Scott, A. C. *An Introduction to the Chinese Theatre*. New York: Theatre Arts Books, 1959.
51. Scott, A. C., ed. and trans. *Traditional Chinese Plays*. Madison: University of Wisconsin Press, 1967.
52. Scott, A. C., ed. and trans. *Traditional Chinese Plays*, Vol. II. Madison: University of Wisconsin Press, 1969.
53 Wang Shih-fu. *The Romance of the Western Chamber*, trans. S. I. Hsiung. New York: Liveright Publishing Company, 1936.
54. Wang Shih-fu. *The West Chamber*, trans. Henry H. Hart. Stanford, California: Stanford University Press, 1936.
55. Zucker, A. E. *The Chinese Theatre*. London: Jarrolds, 1925.
56. Zung, Cecelia S. C. *Secrets of the Chinese Drama*. New York: Benjamin Blom, 1964.

JAPANESE

57. Benedict, Ruth. *The Chrysanthemum and the Sword*. Boston: Houghton Mifflin, 1946.
58. Bowers, Faubion, *Japanese Theatre*. New York: Hill and Wang, 1959.
59. Brandon, James and Tamako Niwa, Adapt. *Kabuki Plays*. New York: Samuel French, Inc., 1966.
60. Chikamatsu, Monzaemon. *The Battle of Coxinga*, ed. and trans. by Donald Keene, with preface by Mark Van Doren. London: Taylor's Foreign Press, 1951.

61. Chikamatsu, Monzaemon. *Four Major Plays*, trans. Donald Keene. New York: Columbia University Press, 1961.
62. Chikamatsu, Monzaemon. *The Love Suicide at Amijima*, trans. Donald H. Shively. Cambridge, Mass.: Harvard University Press, 1953.
63. Ernst, Earle. *The Kabuki Theatre*. New York: Grove Press, 1959.
64. Ernst, Earle, ed. *Three Japanese Plays from the Traditional Theatre*. New York: Grove Press, 1960.
65. Haar, Francis. *Japanese Theatre in Highlight; A Pictorial Commentary*. Tokyo and Rutland, Vermont: Charles E. Tuttle Co., 1952.
66. Halford, Aubrey S. and Giovanna M. Halford. *The Kabuki Handbook: A Guide to Understanding and Appreciation*. Tokyo and Rutland, Vermont: Charles E. Tuttle Co., 1956.
67. Hamaura, Yonezo, and others. *Kabuki*, trans. F. Takano. Tokyo: Japan Publications, 1956.
68. *Japanese Noh Drama: Ten Plays Selected and Translated from the Japanese*. Tokyo: Nippon Gakujutsu Shinkokai, 1955.
69. Kawatake, Shigetoshi. *Kabuki, Japanese Drama*. Tokyo: Foreign Affairs Association of Japan, 1958.
70. Keene, Donald. *Bunraku: Art of Japanese Puppet Theatre*. Palo Alto and Tokyo: Kodansha, Int. Ltd, n.d.
71. Keene, Donald. *Japanese Literature: An Introduction for Western Readers*. New York: Grove Press, 1955.
72. Keene, Donald. *No: The Classical Theatre of Japan*. Palo Alto and Tokyo: Kodansha, Int. Ltd, 1966.
73. Kenny, Don. *A Guide to Kyogen*. Tokyo: Hinoki Shoten, 1968.
74. Kincaid, Zoe. *Kabuki: The Popular Stage of Japan*. New York: Benjamin Blom, 1965.
75. Komiya, Toyotaka. *Japanese Music and Drama in the Meiji Era*, trans. and adapt. Edward G. Seidensticker and Donald Keene. Tokyo: Obransha, 1956.
76. Kusano, Eisaburo. *Stories Behind Noh and Kabuki Plays*. Tokyo: Japan Publications, 1962.
77. Lombard, Frank. *An Outline History of the Japanese Drama*. Boston and New York: Houghton Mifflin Co., 1929.

78. Malm, William P. *Nagauta; The Heart of Kabuki Music.* Tokyo and Rutland, Vermont: Charles E. Tuttle Co., 1963.
79. Miyake, Shutaro. *Kabuki Drama.* Tokyo: Japan Travel Bureau, 1963.
80. O'Neill, P. G. *A Guide to No.* Tokyo and Kyoto: Japan Publications, 1963.
81. Pound, Ezra L., and Ernest Fenollosa. *The Classic Noh Theatre of Japan.* New York: New Directions, 1959.
82. Sadler, Arthur L., trans. *Japanese Plays. No-Kyogen-Kabuki.* Sydney: Angus & Robertson, Ltd, 1934.
83. Scott, A. C., trans. *Genyadana.* Tokyo: Hokuseido, 1953.
84. Scott, A. C. *The Kabuki Theatre of Japan.* New York: Macmillan, 1966.
85. Scott, A. C. *The Puppet Theatre of Japan.* Tokyo and Rutland Vermont: Charles E. Tuttle Co., 1965.
86. Toki, Zemmaro. *Japanese Noh Plays.* Tokyo and Rutland, Vermont: Charles E. Tuttle Co., 1954.
87. Tsubouchi, Shoyo, and Jiro Yamamoto. *History and Characteristics of Kabuki*, trans. Royozo Matsumoto. Yokohama: H. Yamagata, 1960.
88. Ueda, Makoto, ed. and trans. *The Old Pine Tree and Other Noh Plays.* Lincoln: University of Nebraska Press, 1962.
89. Waley, Arthur. *The No Plays of Japan.* New York: Grove Press, 1957.
90. Watanabe, Miyoko, and Donald Richie, trans. *Six Kabuki Plays.* Tokyo: Hokuseido, 1963.

SELECTED LIST

OF

PLAYS IN TRANSLATION

for further reading and production

The numbers following the plays refer to the sources listed in the Selected Bibliography.

INDIAN

Play	*Playwright*	*Source*
The Adventure of the Boy Krishna (*Bála-Caritam*)	Bhasa	15
The Broken Thighs (*Urubhangam*)	Bhasa	15
Carudatta in Poverty (*Darida-Cárudattam*)	Bhasa	15
The Consecration (*Abhisheka-Nátakam*)	Bhasa	15
The Embassy (*Dútauākyam*)	Bhasa	15
The Five Nights (*Pañcarátam*)	Bhasa	15
Karna's Task	Bhasa	15
(*Karna-Bhāram*)	Bhavabhuti	27,34
The Later Story of Rama	Bhavabhuti	27,34
The Little Clay Cart (*The Toy Cart*)	King Shudraka	2, 17, 25, 26, 27, 34
Mālavikāgnimitram	Kalidasa	23
The Middle One	Bhasa	15
The Minister's Vows	Bhasa	15
Nagananda	Harsha	34

CHINESE

The Butterfly Dream (*Hu Tieh Mêng*)	Lieh Kuo (*period*)	38, 51
The Capture and Release of Ts'ao (*Cho Fang Ts'ao*)	San Kuo (*period*)	38
Chuang Yüan's Record (*Chuang Yüan P'u*)	Sung (*period*)	38
The Cinnabar Mole (*Chu Sha Chih*)	Sung (*period*)	38
The Chalk Circle (*The Circle of Chalk*)	Li Hsing-tao	6, 47
The Day of Nine Watches (*Chiu Keng T'ien*)	Sung (*period*)	38
A Double Handful of Snow (*I P'êng Hsùeh*)	Ming (*period*)	38
An Extraordinary Twin Meeting (*Ch'i Shaung Hui*)	Ming (*period*)	38
The Five Flower Grotto (*Wu Hua Tung*)	Sung (*period*)	38
The Golden Locket Plot (*Chin So Chi*)	Ming (*period*)	38
The Green Jade Hairpin (*Pi Yü Tsan*)		38
The Happy Hall of Jade (*The Faithful Harlot*) (*Yü T'ang Ch'un*)	Ming (*period*)	38, 44
Jade Screen Mountain (*Ts'ui P'ing Shan*)	Sung (*period*)	38
Lady Precious Stream	Wang Pao-ch'uan	46
Li Ki Uei Carries Thorns	K'ang Chin-chih	42
The Lucky Pearl (*Ch'ing Ting Chu*)	Sung (*period*)	38
The Mating at Heaven's Bridge (*T'ien Ho P'ei*)	Ming (*period*)	38
The Meeting of the League of Heroes (*Ch'un Ying Hui*)	San Kuo (*period*)	38

JAPANESE

Noh

The Lady Aoi Princess Hollyhock (*Aoi No Uye*)	Zenchiku Ujinobu	2, 80, 89
Atsumori	Seami	89
Basho	Zenchiku Ujinobu	68
The Battle of Yashima	Seami	88
Benkei in the Boat (*Funa-Benkei*)	Nobumitsu	58, 68
Benkei on the Bridge (*Hashi-Bankei*)	Hiyoshi Sa-ami Yasukiyo	89
Chorio	Nobumitsu	80
The Cormorant-Fisher (*Ukai*)	Enami No Sayemon	89
The Damask Drum (*Aya No Tsuzumi*)	Seami	1, 89
Dojoji		82
The Dwarf Trees (*Hachi no Ki*)	Seami	89
Early Snow (*Virgin Snow*) (*Hatsuyuki*)	Kamparu Zembo Motoyasu	2, 82, 89
Equchi	Kannami Kiyotsugu	68
The Feathered Robe (*Hagoromo*)	Seami	80, 89
Genjo	Kongo	80
The Great Shrine (*Oyashiro*)		82
Haku Ratuten	Seami	89
The Hatmaker (*Eboshi-ori*)	Miyamusa	2, 89

The Hoka Priests (*Hoka-zo*)	Zenchiku Ujinobu	89
Ikeniye	Seami	89
Ikuta	Kamparu Zembo Motoyasu	89
Iwabune		82
Jinen the Preacher	Kannami Kiyotsugu	88
Kagekiyo	Motokiyo	80, 89
Kakitsubata	Motokiyo	80, 82
Kamo No Chomei		82
Kantan	Seami	89
Kayoi Komachi		80
Kinuta		80
Kiyotsune	Seami	68
Kokaji		82
Kumasaka	Zenchiku Ujinobu	80, 89
The Lady Within the Cypress Fence	Seami	88
The Maple Viewing (*Momi Jigari*)	Nobimitsu	64
The Mirror of Pine Forest		88
Nakamitsu	Seami	6
Nishigiki	Motokiyo	80
The Old Pine Tree	Seami	88
Sanemori	Seami	68
Shojo		80
Shojo and the Big Jar		82
Sotaba Komachi	Kannami Kiyotsugu	9, 71, 80, 89
Suma Genji		80
The River Sumida (*Sumidagawa*)	Juro Motomasa	68
Tadanori		82
Taihei Shojo		82
Takasago		68

Tamaru	Seami	68, 80, 82
Toboku	Seami	68
Tomoe		82
Tsunemasa	Seami	89
The Valley-Hurling (*Taniko*)	Zenchiku Ujinobu	89
Well-curb (*Izutsu*)	Seami	68

Kabuki

The Battle of Coxinga (*Kokusenya Kassen*)	Chikamatsu	71
Benten the Thief (*Benten Kozo*)	Kawatake Mokuami	64
The Cherry Shower		82
The Courier from Hell (*Meido No Hiyeka*)	Chikamatsu	2
The Courtesan (*Kagotsurube*)	Kawatake Sinichi III	90
The Forty-seven Ronin (*Chushingura*)	Takeda Isumo, Miyoshi Shoraku, Namiki Senryú	90
Gappo and His Daughter Tsuji (*Sesshu Gappo No Tsuji*)	Suga Sensuke	58
Genyadana	Seqawa Joko III	83
The House of Sugawara (*Sugawara Denju Tenabai Kagami*)	Takeda Izumo, Miyoshi Shoraku, Namiki Senryū	64
The Love Suicide at Amijima (*Shinjiten no Amijima*)	Chikamatsu	61, 72
The Love Suicide at Sonezaki (*Sonezaki Shinju*)	Chikamatsu	61, 72
The Maiden at the Dojo Temple (*Musume Dojoji*)		90

BIOGRAPHIES OF CONTRIBUTORS

JOHN Y. H. HU is an Assistant Professor in the Department of Theatre at Michigan State University. He received his Ph.D. in theatre at Indiana University in 1969. Particularly interested in directing, he has done extensive research on ancient Chinese drama. His doctoral dissertation, *Ts'ao Yu*, will soon be published.

VERA RUSHFORTH IRWIN is Professor of Theatre Arts at State University College, New Paltz, New York. She holds degrees from New York University and did advanced graduate work in theatre and dramatic literature at the University of Colorado and at Columbia. In addition to professional training with Margaret Webster and at the Institute of Advanced Studies in the Theatre Arts, she has delved into the work of both American and European directors. She received a Ford Fellowship in 1955 for the study of American theatre and, in 1962–3, went abroad for intensive practice with European directors. At New Paltz, Professor Irwin has designed and directed more than eighty theatrical productions.

WILLIAM PACKARD is Assistant Professor of Poetry at New York University. Since 1957, when he won the Robert Frost poetry award, he has divided his free time between his own poetry and writing for the theatre. His adaptation of *Ikkaku Sennin* was done in 1964 for the Kita troupe of the Noh in Tokyo, which was then preparing for an American tour. In 1965, he completed an English translation of Racine's *Phèdre*, performed off-Broadway by an American cast that included Beatrice Straight and Mildred Dunnock. Among Mr Packard's own plays are *In the First Place*, *Once and For All*, *From Now On*, and *Sandra and the Janitor*, all of which were produced in New York.

LEONARD C. PRONKO is Professor of Romance Languages at Pomona College, Claremont, California. Recipient of a Guggenheim Fellowship, 1963–4, for research in the Orient, he is the author of *Theatre East and West: Perspectives Toward a Total Theatre* and of numerous articles on the Japanese drama. He has directed and acted in Kabuki plays at Pomona College and has experimented with Kabuki styling in a production of Marlowe's *The Jew of Malta*.

MRINALINI SARABHAI is acclaimed throughout the world of dance. She began her training at an early age in her native India, perfecting herself in the purest forms of Bharata Natyam. Later, in Java, she studied the most ancient school of Javanese dancing, and was the first Indian to receive such instruction. In 1948, she founded Darpana, an academy of dance, drama, and music in Ahmedabad. Her troupe has performed in Europe, South America, Mexico, Egypt, Lebanon, South-east Asia, and Japan. Madame Sarabhai's published writings include a verse play, a novel, books for young readers, and numerous articles on the dance, drama, music, and cultural history of India.

ROY E. TEELE is Director of the Center for Asian Studies at the University of Texas and editor-in-chief of *Literature East and West.* He has taught English at Kwansei Gakuin University in Nishinomiya, Japan, and at Nanking University in China. His translations of Noh plays are widely admired, and he is the author of numerous articles on Noh drama.

MIYOKO WATANABE is on the faculty of the Institute of Advanced Studies in the Theatre Arts. Her training began when she was six years old with intensive study of Kabuki acting, choreography, and music in Tokyo. Later, as a leading member of an all-girl Kabuki troupe, she played roles ranging from young maidens to toothless old men. She has the unusual distinction of having received three professional titles. Miss Watanabe came to the United States in 1960 to serve as interpreter-announcer for the first Kabuki troupe to tour the country.

HENRY W. WELLS is Professor of Asian Poetry, Drama, and Art in the Graduate Department of C.W. Post College, Long Island University. For twenty-five years, he was on the faculty of Columbia University, where he taught comparative literature. In the decade since leaving Columbia, he has concentrated chiefly on Chinese studies, aiming to render Chinese poetry into readable English. Books to his credit include *An Introduction to Wallace Stevens*, *Emily Dickinson*, *Poetic Imagery*, and, more recently, *Ancient Chinese Humor*, *The Classical Drama of the Orient*, and *Ancient Poetry from China, Japan, and India*.

DANIEL S. P. YANG is Assistant Professor of Communication and Theatre at the University of Colorado in Boulder. He is the author of *An Annotated Bibliography of Materials for the Study of the Peking Theatre* as well as of articles on Peking drama. In 1963, he directed and designed a full-length Peking opera, *Twice a Bride*, at the University of Hawaii. More recently, at the University of Colorado, he has prepared a full-length production of another Peking opera, *Black Dragon Residence*.